EDUCATING ENTREPRENEURS

As entrepreneurship programs proliferate—from classes in higher education to incubators, accelerators, open innovation platforms, and innovation factories—our understanding of the advantages and challenges of different modes of learning becomes increasingly obscured. In *Educating Entrepreneurs*, Kariv provides an impressively broad and thorough overview of the field of entrepreneurship education, along with practical tools for students to be able to evaluate the strengths and weaknesses of the different options that exist, as well as for these programs' developers and managing teams to be able to plan and manage such processes.

Examining these programs, which are found both within and outside of academia, along with insights into their challenges and opportunities, should help students grasp the entrepreneurship education field, its goals, target audience, and ecosystem involvement. Kariv supplements this comprehensive evaluation with case studies and examples that tie the theory to practical applications. Students can read about contemporary ventures, such as Y Combinators, Techstars, and SOSA, giving them concrete examples to relate to. Interviews with program stakeholders around the world complete the view, with an exploration of the cultural and country-based dynamics related to programs developed in specific countries.

Being both thorough and informative, this book will serve students and faculty of entrepreneurship courses, as well as practitioners looking to understand their entrepreneurship education options.

Dafna Kariv is Vice President for Global Initiatives at the College of Management (COLLMAN), Israel; the Chair of Novus Entrepreneurship Center, and Co-Chair of ACTO, Academic Center for Impact Investing and Entrepreneurship. She is also Academic Manager of the MBA/MS collaboration at Baruch College, USA. Kariv is the author of many research publications, focusing on entrepreneurship, education, and gender. She is a recipient of several European Commission prize funds; involved in academic boards; affiliate professor at HEC, Montreal; and the 'German–Israeli Startup-Exchange Program' ambassador.

"Dafna Kariv has done it again, this time by presenting entrepreneurship education in a global, multi-faceted way that is easily accessible to everyone."
—*Louis Jacques Filion, HEC Montreal, Canada*

"This is a comprehensive textbook that fills a gap in the literature of entrepreneurship. It covers a rich curriculum and reviews diverse methods for teaching, learning, and experiencing entrepreneurship, blended with case studies, illustrations, and many other innovative elements and ideas for enriching the learning process of entrepreneurship in both theory and in practice."
— *Oren Kaplan, College of Management Academic Studies, Israel*

EDUCATING ENTREPRENEURS

Innovative Models and New Perspectives

Dafna Kariv

NEW YORK AND LONDON

First published 2020
by Routledge
52 Vanderbilt Avenue, New York, NY 10017

and by Routledge
2 Park Square, Milton Park, Abingdon, Oxon, OX14 4RN

Routledge is an imprint of the Taylor & Francis Group, an informa business

© 2020 Taylor & Francis

The right of Dafna Kariv to be identified as author of this work has been asserted by her in accordance with sections 77 and 78 of the Copyright, Designs and Patents Act 1988.

All rights reserved. No part of this book may be reprinted or reproduced or utilised in any form or by any electronic, mechanical, or other means, now known or hereafter invented, including photocopying and recording, or in any information storage or retrieval system, without permission in writing from the publishers.

Trademark notice: Product or corporate names may be trademarks or registered trademarks, and are used only for identification and explanation without intent to infringe.

Library of Congress Cataloging-in-Publication Data
Names: Kariv, Dafna, author.
Title: Educating entrepreneurs : innovative models and new perspectives / Dafna Kariv.
Description: New York : Routledge, 2019. | Includes bibliographical references and index.
Identifiers: LCCN 2019005042| ISBN 9781138542839 (hardback) | ISBN 9781138542846 (pbk.) | ISBN 9781351008006 (ebook)
Subjects: LCSH: Business education. | Businesspeople—Training of. | Entrepreneurship.
Classification: LCC HF1106 .K377 2019 | DDC 338/.040711—dc23
LC record available at https://lccn.loc.gov/2019005042

ISBN: 978-1-138-54283-9 (hbk)
ISBN: 978-1-138-54284-6 (pbk)
ISBN: 978-1-351-00800-6 (ebk)

Typeset in Bembo
by Swales & Willis Ltd, Exeter, Devon, UK

 Printed in the United Kingdom by Henry Ling Limited

CONTENTS

List of Tables xi
List of Figures xii
Acknowledgments xiv
Preface xvii

Introduction 1

1 A Contextual Overview of Entrepreneurship Education Programs 7

Education through an Entrepreneurial and Contextual Framework 9
The Whole-person Pedagogy 11
Summary 12
Takeaways 13
Case Study 1 – Innovation and Education: The Startup Grind Worldwide Community 14
Questions on the Case Study 16
Reflective Questions 16
Notes 17
References 17

2 What Does Education Entail for Entrepreneurs? 20

The Complexity of Teaching Entrepreneurship 21
Entrepreneurship Education (EE) 23

Entrepreneurship Learning (EL) 24
Entrepreneurship Teaching (ET) 26
Teaching Entrepreneurially 29
Entrepreneurship as a Career Choice 30
Summary 30
Takeaways 31
Case Study 2—An Entrepreneurial Look into EE, the Case of Art-preneurs 32
Questions on the Case Study 33
Reflective Questions 34
Notes 35
References 35

3 The *What, Why* and *How* of Entrepreneurial Education   42

Modernizing the Prevailing Approach 45
Reciprocal Relations between Exceptions and the Mainstream 48
The What 49
The Why 50
The How 53
Summary 54
Takeaways 55
Case Study 3 – NOVUS, the Academic Accelerator 55
Questions on the Case Study 58
Reflective Questions 58
Notes 58
References 59

4 There Is No 'One Size Fits All': New Concepts in Educating Entrepreneurs   62

The Entrepreneurial Learning Cycles 63
The Blended-value Approach to Learning 64
The Personalized Approach 68
Summary 76
Takeaways 76
Case Study 4 – Venture Building: A New Blended-value Type of Education to Assist Entrepreneurs 77
Questions on the Case Study 78
Reflective Questions 79
Notes 80
References 80

5 The Entrepreneur's Perspective   84

   Why Do Entrepreneurs Enroll in Entrepreneurship Programs? 84
   Psychological Perspectives in EE: The Meeting Point of
      Psychology–Entrepreneurship–Education 87
   A Process-driven View 91
   An Outcome Outlook 94
   The Individual and the Stakeholders 95
   Summary 98
   Takeaways 99
   Case Study 5 – "Living in a Nursing Home to Get Closer to
      my Customers": Insights from the Y Combinator Accelerator
      Experience 100
   Questions on the Case Study 103
   Reflective Questions 103
   Notes 105
   References 105

6 The Sharing Economy and Shared Entrepreneurial
   Spaces Nexus   108

   The Sharing Economy in the Entrepreneurial Context 108
   Digital Content 112
   Shared Spaces 115
   Crowdfunding 119
   Summary 121
   Takeaways 122
   Case Study 6—The Nexus of a Co-working Space: Diversity
      and Multisectoriality, the Canadian Experience of entrePrism,
      Montreal, Canada 123
   Questions on the Case Study 125
   Reflective Questions 125
   Notes 126
   References 126

7 The New Breed of Programs and Academia's Role   129

   'Entrepreneurship Can Be Taught!' 129
   Gamification 130
   Practice, Internship 133
   Virtual, Digitalized Learning (Figure 7.1) 134
   Summary 137
   Takeaways 138

viii Contents

    Case Study 7—INNOVATING, Accelerator Program in a Technological Academic Institution 139
    Questions on the Case Study 141
    Reflective Questions 142
    Note 142
    References 142

8 Portraying the Enabling Platforms: Incubators   145

    The Landscape of Incubators 145
    Internal Resources 146
    External Resources 146
    Incubators: Models and Approaches 147
    The Journey 149
    The Institutionalizing Perspective 149
    Summary 154
    Takeaways 155
    Case Study 8 – From a Musical Journey to 2018 Incubator of the Year: The Case of Neotec HUB, Kolkata, India 156
    Questions on the Case Study 159
    Reflective Questions 159
    Notes 160
    References 160

9 The Rise of the Acceleration Model   162

    Models and Trends 163
    Scaleup Accelerators 172
    Corporate Accelerators 173
    Institutional Accelerators 174
    Summary 174
    Takeaways 175
    Case Study 9—Techstars 176
    Questions on the Case Study 179
    Reflective Questions 179
    Notes 180
    References 181

10 The Evolution of Innovative Enabling Platforms   183

    Open Innovation Platforms (OIPs) 183
    Individuals' Personalized Platforms 187
    Innovation Factory 187

Venture Builders 189
Startup Factory 189
Impact Hubs 190
Startup Studios 190
Venture Labs, Co-labs 191
Boot camps 191
Summary 193
Takeaways 194
Case Study 10—SOSA NYC: A Disruptive Concept of an OIP 195
Questions on the Case Study 196
Reflective Questions 197
Notes 197
References 198

11 The Role of the Environment in Fostering Entrepreneurship   200

The Reciprocal Impact of the Ecosystem on Entrepreneurship 200
How Is Value Created in an Ecosystem? 201
Venture Capital and Investing Companies 206
Banks Embedded in the Entrepreneurial Offerings 208
Public Sector Participation 209
Private Sector Outreach 212
The International Perspective on Entrepreneurship Support 213
Entrepreneurial Cities and Communities 214
Summary 216
Takeaways 217
Case Study 11—A One-stop Shop for Innovation: J. P. Morgan's In-Residence Startup Program 218
Questions on the Case Study 219
Reflective Questions 220
Notes 221
References 221

12 Evaluation, Implications and Future Avenues   225

Evaluation of EE and Enabling Systems 225
The Value of the Outcome 226
Evaluation of the Educational Process 229
Summary 231
Beyond the Here and Now 236

Sharing and Mapping 237
Summary 238
Takeaways 238
Case Study 12 – Accelerating Startups for the Chinese Market: Beijing, China 243
Questions on the Case Study 244
Reflective Questions 244
Notes 245
References 245

Index 247

TABLES

3.1	Demarcating entrepreneurship for suitable education	43
4.1	Planning and pre-routinizing steps to programs reflecting the edu-preneurship approach	73
5.1	Reasons to join entrepreneurial programs: a push/pull perspective	88
5.2	Interested groups, how they are affected by, and affect, EE	96
6.1	Opportunities and hurdles	110
6.2	The challenges of a sharing economy	111
6.3	Insights from shared-space tenants	116
7.1	Opportunity-driven streams in EE, education forms and expected results for the learners	131
9.1	Accelerator activities and platforms	166
12.1	Evaluation factors and the level of measurement	230
12.2	Evaluating the process through different views	232
12.3	A summative framework for enabling systems' conceptual organization—creation of a smart map	240

FIGURES

1.1	The whole-person pedagogy	11
2.1	A simple EE-acceleration model	21
2.2	Forces influencing EL	25
2.3	An innovative look at teaching methods	27
3.1	The 'learning about' map	44
3.2	Diffusing EE foci	46
3.3	The value 'buffet': example of a health and medicine accelerator program	52
4.1	Leading models of learning cycles	63
4.2	Agile view of entrepreneurial learning basics	65
4.3	The blended-value approach—bridging the principles	66
4.4	The personalized approach	69
4.5	Relations between the blended-value approach and personalized approach in edu-preneurial learning	75
5.1	Reciprocal relations of EE and attitudes	92
5.2	The EE user–client relationships	95
6.1	The digital entrepreneur—need for a changing skill set	111
6.2	New EE skills to be developed to leverage the digital content trend	114
6.3	Crowdfunding in the context of EE	120
7.1	Virtual learning perspectives—the illusion of being in a different space and time	134
7.2	Synchronous and asynchronous approaches to EL	137
7.3	Types of learning tools	139
8.1	Incubators' focus and development	148
8.2	The twofold perspective of the journey	150

8.3	Incubators' strategic connections	152
9.1	The accelerator process	171
10.1	The main factors categorizing enabling systems for entrepreneurs	184
10.2	The revolutionary evolution of enabling systems	186
11.1	A full-range ecosystem	203
11.2	Structure and processes—the ecosystem's performance	205
11.3	Banks' directions in supporting entrepreneurship	209
12.1	Conceptual organization for evaluating enabling systems	226
12.2	A 'diamond-sided' evaluation of the EE process	231
12.3	A smart-mapping skeleton	239

ACKNOWLEDGMENTS

Six years ago I founded an academic program for student entrepreneurs that I termed 'accelerator', with the vision of enabling anyone who wants to 'touch' entrepreneurship to dare, initiate, ideate and, beyond the opportunity to start a company, to gain personal encouragement and empowerment to implement any entrepreneurial dream. I believe in introducing a large scope of resources, to be rigorously transferred to the student entrepreneurs, then mobilized by them along their subsequent entrepreneurial journey. In my constant search to obtain more insight into the acceleration process and fortify the program, I have been confounded with various models, from research and practice, on entrepreneurship education (EE); some have been sporadically discovered, though worth a thorough look, others have shared similar titles (e.g., accelerator, incubator) but with different foundations. Linking my enthusiasm for deepening my knowledge with my multiple roles—teaching professor, researcher, judge of various competitions, and board member—I have been confronted with the different views held by each 'player' on EE. This book's premise lies in detecting and organizing the multiple EE programs, by developing a better understanding of the ways in which each program envisions value delivery to the learner, as well as to the various other players affected by EE; specifically, how does each program refresh their conveyance of a bundle of resources so that they can keep pace with a changing environment? This is a challenge that can only be met by touching the field. I interviewed approximately 20 founders and managing teams of various EE programs around the world, both by targeting the best-known programs, such as Y Combinator, Techstars and SOSA, and delving into the key success factors of EE; and by aiming to obtain a comprehensive scope across countries and players, such as alumni/tenants, banks, corporate companies, academia, etc., to understand the outlooks of the different players who are directly involved in EE. This was one of the most interesting journeys that I have taken, both academically and emotionally. Writing this book was made possible by the support and encouragement that I have received from so many people.

My thankful appreciation goes to Meredith Norwich, Senior Editor, Routledge, and Alston Slatton, Editorial Assistant, Routledge, Taylor & Francis, New York, for their continual support, valuable feedback, constant attention, and highly professional approach that enabled me to bring this book to its meticulous fruition. I am grateful to the amazing people in the field whom I interviewed for this book's cases studies and at-a-glance segments—the initiators, founders, managing teams, alumni, and students of various EE programs around the world. Some of them garnered remarkable achievements during this book's writing, such as Guy Franklin and his team at SOSA NYC, who were chosen by the city of New York, in October 2018, to build the city's official Global Cyber Center, and Shahar Matorin and his team at Startup Grind, who were recently informed that the Mayor of Berkeley had signed a proclamation from the city honoring their startup community. Through these interviews, my knowledge and understanding of the EE phenomenon were greatly enhanced, and I was enormously inspired by their vibrant spirit and tenacity to pursue my dream and intensify my quest to delve into the topics of EE. I feel so privileged to have met with these extremely enthusiastic, visionary and professional individuals, who add exceptional flavor to the entrepreneurial landscape.

I am grateful to the College of Management, Academic Studies (COLLMAN), Rishon Lezion, Israel, which provided me with the financial support, and the administrative and technical input for the work on which this book is based. Special thanks to my team, and especially Hila Aharoni, for their assistance in connecting the dots, and to my colleagues from around the world for providing me with constructive comments on my work. My deepest thanks and appreciation go to Professor Oren Kaplan, the president of COLLMAN, for his limitless support during my writing journey. His accuracy in the research process, his constructive observations and helpful ideas, embedding psychological aspects into the education process, have considerably deepened my reflections on the essence and dynamics of the educational process and have accelerated my pursuits in the EE field.

I would like to offer special thanks to Professor Norris Krueger for his insightful and valuable contributions to this book in writing the preface.

Last, and most importantly, to the most meaningful anchor in my life, my beloved family, Raanan, my husband, Tomer and Maayan, Ofir and Shir, my children, I send you my deepest thanks. Dear family, your absolute confidence in me, your endless encouragement of my work, and your obvious pride in my achievements are the source of my inspiration and my foundation; these are the building blocks of my drive and passion for my academic work. I am thankful to my mother, Bianca Barel, for her unflagging emotional support and faith in me and my work. I wish my father could have taken part in this moment.

I would like to express my indebtedness to Camille Vainstein for her most appreciated assistance in the copy-editing of this manuscript, and for considerably impacting and adding so much value to my writing and to the way in which I articulate my views. This is the fourth book for which Camille has accompanied me in the writing process, and I feel fortunate to be able to harmonize her language- and word-shaping capabilities with my thoughts and views, resulting in such a great finalized version of this endeavor.

Dafna Kariv

PREFACE

As someone immersed in a major EU project to build a robust, comprehensive protocol and tool kit to assess the impact of entrepreneurial training,[1] a major question is: what if we find relatively little impact in higher education programs? As an entrepreneur immersed in helping build entrepreneurial ecosystems, that community makes it clear that the best training is happening outside academe. Even within academe, their best tools have been adopted from outside sources. It was not universities *per se* who invented lean startup or design thinking, even though they might have been involved (e.g., Stanford and Berkeley convincing Steve Blank that lean startup could actually be taught within the confines of academic settings; design thinking was born partly in Stanford's own stand-alone d.school and partly in design education[2]). While the smart schools figured out the potential of such tools, they are scarce. However, the crucial point is that it is clear that the entrepreneurial community sees that academic offerings so often fall short.

Instead, the entrepreneurial community sees that the best entrepreneurial learning takes place via entities such as Techstars, Y Combinator, and the like. The sterling reputation and superior performance of Techstars and Y Combinator are testimony to their doing something right. Ventures who participate in these certainly perceive the learning as immense.

So what *is* it that they are doing right to promote great entrepreneurial learning? (And what can they do that universities often cannot?) Because of all this, it is more than timely to see work such as this one that explores multiple best practice programs to answer these questions. Dr. Kariv is herself a strong educator and has studied entrepreneurship programs around the globe. She is perfect to compare and contrast these great programs to each other, to a range of other existing programs, and to more traditional academic programs.

Rigorous research to assess entrepreneurship education has been painfully sparse (Nabi et al., 2017), but there are tantalizing hints that deep experiential learning matters, and matters greatly. Any reading of education theory can tell you that; the most important impact of any training program is to help prospective entrepreneurs move from thinking like a novice entrepreneur toward thinking like an expert entrepreneur (Krueger, 2015). Traditional behavioristic pedagogies simply do not suffice.

When we try to assess any training program, there are two ways to map the assessment tools. First, while we want to assess the outputs, those outputs may be difficult or contentious, thus we also need to look at the throughput—what are programs doing skillfully?—and the inputs. For example, Techstars and Y Combinator draw from a large pool of the very best entrepreneur prospects and deploy experienced facilitators and excellent mentors. From those inputs, it would be shocking if the results were poor. But 'results' can be in the eye of the beholder; great programs work hard at 360° evaluation.[3]

Education assessment suggests at least five categories of metrics: Behaviors (do they launch?), Knowledge (what do they know?), Skills (know how to do), Mindset (that deep cognitive change), and External Impact (do graduates impact the community?). None of these is particularly easy to measure and formal metrics are fraught with risk. One thing that the reader will enjoy in this volume is to see how these non-academic programs assess their performance. It is no secret in education that great programs in any domain work hard at rigorous assessment.

Similarly, the programs chronicled here share other key ingredients of any effective training program, such as insisting on leadership from the trainees themselves (just as any competent academic project-based learning program is largely student led, even student designed) and very deep engagement with the community. For organizations like Techstars and Y Combinator, the line between them and the community is often beyond blurry. It is not that they are immersed deeply in the community, but that they and the community are deeply co-immersed. Could this be their 'secret sauce'?

Why is all this important? There is an old expression: "you get what you measure"; the metrics that any program chooses should be influential. The programs discussed here are very much market-driven. If they do not create growth ventures, do not raise serious equity capital, etc., those metrics will make it painfully evident. However, one thing that these programs also have is the less obvious Key Performance Indicators (KPIs), such as embracing the model that most universities say they are doing: not teaching about entrepreneurship, but teaching to think and act entrepreneurially. Easy to say, hard to do. But easier to do with deep co-immersion (part 2 of their 'secret sauce'?).

Can universities learn? The short answer is yes. However, what makes these programs so effective is less easy to do in academic settings. Having great instructors/facilitators who get experiential learning at a deep level is something universities rarely have. As you read this volume, you will see example after example of how these programs do things in ways that are challenging for academic settings.

But let me close with two optimistic notes. First, if we can have brilliant entrepreneurial training in secondary, even primary schools, universities can learn from them.[4] Second, consider the still-valid maxim of venture capitalist–entrepreneur Brad Feld (2012) that to grow the ecosystem requires that everything be bottom-up, entrepreneur-led. One country that has embraced this for educational training is the Netherlands (OECD, 2018). Entities such as Startup Delta, ensuring programs such as Venture Lab (Twente, Groningen) and the Erasmus Centre, have been able to be fully co-immerse in their local entrepreneurial ecosystems and are free to do gold-standard level project-based learning. One cannot underestimate the difficulty for academic programs to do the right things in the right way. The Dutch example may be quite instructive. However, one key takeaway is that they have worked very hard to give everyone the kind of training that they get in programs like those celebrated in this much overdue volume. My colleagues in both academe and the ecosystem stand ready to help any program.

Norris Krueger, Ph.D.
Entrepreneurship Northwest

Notes

1 Evaluating Entrepreneurship Education Programs in Higher Education Consortium (EEEPHEIC, aka EPIC; http://epic.ecorys.com. Dr. Gabi Kaffka, program manager).
2 For example, the pioneering work of Andrew Penaluna and colleagues (e.g., Penaluna & Penaluna, 2015).
3 www.HEInnovate.eu
4 www.oecd.org/site/entrepreneurship360/

References

Feld, B. (2012). *Startup Communities: Building an Entrepreneurial Ecosystem in Your City*. Hoboken, NJ: John Wiley.
Krueger, N. (2015). *Entrepreneurial Education in Practice Part 1: The Entrepreneurial Mindset*. Paris, France: OECD. www.oecd.org/cfe/leed/Entrepreneurial-Education-Practice-pt1.pdf
Jones, C. (2018). *How to Teach Entrepreneurship*. Cheltenham, UK: Edward Elgar.
Nabi, G. Liñán, F., Fayolle, A. Krueger, N., & Walmsley, A. (2017). The impact of entrepreneurship education in higher education: A systematic review and research agenda. *Academy of Management Learning & Education, 16*(2), 277–299.
OECD/EU (2018). *Supporting Entrepreneurship and Innovation in Higher Education in The Netherlands*, OECD Skills Studies. Paris, France: OECD.
Penaluna, A., & Penaluna, K. (2015). *Entrepreneurial Education in Practice Part 2: Building Motivations & Competencies*. Paris, France: OECD. www.oecd.org/cfe/leed/Entrepreneurial-Education-Practice-pt2.pdf

INTRODUCTION

In entrepreneurship, rapid, dynamic realities frequently develop and breed extensively, while research and practicalities lag behind. The first US startup incubator, the Batavia Industrial Center in New York, opened in 1959, to provide support to early-stage companies under one roof. However, the associated concept of 'sharing' was only embraced in the late 1970s, followed by the rapid and intensified emergence of startup incubators across the US in the 1980s, accompanied by a shift to seeking innovation and disrupting the global economy. It was only in 1985 that the first academic papers on incubators were published in academic journals, defining them as 'a facility', 'a collective and temporary place for accommodating companies', or a place to 'leverage entrepreneurial talent'. Incubators have since moved beyond their massive proliferation stage into new, agile, well-matched, bottom-up-driven models, which have evolved to provide a set of responses, although not necessarily solutions, for a real need.

About 60 years have passed since the incubator's inception, and while most of the key ingredients still seem to be necessary for successful incubation—mentoring, engagement with local entrepreneurs, networking, among others—and the realm of incubators and other support systems has matured, systematic assessments and theory building around this phenomenon are limited and mostly localized, that is, descriptions of individual experiences. The 60-year evolution in the vision, activity and models of 'incubators' is critically important to the message that incubators are required for entrepreneurial businesses progress; at the same time, a phenomenon cannot sustain itself or grow while being dependent on a single part, that is, the entrepreneurial business; its growth to other countries and in new directions proves that the ecosystem finds value in it, and thus supports it (Albert, 1986; Allen & McCluskey, 1991; Allen & Rahman, 1985; Plosila & Allen, 1985; Smilor & Gill, 1986).

It is surprising that such a gap exists between the 'incubation' phenomenon and research, specifically with respect to the holistic perspective, which leaves this research area sparse, and hinders a delineation of the reciprocal roles, that is, the value delivered and the impact of incubators on entrepreneurial companies and vice versa. Furthermore, keeping abreast of the changes in this realm, as presented above, that is, the new, more complex models of 'incubators' and the compounded effects on entrepreneurial companies, requires comprehensive academic and practical attention.

One of the most salient gaps between the incubation phenomenon and research is in establishing a *name* or an accepted *term* for the phenomenon. Incubators, presumably the pioneering 'facility' for entrepreneurial businesses, have become only one part of this realm, while the next generations of incubators are bourgeoning: accelerators, open innovation platforms (OIPs), co-working spaces, innovation factories, and venture builders, among others, hold different names and draw on much more elaborate conceptual backbones. Hence, terming the whole phenomenon as an 'incubation process' is not suitable, as it is biased toward a specific model. Moreover, the predominant research in this area defines incubators as a process, rather than a facility, emphasizing the creation of value; this was not the focus of previous research in this area. The transfer from the concept of 'facility', providing mere physical and financial resource support, to models with a focus on a broad range of intangible high-value offerings, followed by a more recent shift that touches upon knowledge-intensive business services, almost entirely abandoning the original services upon which the incubation models were founded, clearly confirms the need to create a new term which will include the different systems and programs. The emergence of accelerators stimulated the nexus to education research, mainly as accelerators are considered providers of intangible services, such as mentoring, education and networking, focused on intense interactions, monitoring and education to enable rapid progress, including continued education beyond a limited time, or cohort-based program. Research into the entrepreneurship–education link has brought about astute insights and new directions in the heuristic enquiry of incubation and acceleration processes, along with a new term for the phenomenon: entrepreneurial education (EE) programs. This term may correct the error of using 'incubators' as a generic term, yet it limits the search to 'education' and 'programs', while the phenomenon is larger, and includes various systems that converge to support entrepreneurship in many ways, delivering value to entrepreneurs and to the ecosystem (Bruneel, Ratinho, Clarysse, & Groen, 2012; Clarysse & Bruneel, 2007; Cohen & Hochberg, 2014; Grimaldi & Grandi, 2005; Isabelle, 2013; Soetanto & Jack, 2013; Wise & Valliere, 2014).

This book aims to complement the budding research and accumulated knowledge on EE programs, and to introduce a term: enabling systems, and a smart mapping outline (introduced in Chapter 12), to urge a rigorous, but also agile, pursuit of the continually emerging systems for entrepreneurial companies.

Academic research in this area is still embryonic and focused mainly on systems based in the US, while recent reports[1] on the number of accelerators[2] worldwide show that more than 3,700 accelerators are located in Europe, around 1,800 in Latin America, around 1,400 in Asia, and approximately 1,200 in the Middle East and Africa, compared to 3,300 in the US and Canada. Hence, it seems imperative to gain a wider perspective on this phenomenon.

This book draws on the theoretical foundation of entrepreneurship, basing its insights on the conceptual models of the resource-based view and the dynamic capabilities model. To capture the new directions and evolution of the phenomenon of 'incubators' toward the shift to 'enabling systems', it introduces a case study for each of the topics debated in the chapters. To build the rationale for the new term—enabling systems—and an outline to chase down research and practice in this abundant area, the term 'smart map' will be introduced first, to encapsulate the various systems, for example, incubators, accelerators, virtual communities, innovation factories, as EE programs; in the final chapter, the term 'enabling systems' will be introduced.

The case studies presented in each chapter are based on interviews that were personally conducted by the author, with players who are directly related to EE programs. The interview with Shahar Matorin, the founder of the Israeli chapter of *Startup Grind*, a global startup community powered by Google for Entrepreneurs and connecting networks of vibrant startup communities to educate, inspire and fuel innovation at the local level, is presented in Chapter 1, which discusses the reciprocal roles of entrepreneurial business success and development of EE programs, and takes an international look at the ecosystem, introduced innovation, and dynamic trends. The quest for what education entails for entrepreneurs, presented in Chapter 2, is complemented by a case study on an innovative, *artist-centric graduate degree program*[3] for cultural entrepreneurs, attesting to the need for innovative, creative and artistic ways to achieve experiential learning, by seizing the founder's views on the center's mission and activities, and the alumnus entrepreneurs' approaches to the learning gained. *NOVUS* is an academic center of entrepreneurship located in an academic institution in Israel; a founder's view and a mentor's view are presented to exemplify 'meaningful learning' and its content and structural constituents—the *'what'*, *'why'* and *'how'*—discussed in Chapter 3. Chapter 4 explores the underlying conception is that there is no 'one size fits all' in educating entrepreneurs; the accompanying case study is of a *venture builder*, located in Hangzhou, China. The founder, Xiabo Zhōngháng, and Canadian angel investor, Pierre Leblanc, demonstrate an innovative education model, developed through an entrepreneurial journey, and complementing the edu-preneurial approach introduced in the chapter. This is followed, in Chapter 5, by an intriguing interview with Dr. Tim Peck, MD, the co-founder and CEO of *Call9*, and alumnus of *Y Combinator (YC)*, the first and a leading accelerator in the US and, presumably, worldwide. Gaining insights from the co-founder of a successful business who attributes much of his business's success and his entrepreneurial mindset to his time at YC is of significant value; YC's approach of addressing the individual, the entrepreneur, by offering a smart, personalized program that enables the individual, the tenant, to choose from the proposed deliveries, underpins the ideas discussed in Chapter 5, of paying more attention to the learners' specific personality traits and their personal styles of absorbing knowledge, as well as to the necessity of developing entrepreneurs in a context and ecosystem that direct them to success. The co-working space *entrePrism*, located in Montreal, Canada, is presented in Chapter 6 through the eyes of its two co-founders, along with some insights from alumni, demonstrating the significance of shared space and shared content in delivering value, expanding connections and unleashing creativity. The uniqueness of entrePrism in supporting entrepreneurs from all backgrounds, with a particular focus on immigrants in the Quebec business ecosystem, fortifies the conceptual premise of a shared economy, by embracing diversity and inclusion. Chapter 7 debates on innovative ways to educate entrepreneurs by introducing a parallel journey—education/ learning and entrepreneurial—to a more fine-tuned preparation for the entrepreneurial world; the case study on the *INNOVATING* acceleration program, located in Germany, complements the discussion in Chapter 7 on innovative tools, use of new technologies, and interesting ways to connect with the ecosystem. Chapter 8 is focused on incubators, and discusses the evolution of their models with time, supported by the case study of *Neotec HUB*, in Kolkata, India, presented through the eyes of Sanjay Sarda, the director of this incubator. The renowned and leading accelerator *Techstars* is presented in Chapter 9, through an interview with its co-founder, David Brown, who shares the fundamental ideas and building blocks from which Techstars originated and how it has educated a market and delivered value to and from its expanded network. Feedback from alumni who have participated in the program complete the case study, giving a two-sided perspective of the new paths of acceleration activity presented in that chapter. Chapter 10 probes the various enabling platforms, collecting insights from various sources on OIPs, individuals' personalized platforms, innovation factories, venture builders, startup factories, impact hubs, startup studios, venture labs, co-labs, and boot camps. These are exemplified by the case study of *SOSA*, located in New York City, one of the leading places for entrepreneurs; this is an OIP that 'matches' innovation 'from outside' the corporation through the startups' capacity for creating valuable innovation. The unique concept, along with a disruptive implementation that has gathered a substantial ecosystem around it, evidences the significance of new enabling platforms in the entrepreneurial landscape. To delve into the role of the environment through the eyes of the various collaborators, financial institutions, banks, public sector, private sector, international bodies, communities and cities, among others, in Chapter 11, the case of J. P. Morgan's In-Residence startup program in its New York City office is presented, demonstrating the views of financial strategic collaborators in developing innovation and entrepreneurship. Chapter 12 concludes with the case of an internationally based accelerator program, opened in Beijing with the support of the Israeli government, and introduces and discusses enabling systems and smart mapping.

Rich, empirical coverage of the most up-to-date enabling systems can expand our insights into entrepreneurial-enabling systems across different countries, for different verticals and sectors, capturing various companies at different stages of development, and introducing innovative, disruptive contents, tools, and technological platforms, supported by a fertile ecosystem.

At-a-glance cases are presented in some chapters to complement the discussed topics with real-life illustrations. Finally, to produce more value, each chapter includes 'takeaways' for the various players: EE program developers, entrepreneurs looking for a place to enroll, and tenant entrepreneurs, among others. The chapters conclude with five contemplative case study questions to allow the readers to reflect on the chapters' models and concepts through the case study's dynamics; these are followed by five reflective questions that harmonize with the chapter's topics, while requiring creative, independent thinking, to pave the readers' way to embedding the insights into their own entrepreneurial action.

Notes

1 See at: http://gust.com/accelerator_reports/2016/global/
2 Information provided on accelerators only, hence, there may be more 'enabling systems' such as OIPs, innovation factories, corporate programs for entrepreneurship, and more, that are not included in these numbers.
3 This is the only case study in this book that was developed without any personal interview by me of the program's stakeholders.

References

Albert, P. (1986). Enterprise incubators–An initial diagnosis. *Revue Francaise de Gestion*, Sept–Oct, 27–30.

Allen, D. N., & McCluskey, R. (1991). Structure, policy, services, and performance in the business incubator industry. *Entrepreneurship Theory and Practice*, 15(2), 61–77.

Allen, D. N., & Rahman, S. (1985). Small business incubators: a positive environment for entrepreneurship. *Journal of Small Business Management* (Pre-1986), 23(000003), 12.

Bruneel, J., Ratinho, T., Clarysse, B., & Groen, A. (2012). The evolution of business incubators: Comparing demand and supply of business incubation services across different incubator generations. *Technovation*, 32(2), 110–121.

Clarysse, B., & Bruneel, J. (2007). Nurturing and growing innovative start-ups: The role of policy as integrator. *R&D Management*, 37(2), 139–149.

Cohen, S., & Hochberg, Y. V. (2014). Accelerating startups: The seed accelerator phenomenon. *SSRN Electronic Journal*. https://doi.org/10.2139/ssrn.2418000

Grimaldi, R., & Grandi, A. (2005). Business incubators and new venture creation: An assessment of incubating models. *Technovation*, 25(2), 111–121.

Isabelle, D. A. (2013). Key factors affecting a technology entrepreneur's choice of incubator or accelerator. *Technology Innovation Management Review*, 3(2), 16–22.

Plosila, W. H., & Allen, D. N. (1985). Small business incubators and public policy: Implications for state and local development strategies. *Policy Studies Journal, 13*(4), 729–734.

Smilor, R. W., & Gill, M. D. (1986). *The New Business Incubator: Linking Talent, Technology, Capital, and Know-How.* Lexington, MA: Lexington Books.

Soetanto, D. P., & Jack, S. L. (2013). Business incubators and the networks of technology-based firms. *Journal of Technology Transfer, 38*(4), 432–453.

Wise, S., & Valliere, D. (2014). The impact on management experience on the performance of start-ups within accelerators. *Journal of Private Equity*, 9–19.

1
A CONTEXTUAL OVERVIEW OF ENTREPRENEURSHIP EDUCATION PROGRAMS

Incubators, accelerators, academic programs, boot camps, co-working spaces, corporate-based innovation centers, impact hubs, scaling accelerators, startup factories, venture builders, startup studios, venture labs, government programs—these are just some of the programs designed for adult entrepreneurs. The burgeoning interest in, and proliferation of, the number of programs for entrepreneurs validate the importance of education for the success of existing and potential entrepreneurs (Matlay, 2006; Politis, 2005).

The more programs that are offered, the less their natural audience and stakeholders know about what they offer and their competitive advantages or distinguishing features compared to all other programs. The programs are diverse, emerging from different bodies (private, governmental, local, national), and stem from different goals and interests. The hidden promise that such programs will 'create' the most successful entrepreneurs captivates the entrepreneur, who may choose any one program at random, even if it is not best suited to his/her needs or expectations. Thus, despite the presumed benefits, the proliferation of such programs may, in fact, be counterproductive. In reality, the multiplicity of programs has attracted its share of criticism, given the dearth of research scrutinizing their goals, structures, delivery, teachers, content, etc.

Programs for entrepreneurs have thrived in the past decade within the intertwined contexts of entrepreneurship–education–environment (ecosystem). Three main insights have been linked to their proliferation: (a) research in the broad field of EE has flourished; (b) the role and impact of entrepreneurship have intensified at both the macro and micro levels; (c) in practice, EE has not undergone the anticipated significant changes, while the entrepreneurship and education fields have matured and have undergone such changes (Covin, Green, & Slevin, 2006; Kuratko, 2005; Mintzberg, 2004).

The vast interest in EE goes beyond special issues in leading academic conferences or the development of flagship academic programs to educate entrepreneurs. The World Bank[1] has dedicated funds to thoroughly investigate the dimensions of EE the world over; the European Commission has devoted funds to this area of investigation as well, and is calling for research and practice to contribute to EE, training and teaching[2]; global companies are subsidizing and implementing entrepreneurship programs. According to the Global Accelerator Report 2015 (Brunet, Grof, & Izquierdo, 2016), the accelerator industry has undergone vast development worldwide: in the US, there are 2522 accelerators, 1124 in the UK, 568 in India and 430 in Israel, together with a total amount invested worldwide of almost US $200,000,00.[3] The same exponential growth trends emerge from a report on incubators[4] that delineates their role in providing better value for the ecosystem and startups.

Turning to a test case, WeWork, a co-working space for entrepreneurs, has raised $969 million in funding at a $10 billion valuation, and it is the 11th most valuable startup in the world;[5] it is growing exponentially, expanding to various locations worldwide. Its goal is to provide co-working spaces, community and services by enabling the startups that are working under the same roof to become reciprocal service providers and eventually create a community. Entrepreneurs benefit from the shared space, which allows them to learn, adapt and adjust their ideas and operation through their community's service, feedback, networks, assistance, and more. Drawing on the concept of a venue to support entrepreneurs, different co-working spaces have arisen for craftsmen, artists and the culinary field, confirming the influence of such programs on a growing array of stakeholders. WeWork is mentioned here as an example of a co-working space that can be regarded as a revolutionary concept for entrepreneurial learning, as entrepreneurs can proactively satisfy their most immediate needs by sharing, collaborating, partnering and establishing mentorships, mainly informally through practical trial and error experience, rather than traditional education. This is a personalized concept that is catching on worldwide.

RockaLabs[6] from Colombia is another leading edge, innovative concept for entrepreneurs—the venture builder. The vision behind this concept lies in developing businesses through a combination of startup development, shared resources and other integrative processes, including design, development of a customer base, business development and market research, among others. At RockaLabs, the approach draws on the shared operation of the most talented experts in different areas of the entrepreneurial businesses' stages of development: from finding opportunities, resources and prototyping, to ideation, analysis, production and growth. Khan Academy[7] is another enabling program for people who wish to gain and exercise knowledge. It was not meant for entrepreneurs at the outset, but as a complete learning dashboard to guide students through courses on a wide variety of topics. However, it inspired the development of a personalized learning dashboard that enables entrepreneurs to gain knowledge relevant to their needs at their own pace, including virtually in 'international classrooms', thereby benefiting from international networks.

These examples reflect the desire for a platform that offers innovative enablers for entrepreneurs to operate, share, learn, gain relevant knowledge, expand networks, and much more. However, there is a real lack of smart lists, reports and meticulous research on the variety of programs for entrepreneurs. The aforementioned reports on accelerators and incubators touch upon only a fragment of the widespread realm of 'bodies' aimed at bringing customized value to entrepreneurs, their businesses and their ecosystem, via innovative, more personalized programs.

Education through an Entrepreneurial and Contextual Framework

AT-A-GLANCE

Spending time in a graduate student exchange program in Europe, Reach and Montha, two Cambodian school teachers, figured out that 'creativity' is differently interpreted in Cambodia, Taiwan and Thailand, where they spent most of their lives, as compared to France and the Netherlands, where they have been staying for the exchange programs. They are in the midst of developing a program aimed at introducing creativity to entrepreneurial businesses by involving experienced business people virtually, in a cross-cultural way. Their first pilot has been enthusiastically received by a 'pair' who have been virtually matched to induce more creativity in their startup. The founding team from Cambodia, developing a real-time data analysis platform, in a very early stage, were paired with Jean-Claude, the head of the innovation department at an international high-tech company in France. Jean-Claude and his team worked with the founders to grasp the idea's cutting-edge market opportunities. Reach and Montha are now developing teaching material to allow the startups that have gone through the pairing process to document and make use of their virtual creativity mentoring.

Food for thought:

What are the main challenges that 'international' programs such as this may encounter?

Ecosystem—Entrepreneurship is nurtured in, and fueled by, its ecosystem. Entrepreneurship evolves in a context, and is consequently shaped by the mindsets, habits, perceptions, interests, exchanges, collaborations and strategies sought to introduce sustainable value with its shareholders. Therefore, EE is affected by, and simultaneously affects, not only the participants of the programs, but also the community, sector, industry, suppliers, and potential or existing customers and investors, among others.

An international outlook—A global view of education and learning has continually been considered a leading subject of research in affecting individual knowledge, attitudes and performance, among others (Hunter-Jones, 2012; Jonsson & Rudolphi, 2011; Ogbu, 1992); on the other hand, within the research on EE, emphasis has been devoted to specific topics, such as opportunity exploitation and entrepreneurial-related capabilities (Rae, 2007), covered by programs devoted to entrepreneurs. Because entrepreneurship and education both occur in their respective contexts, it seems natural to enquire into EE within a context. Kolb's (1984) leading model stresses that learning requires a transformation of experiences into a process that brings meaning to the experiences through a process of learning assimilation. This is a process of making sense of the material and practices offered in the programs. Thoroughly understanding EE requires broadening the research scope to cultural, regional and national aspects (Holcomb, Holmes Jr., & Connelly, 2009). Cultural and national differences may be reflected in various dimensions, for example, cross-cultural differences in proneness to entrepreneurship, approaches to competitive issues, core competencies, resource exploitation, strategic and financial aspects of the business, the starting points of new venture creation, as well as objective measures such as political aspects, legal systems, regulatory matters, market dynamics, viability of capital markets and availability of institutional funds. This book aims to embrace the effects of the environment and the ecosystem and illuminate the diversity of the entrepreneurship programs' processes in different countries. The conducted interviews that are presented as case studies will illustrate a large scope of programs across countries.

Innovation—While EE is attracting a great deal of attention, there is still a dearth of integrated knowledge in this field, which is both well-established in research and reflects the national and cultural effects of EE on adult entrepreneurs. The promise of entrepreneurship is more than developing technological gadgets; it encapsulates practical, innovative responses to obstacles through fresh thinking, new technology, and a blend of existing models and mindsets for a new product or service.

Social and economic stimuli—The education–industry–government relationship holds the key to the development of knowledge-based societies, by dynamically allocating knowledge and non-academic life skills and capabilities to peripheral enclaves. As such, EE programs that are properly linked to social and economic needs, contribute to, and can be enhanced by, each segment: education, industry and government. Social and economic stimuli are also imperative to improving the organizational arrangements and incentives that foster innovation.

Content and trends—EE can be encapsulated in terms of whether it is aimed *for* entrepreneurship or *about* entrepreneurship, resonating the educational trends, but, more broadly, the general social and generational trends. The 'for' orientation takes an activity-based perspective to learning, and therefore delivers practices that are useful for the business creation stages and processes, which can then be implemented by the learners; it can emphasize capabilities and mindsets, and coach actual practices and actions. The 'about' perspective uses the infrastructure of knowledge, inspiration, successful entrepreneurial experiences, renowned achievements and well-established models, for example (Fiet, 2001a, 2001b; Gibb, 2002; Harmeling & Sarasvathy, 2013; Levie, 1999; Neck & Greene, 2011).

The Whole-person Pedagogy

This holistic view addresses the role of education for entrepreneurs by looking concurrently at individuals' entrepreneurial capabilities over time and their evolution, that is, past, present and potential, and through spheres, for example, emotional, behavioral, cognitive, professional. The pedagogy is regarded as the core of experiential learning (Hoover, 1974), involving "learning of a unified sort, at the cognitive, feeling and gut levels, with a clear awareness of the different aspects of this unified learning" (Rogers, 1995).

Past experience and accumulated knowledge, along with concurrent main activities and future ambitions and vision (potentiality) are interpreted through a holistic view, encompassing emotion, behavior, cognition and other domains. Similar to Bernd Schmitt's (2011) model of Sense, Feel, Think, Act, React, this holistic approach looks at ways to create the full entrepreneurial and educational experience by employing a combined sensory, affective, and creative approach. As shown in Figure 1.1, education can be customized by constructing content, method or engagement through the learners' relevant characteristics.

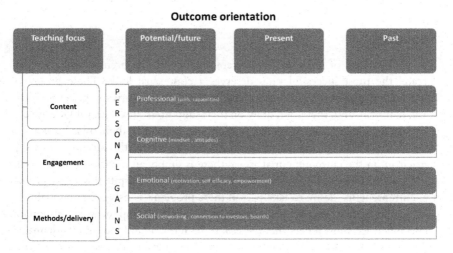

FIGURE 1.1 The whole-person pedagogy

The techniques used in this approach are aimed at creating high-involvement learning, including skill practice, learning by doing, and learning by observing, to enable the learners to gain capabilities related to team building and management, leadership, group facilitation and ethical decision-making, among others, or, as Lengnick-Hall and Sanders (1997) noted, "To create a high-involvement learning system, student coproducers can be provided with information, knowledge, power, and rewards that enable them to more effectively manage learning transformations" (Lengnick-Hall & Sanders, 1997: 1339).

The whole-person pedagogy enables students to interpret, integrate and make sense of their educational experience. Unlike the more connectional pedagogy, the holistic view touches different senses, and is, therefore, expected to be pertinent for a large scope of entrepreneurial students, for example, covering a range of demographic characteristics, experiences, business industry or level of development of the business idea. In a business context, this pedagogy is associated with the attainment of leadership, entrepreneurial abilities and relevant capabilities that will play an important role in the learner's future success (Boyatzis, Stubbs, & Taylor, 2002; Doh, 2003; Eriksen, 2009; Hoover, Giambatista, Sorenson, & Bommer, 2010; Motschnig-Pitrik & Mallich, 2004; Waddock, 2007; Waddock & Lozano, 2013; Yorks & Kasl, 2002). Its relevance to entrepreneurship is, therefore, evident; it postulates sequential learning processes that are based on the installed infrastructure, for example, content, practices, settings, but adds engagement by enabling the learners to translate their learning outcomes in their own ways and at their own pace, thus providing them with a sustainable format for EE. Entrepreneurs are recognized as independent, free-spirited, self-regulating personalities, who start their businesses through their own ideas and dreams, which they deem feasible and valuable. As such, a pedagogy that respects their personality traits is expected to be more appropriate to their needs.

Summary

The proliferation of programs for entrepreneurs with the premise that they can 'create' the most successful ones deserves a contextual look. These programs are diverse, supported and promoted by different bodies (private, governmental, local, national), and, therefore, draw on their supporters' interests. Obviously, the developed programs aim to enable entrepreneurs to start their own businesses. There is no formal guarantee of the imminent success of the business or of the participant in the entrepreneurial arena; there is simply an indication of the tools and strategies that can be acquired from these programs. Despite this vague promise, entrepreneurs' desire to take part in these programs is rising exponentially.

To capture the contextual framework of EE, several components are important to decipher. EE must reflect the *ecosystem* to be relevant and introduce sustainable value to its stakeholders. An *international outlook* is crucial to EE; because entrepreneurship occurs in a context, and education occurs in a context, EE is the result of a context; hence, to release EE from its local context, it has to broaden its practical and research scopes to cultural, regional and national aspects. Entrepreneurship is the backbone of the disruption that forms a new solution, idea or even situations or processes. Hence, *innovation* should be a leading principle in EE, to be mirrored within the program's structures and content, while the entrepreneurs' and stakeholders' expectations and agendas are matched. *Social and economic stimuli* reciprocally form EE but also change through EE outcomes; while social and economic needs or hardships enhance the creation of programs that can provide innovative solutions; these needs are then affected by the solutions developed through EE— they may diminish or be altered, or new and unexpected needs may evolve from the solutions. The triple relationship of education–industry–government enables EE to develop in ways that can be most relevant to entrepreneurs and their ecosystems; moreover, the dissemination of information by each of these parts can create a stronger impact of EE. Finally, *content and trends* look at the different ways in which people learn and study, with an eye on the trends in the field and in education; for example, teaching innovation through traditional structures can be bewildering, as participants might be confused by the presented teaching model; 'teach what you preach' is the ground rule. Whole-person pedagogy adds to the contextual understanding by accounting for the person's experience in interpreting, integrating and being compatible with the processes and educational experience, by touching different senses in the learner.

Takeaways

For educators and teaching developers:

- EE requires a familiarization with the ecosystem to develop the most compatible programs.
- The aspects of the field (e.g., social entrepreneurship, health-related entrepreneurship, finance-related entrepreneurship) should be thoroughly studied, as should their global distinctions.
- EE programs should touch as many stakeholders as possible to be relevant, supported and disseminated.

For EE participants:

- The emergence of EE programs for entrepreneurs affords a larger array of choices; it is imperative to find the best match, not necessarily the most popular or branded program.
- EE should provide sustainable value; it should be relevant to your needs and expectations, and meet the program's stated guarantee.
- Refer to 'whole-person pedagogy' to gain more insights on the personal experience that you can expect from the EE process.

- A global perspective of the EE program is imperative, regardless of the business or idea's orientation; even local ideas may evolve into international or global ones.

Case Study 1 – Innovation and Education: The Startup Grind Worldwide Community

Shahar Matorin,[8] Israel Country Manager and Tel Aviv Director at Startup Grind Inc. says that when you look around at the Startup Grind conference, and see 300 speakers and so many entrepreneurs gathered, talking to each other, creating friendships, telling you about the huge impact the Startup Grind community provides personally and to their peer entrepreneurs, this is a mind-blowing moment.

Startup Grind is operated in 450 cities in 120 countries, with 5200 volunteers, and 1,500,000 members and attendees at 6500 monthly events around the world since 2010. Startup Grind[9] is the largest and most impactful independent startup community, dedicated to its vision of reaching any entrepreneur, worldwide, to benefit from its global community, intertwined with its triple mission to: educate – by delivering authentic content; inspire—by engaging entrepreneurs personally and emotionally, through the introduction of a personal look at the startup journey, and allowing a 'behind the scenes' perspective, driven by a founder-to-founder method; and connect—locally and globally, to hasten the learning and consequent entrepreneurial success. Matorin says,

> As an entrepreneur, you frequently experience loneliness; contacts are sporadic and short-term; yet, we figured out that by motivating entrepreneurs to get together, 'under one roof', their presence together stimulates friendship, and the loneliness is mitigated. Then, giving, sharing, helping, all naturally spring from entrepreneurs. Hence, we have agreed on the following values: give first – take less; we therefore do not encourage pitch meetings or 'business card' encounters, rather, we commit to the authentic 'look at each other' approach, which stimulates reciprocal help; make friends not just contacts—targeting long-term relationships; and help others as a leading motif, even prior to helping yourself, to create deep links. The idea is to educate entrepreneurs, by delivering authenticity, through stories on entrepreneurs' journeys. Our blog encompasses the documentation and valuable storage of founders' narratives from entrepreneurs.

A TED talk-based format enabled Startup Grind to share the inspirational videos with a large audience, from Silicon Valley throughout the world to Japan. Powered by partnerships with organizations such as Google for Entrepreneurs, the yearly global conferences are of immense value; speakers[10] such as Michael Seibel, CEO, partner of Y Combinator; Joe Gebbia, co-founder, CPO at Airbnb; Reid Hoffman, co-founder, partner at LinkedIn and Greylock Partners; Aaron

Levie, co-founder, CEO at Box, among others, discuss lessons learned and share their genuine stories, prior to their vast successes, to prove that entrepreneurship is a way of life, a mindset, a passion. Startups accepted to the global conference enjoy the exposure of their company's demo to a large scope of investors and potential customers. Backed by its vision to engage any entrepreneur in the world to the Startup Grind community and values, local monthly events have been held in central cities worldwide; as a forceful platform to make connections, these events have gradually attracted local entrepreneurs to join Startup Grind, as well as partners such as Google, Oracle, Intuit, and Silicon Valley Bank that consider the community to be a resourceful source to meet entrepreneurs, 'touch' the trends, and use Startup Grind's values to bridge their companies to the emerging, entrepreneurial scene.

Research shows that innovation in educating entrepreneurs globally is taking many directions, although all are grounded in the dual educational approach for the new generation of entrepreneurs: to attain practical deliveries and to have their 'space' to use those deliveries in their own time, and at their own pace and business stage. Conservative education combines practical deliveries with operating instructions, which are less relevant to today's entrepreneurs' needs. The education introduced by Startup Grind relies on the premise of educating through inspiration from authentic stories, and engaging through values and missions. New generations are learning through their emotional attachment to the content. Moreover, EE scholars stress that both emotional and experiential events are effective in entrepreneurship learning; values that tap into the emotional aspects of learning are holding a more and more explicit place in learning and teaching; the OECD report, 2015[11] addresses emotions as key components in the learning experience, by "using emotional and critical learning events as a link between educational design and developed entrepreneurial competencies . . . yielded some insights into the 'black box' of entrepreneurial learning in education" (p. 20). Startup Grind thus presents an interesting, up-to-date, innovative form of education (Cope, 2003; Rae, 2005). The global proliferation of Startup Grind's communities has been swift and gigantic. By reaching 1.5M entrepreneurs involved in Startup Grind in central cities around the world, and fueled by the proven concepts that education and globalization are critical key success factors for entrepreneurs, Matorin describes,

> the Startup Grind initiated two programs aimed at bridging local to global, through SGx for smaller, peripheral cities of less than 300,000 residents, designed to build an active, local startup community, that can either reinforce or set in motion a regional, entrepreneurial culture, and act as a channel to grasp the global Startup Grind community, thus enabling smaller cities to scale up their entrepreneurial presence; and SGu, attracting universities to spark their entrepreneurial communities by engaging founders of entrepreneurial companies to share their stories at monthly events.

16 Entrepreneurship Education Programs

Recently, Jesse Arreguín, Mayor of Berkeley, signed a proclamation from the city in honor of Startup Grind,[12] recognizing its chapter in that city.

Questions on the Case Study

1. What are the 3–4 main characteristics that turn Startup Grind into an educational enabling program for entrepreneurs? In your opinion, is it a learning experience? Explain.
2. Search for 2–3 stories in the Startup Grind blog, at: /www.startupgrind.com/blog/category/stories/, and write down the names and web addresses (for the stories on the blog). Identify the three main educational-based characteristics of the stories. What is your conclusion on the educational contribution of the authentic stories approach? Explain.
3. Search for five communities for entrepreneurs, such as: Google for Entrepreneurs, LinkedIn, Biznik (http://biznik.com/about/), The Funded (http://thefunded.com/), and more. Write down their names and website addresses. List the three main values/missions delivered by each. What is your main conclusion about communities as an innovative, up-to-date educational enabler? Explain your response.
4. In your opinion, and based on your search in question 3, how did Startup Grind attract such a vast number of entrepreneurs to its community? Also address Berkeley's recognition of Startup Grind. What are the values delivered by Startup Grind, and for which ecosystem players?
5. Suppose an association is asking your advice on starting a community for entrepreneurs in your home town. What are the five main questions that you would ask them about their mission, to gain information and plan the community? Explain your answer.

Reflective Questions

1. Look for one center for entrepreneurs in Europe and another one in Asia, and provide their names and web addresses. Identify 2–3 similarities and 2–3 differences in these centers' approaches to: *ecosystem* and *international outlook*. What are your main conclusions?
2. A governmental association asks for your advice in promoting a new center of entrepreneurship that has been active for five months but has still not attracted entrepreneurs. Based on the chapter's content, list the five main questions you would ask the association, in order to provide them with the most appropriate counsel.
3. A woman entrepreneur who has developed an idea to purify water using solar energy wishes to choose an EE program. Based on the chapter's main ideas, write three criteria that you would advise her to consider prior to choosing a program. Explain the relevance of the criteria for this entrepreneur.

Entrepreneurship Education Programs 17

4. Search the internet for a university in Africa that has opened a center for entrepreneurship and write down its name and web address. Describe its goals, vision, audience and structure. List its main strengths as related to Africa's unique challenges; explain why you consider them strengths.
5. Watch 'New opportunities for young Entrepreneurs in Zimbabwe www.youtube.com/watch?v=aZKHGgCPHWk. Through the Zimbabwe:Works initiative, Christine learned critical life skills and practical work training, and had the opportunity to get a loan to expand her business. Watch how this initiative is creating new opportunities for youth in Zimbabwe. Address the 'whole-person pedagogy' with respect to the interviewer's description of the development through the Zimbabwe:Works program. Explain your response.

Notes

1 See at: https://openknowledge.worldbank.org/bitstream/handle/10986/18031/9781464802027.pdf
2 See at: http://ec.europa.eu/index_en.htm
3 See at: http://gust.com/global-accelerator-report-2015/
4 See at: http://ubi-global.com/research/ranking/rankings-2015/
5 See at: "How WeWork became the most valuable startup in New York City", Maya Kosoff, Oct. 22, 2015, 12:25 PM. www.businessinsider.com/the-founding-story-of-wework-2015-10
6 See at: http://rockalabs.com/index.html#/home
7 See at: https://www.khanacademy.org/
8 Personal and telephone meetings and interviews with me.
9 See at: https://www.startupgrind.com/
10 See at: https://www.startupgrind.com/conference/
11 Lackéus, M. 2015, Entrepreneurship in Education. OECD. See at: https://www.oecd.org/cfe/leed/BGP_Entrepreneurship-in-Education.pdf
12 See at: file:///C:/Users/user/Downloads/9.25.18%20Startup%20Grind%20(1).pdf

References

Boyatzis, R. E., Stubbs, E. C., & Taylor, S. N. (2002). Learning cognitive and emotional intelligence competencies through graduate management education. *Academy of Management Learning & Education*, *1*(2), 150–162. https://doi.org/10.5465/amle.2002.8509345

Brunet, S., Grof, M., & Izquierdo, D. (2016). *Global Accelerator Report 2015.* Retrieved from http://gust.com/global-accelerator-report-2015/

Cope, J. (2003). Entrepreneurial learning and critical reflection. *Management Learning*, *34*(4), 429–450. https://doi.org/10.1177/1350507603039067

Covin, J. G., Green, K. M., & Slevin, D. P. (2006). Strategic process effects on the entrepreneurial orientation–sales growth rate relationship. *Entrepreneurship Theory and Practice*, *30*(1), 57–81. https://doi.org/10.1111/j.1540-6520.2006.00110.x

Doh, J. P. (2003). Can leadership be taught? Perspectives from management educators. *Academy of Management Learning & Education*, *2*(1), 54–67. https://doi.org/10.5465/amle.2003.9324025

Eriksen, M. (2009). Authentic leadership. *Journal of Management Education, 33*(6), 747–771. https://doi.org/10.1177/1052562909339307

Fiet, J. O. (2001a). The pedagogical side of entrepreneurship theory. *Journal of Business Venturing, 16*(2), 101–117. https://doi.org/10.1016/S0883-9026(99)00042-7

Fiet, J. O. (2001b). The theoretical side of teaching entrepreneurship. *Journal of Business Venturing, 16*(1), 1–24. https://doi.org/10.1016/S0883-9026(99)00041-5

Gibb, A. (2002). Creating conducive environments for learning and entrepreneurship. *Industry and Higher Education, 16*(3), 135–148. https://doi.org/10.5367/000000002101296234

Harmeling, S. S., & Sarasvathy, S. D. (2013). When contingency is a resource: educating entrepreneurs in the Balkans, the Bronx, and beyond. *Entrepreneurship Theory and Practice, 37*(4), 713–744. https://doi.org/10.1111/j.1540-6520.2011.00489.x

Holcomb, T. R., Holmes Jr., R. M., & Connelly, B. L. (2009). Making the most of what you have: Managerial ability as a source of resource value creation. *Strategic Management Journal, 30*(5), 457–485. https://doi.org/10.1002/smj.747

Hoover, J. D. (1974). Experiential learning: conceptualization and definition. In J. Kenderdine & B. Keys (Eds.), *Simulations, Games and Experiential Learning Techniques: On the Road to a New Frontier*. Norman, OK: University of Oklahoma Press.

Hoover, J. D., Giambatista, R. C., Sorenson, R. L., & Bommer, W. H. (2010). Assessing the effectiveness of whole person learning pedagogy in skill acquisition. *Academy of Management Learning & Education, 9*(2), 192–203. https://doi.org/10.5465/AMLE.2010.51428543

Hunter-Jones, P. (2012). The continuum of learner disengagement. *Journal of Marketing Education, 34*(1), 19–29. https://doi.org/10.1177/0273475311430801

Jonsson, J. O., & Rudolphi, F. (2011). Weak performance–strong determination: school achievement and educational choice among children of immigrants in Sweden. *European Sociological Review, 27*(4), 487–508. https://doi.org/10.1093/esr/jcq021

Kolb, D. A. (1984). *Experiential Learning: Experience as the Source of Learning and Development*. Englewood Cliffs, NJ: Prentice-Hall. Retrieved from www.researchgate.net/publication/235701029_Experiential_Learning_Experience_As_The_Source_Of_Learning_And_Development

Kuratko, D. F. (2005). The emergence of entrepreneurship education: development, trends, and challenges. *Entrepreneurship Theory and Practice, 29*(5), 577–598. https://doi.org/10.1111/j.1540-6520.2005.00099.x

Lengnick-Hall, C. A., & Sanders, M. M. (1997). Designing effective learning systems for management education: student roles, requisite variety, and practicing what we teach. *Academy of Management Journal, 40*(6), 1334–1368. https://doi.org/10.2307/257036

Levie, J. (1999). Entrepreneurship education in higher education in England: A survey. Retrieved from www.researchgate.net/publication/228796374_Entrepreneurship_Education_in_Higher_Education_in_England_A_Survey

Matlay, H. (2006). Entrepreneurship education: more questions than answers? *Education + Training, 48*(5).https://doi.org/10.1108/et.2006.00448eaa.001

Mintzberg, H. (2004). *Managers, not MBAs: A Hard Look at the Soft Practice of Managing and Management Development*. Oakland, CA: Berrett-Koehler.

Motschnig-Pitrik, R., & Mallich, K. (2004). Effects of person-centered attitudes on professional and social competence in a blended learning paradigm. *Journal of Educational Technology & Society, 7*(4), 176–192. https://doi.org/10.2307/jeductechsoci.7.4.176

Neck, H. M., & Greene, P. G. (2011). Entrepreneurship education: known worlds and new frontiers. *Journal of Small Business Management, 49*(1), 55–70. https://doi.org/10.1111/j.1540-627X.2010.00314.x

Ogbu, J. U. (1992). Understanding cultural diversity and learning. *Educational Researcher*, *21*(8), 5. https://doi.org/10.2307/1176697

Politis, D. (2005). The process of entrepreneurial learning: a conceptual framework. *Entrepreneurship Theory and Practice*, *29*(4), 399–424. Retrieved from www.sciepub.com/reference/96141

Rae, D. (2005). Entrepreneurial learning: a narrative-based conceptual model. *Journal of Small Business and Enterprise Development*, *12*(3), 323–335. https://doi.org/10.1108/14626000510612259

Rae, D. (2007). *Entrepreneurship: From Opportunity to Action*. Basingstoke, UK: Palgrave Macmillan.

Rogers, C. R. (1995). *Client-centered Therapy*. London, UK: Constable (original work published 1951).

Schmitt, B. (2011). *Experiential Marketing: How to Get Customers to Sense, Feel, Think, Act, and Relate to Your Company and Brands*. New York: Free Press.

Waddock, S. (2007). Leadership integrity in a fractured knowledge world. *Academy of Management Learning & Education*, *6*(4), 543–557. https://doi.org/10.5465/amle.2007.27694954

Waddock, S., & Lozano, J. M. (2013). Developing more holistic management education: lessons learned from two programs. *Academy of Management Learning & Education*, *12*(2), 265–284. https://doi.org/10.5465/amle.2012.0002

Yorks, L., & Kasl, E. (2002). Toward a theory and practice for whole-person learning: reconceptualizing experience and the role of affect. *Adult Education Quarterly*, *52*(3), 176–192. Retrieved from www.uwyo.edu/aded5050/5050unit9/toward_a.pdf

2
WHAT DOES EDUCATION ENTAIL FOR ENTREPRENEURS?

Researchers reviewing some of the pioneering universities that include EE have concluded that while entrepreneurship drives innovation and outside-the-box thinking and behavior, its educational model is conservative. It is taught at the university level mainly in business schools, eliciting management and business contents. In non-academic institutions, it is limited to practical education only. Researchers are pushing to develop new educational forms for EE by transforming teachers' and educators' approaches to their role in the classroom, as well as the student entrepreneurs' expectation of a traditional, relatively passive role there. In meeting 21st century challenges, EE should move toward innovative concepts that will make an impact in the world (Hitt, Duane Ireland, Camp, & Sexton, 2001; Katz, 2003; Kuratko, Ireland, & Hornsby, 2001; Kuratko, Ireland, Covin, & Hornsby, 2005; Miles, Munilla, & Covin, 2002; Morris, Kuratko, & Covin, 2010; Zahra, Kuratko, & Jennings, 1999). A simple EE-accelerating model is presented in Figure 2.1, showing that EE can be accelerated by integrating knowledge derived from academia and practice, as well as from the social networks which have a substantial role in founding that knowledge, then delivering the content through the performance of methods and pedagogy, and finally establishing the 'right' EE and introducing new knowledge or new methods into the mainstream. This model should be constantly fueled with expert feedback to adjust and improve it, and then it should be scaled up, when transformational learning is achieved. Transformational learning triggers a change in individuals' frame of reference through critical reflection on their assumptions and the introduction of new ways of defining their worlds, through a fundamentally rational and analytical process (King, 2002; Mezirow, 1991, 2000; Taylor, 2007).

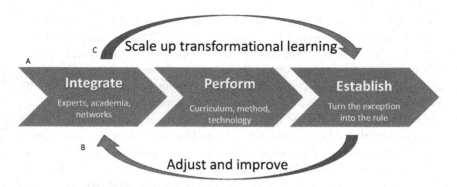

FIGURE 2.1 A simple EE-acceleration model

The Complexity of Teaching Entrepreneurship

How can we delineate the role of education in enabling and improving entrepreneurs' capabilities or their businesses' creation and growth? Researchers have stressed that programs that simply deliver knowledge, train, convey entrepreneurial capabilities and mindsets, or provide real experience, are insufficient for the promotion of student entrepreneurs and their businesses. A single 'manifestation' of knowledge, training or tools through the program's course of action is inadequate for presenting the whole picture of entrepreneurship. Entrepreneurship is a complex, multifaceted process, requiring non-conventional educational methods to introduce its complexity to learners. For example, learners in programs that emphasize training may benefit from the different capabilities and skills that they obtain, but may lack knowledge regarding where, when or in front of whom (e.g., investors, bankers, co-founders) they should implement their new skills.

Moreover, entrepreneurship takes on various forms, for example, social ventures, technological ventures, virtual businesses and global businesses, among so many others, making it difficult for researchers and teachers to simulate the entrepreneurial reality in its many manifestations. In addition, entrepreneurs are profiled as practical, target-oriented, rebellious, proactive and creative individuals, who tend to break the rules and are constantly innovating. Thus, programs need to be customized for the diverse and distinct types of entrepreneurs to guarantee effective and achievement-oriented teaching. Finally, entrepreneurs consume EE at different stages of their business lives, from the ideation phase, to planning, implementation or scaling stages; some have merely developed a curiosity about entrepreneurship and enroll in EE to see what it entails. Researchers, teachers and program developers are endeavoring to create 'something' that can propel all entrepreneurs, who are basically different in their individual and business characteristics, in their businesses' stage of development, and in their resources, skills, and experience (Cope & Watts, 2000; Fleming, Yang, & Golden, 2010; Gruber, 2007; Honig & Samuelsson, 2012; Karlsson & Honig, 2007; Lackéus & Williams, 2011; Rasmussen & Sørheim, 2006; Samwel Mwasalwiba, 2010; Siegel, 2009).

Furthermore, entrepreneurship draws on a multidisciplinary perspective, including new venture creation, technology, business, education, etc., with each discipline trying to enforce its values and standards. For example, teaching techniques are important for the field of education, while coding skills are important for the technological fields. A more holistic perspective of EE requires contents and strategies that expose each field's main principles, but also a core motif around which the fields can converge, so that the program ultimately enables a proficiency in multiple disciplines. This is a complicated challenge. As an analogy, an English course teaches English in depth; it would not focus on teaching different languages. As such, different views, or interests, arise between the student entrepreneurs and their ecosystem (favoring multiple contents) and the academic fields' representatives (favoring intensified knowledge and skill acquisition in particular fields). A deeper look into EE content and strategies reveals other variations:

- Specialization and discipline-based perspective—there are various fields relevant to the entrepreneurial business that can be stressed in teaching, for example, finance, strategy, technology and social aspects, among others.
- Entrepreneurial perspective—teaching can include aspects of opportunity exploitation, materializing ideas into real ventures, feasibility tests and agility models, which are relevant to starting a business.
- Business aspects—there are multiple processes to be addressed in teaching, such as team building and management, strategy crafting and implementation, financial aspects, marketing, management issues, etc.
- Teaching methods—for example, learning by doing, experiential learning, vicarious learning, learning by modeling, etc.
- Individual perspective—teaching can cover aspects of motivation, emotional processes, cognitive processes, knowledge acquisition and exploitation, among others

(Baron, 2004; Holcomb, Holmes Jr., & Connelly, 2009; Meyer et al., 2014; Mitchell et al., 2007; Politis, 2005; Rae, 2005; Ravasi & Turati, 2005; Verzat, Byrne, & Fayolle, 2009; Young & Sexton, 2003)

Teaching produces learning, while learning must be aligned with the discipline to which it refers. Entrepreneurship is an applied area, emphasizing the experimental and the practical, and teaching entrepreneurship should reflect this. On the other hand, learning is defined in research as acquisition of knowledge, skills and competencies by observing, organizing and integrating prior knowledge and experience through sense-making, that is, constructing meaning for such prior knowledge (Gibb, 2002; Holcomb et al., 2009; Rae, 2005; Warren, 2004). Thus, an inherent paradox exists between entrepreneurship teaching (ET) and entrepreneurship learning (EL) in their traditional forms (Clarysse & Moray, 2004; Cope, 2003; Corbett & Katz, 2012; Gartner, 2001; Minniti & Bygrave, 2001).

Entrepreneurship Education (EE)

EE is a unique fragment in 'education' that facilitates individuals' development of the skills, knowledge, and attitudes necessary to achieve the entrepreneurial goals that they have set for themselves. Evidence also shows that people with EE are more employable.

EE embodies processes that prepare individuals to set up their own companies using entrepreneurial mindsets and skills that can be effectively developed by hands-on experience and experiential learning, teaching across disciplines and themes through both separate and combined subjects, leading innovation, and promotion beyond the educational institutions to businesses and the wider community.

EE takes different forms. It may focus more broadly on personal development, mindset, skills and capabilities in the specific context of setting up a venture, or it can focus on the business's development through the learner's innovation, discovery, financial management or other business-oriented processes.

Some researchers have proposed a joint term for EE, encompassing both enterprise and the individual's education. In either case, it is characterized by prevailing attention to capacity building, simulating real-life scenarios that entrepreneurs are likely to encounter, and providing a platform for combined theoretical and practical learning in the most representative situations. EE has progressed greatly, with shifting definitions, pedagogical approaches and emphases on practice over theory. Unlike 'general' education, EE should practice what it preaches (Plautus); as such, it should be a creative, agile, flexible, and value-generating platform. EE cannot be traditional while emphasizing entrepreneurs' business innovations; rather, it should convey a model of innovative, agile conduct, and introduce innovation in its content, structure, methods, and planned deliveries. Yet, researchers decry deficiencies in the practical orientation at higher education levels (Bacigalupo, Kampylis, Punie, & Van den Brande, 2016;[1] Erkkilä, 2000; Hannon, 2005; Lackéus, 2015;[2] Mahieu, 2006). The following challenges arise with the new forms of EE:

- Teachers and professors in entrepreneurship must transform their approach to their classroom role from delivering to enabling.
- Viewing education as an experience, a meaningful one, thus daring, taking risks, moving out of one's comfort zone.
- Considering EE as continual innovation and creativity, a long-run learning process and an ongoing practical formula.
- Embracing brand-new educational methods, including distant learning, VR, video conferencing, or streaming of video case studies.

- Embedding technology in education to add richness to the educational experience.
- Eliminating time, distance, and other limitations to transform theoretical education into practical implementation.
- Adopting the new innovative regime of the 21st century by dreaming, imagining, inventing, provoking, creating, and changing.
- Combining various fields and expertise to formulate new courses and programs.

Entrepreneurship Learning (EL)

Learning refers to the traces left by education in students' thoughts, knowledge, curiosity, performance, motivations and more. The various definitions of learning can be recapped as the processes of information acquisition, skill and knowledge procurement, and practicing know-how. EL adds another layer to this by yielding the expected results, for example, exploiting opportunities, ideating, generating relevant resources, producing products/services, and networking, among others. Each capacity as such seems to derive from a different area, such as management, finance, production, engineering, technology, communication, etc.

The European definition of EL refers to the development of entrepreneurial attitudes, skills and knowledge that will enable the individual to turn creative ideas into action while creating value in all areas of life and society in any economic or social situation, for example, value in crises, value in deprived areas, value in abundant times, etc. EL serves to:

- Generate conditions for job creation and a vibrant, dynamic economy.
- Stimulate innovation and capacity building for constant changes and globalization.
- Engage learners through relevant learning experiences in a continual learning process that allows them to be constantly relevant, up to date and more employable.
- Encourage learners to create value for society and economy.

The term EL is often used as an equivalent to enterprise education and this sometimes causes confusion, since the same term is used in research. However, we deem learning as the outcome of education; as such, educators are expected to develop and deliver the material in impactful ways so that learning ensues. The challenge lies in capturing the students' different learning styles under complex conditions, that is, while introducing a coherent, sound educational 'package' that includes a three-pronged process: (a) knowledge, data, and information, (b) entrepreneurial practices, development of skills and capabilities, and (c) enhancement of motivation, aspirations and mindset. The challenges encountered by EE relate to the heterogeneity in, for example, learning styles, entrepreneurial situations to be simulated and educational outcomes. Moreover, entrepreneurship students are eager to gain substantial value from their education, a further challenge to educators in entrepreneurship (Heder, Ljubic, & Nola, 2011;

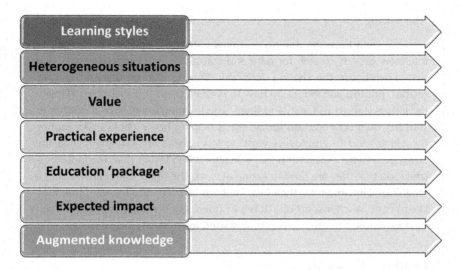

FIGURE 2.2   Forces influencing EL

Leffler & Falk-Lundqvist, 2013; Seikkula-Leino, Ruskovaara, Ikavalko, Mattila, & Rytkola, 2010).

Figure 2.2 shows the various factors that should be taken into consideration in developing EE in order to gain meaningful EL.

Another aspect of EL corresponds to the consequent influence of students' learning on the ecosystem. In fact, learners can be regarded as ambassadors of knowledge, performance or mindsets in the ecosystem, including entrepreneurs and potential entrepreneurs, existing and more advanced companies that embrace entrepreneurship and innovation, investors, and other groups of interest. It is only by adopting EE that learners can disseminate it in their ecosystem.

AT-A-GLANCE

Henrietta Alscher from Germany started her entrepreneurial business as a result of participating in a most inspirational course in 'shared economy'. As a university student in economy, she did not expect to start a business, but to enrich her knowledge in new economy formats; "it was an online course, I had no expectations, but it turned out to be the most inspiring course in my studies . . . the concepts were discussed and analyzed in various ways and through different approaches, enabling us to develop knowledge on, as well as criticize the sharing economy, but also pushing us to sketch responses to the spotted downsides." Alscher was asked to plan an idea that

(continued)

(continued)

would benefit from the sharing economy concepts; she was encouraged to interview experts, search for data and statistics, and practice in ways that would symbolize the sharing economy. She decided to upload her cake recipes, photos, and videos on how to prepare them to a website and invite her virtual class to visit, eat, and share. This learning experience drove her to start her own business and today, she is helping home cooks make money by selling food to employees working long hours in Germany. While the employees benefit from food that is healthier and tastier than the industrialized food that they are used to eating at work, the home cooks are making a meaningful income from their own kitchens by preparing the food that they like to cook. Alscher sums up: "It is a wonderful undertaking, which is nowadays expanding to other areas. It all started from an inspiring course . . ."

Food for thought:

What is the main strength of the inspirational course that Alscher took with regard to EE and teaching?

Entrepreneurship Teaching (ET)

Teaching refers to the processes and ways in which education is conveyed to its audience. As such, it is the bridge between education and learning, by circulating, interpreting and customizing education through methods and forms that will eventually result in meaningful learning. Educators, entrepreneurs and entrepreneurship program developers allocate time and effort to the introduction of teaching that is aligned with the course objectives, environments and types of students in the program (Hannon, 2006; Heinonen & Poikkijoki, 2006; Izquierdo, Caicedo, & Chiluiza, 2007; Jones & Lourenço, 2006; Robertson & Collins, 2003; Smith, 2006; Van Auken, Fry, & Stephens, 2006; K. Verduyn, Wakkee, & Kleijn, 2009).

Much discussion around EE contrasts between 'traditional' and 'entrepreneurial' ways of teaching, advocating for a paradigm shift from traditional teaching to ET. While the traditional form embodies a more content-focused, passive and single-subject-based curriculum, ET is customized, agile, active, process-based, project-centric, collaborative, experiential and multidisciplinary. ET refers to learning based on the following approaches:

- Experiential learning.
- Situational learning.
- Service learning.

- Problem/project-based learning.
- Adult learning.
- Cognitive apprenticeship and social constructivist learning

(Collins, 2006; Cuban, 2007; Helle, Tynjälä, & Olkinuora, 2006; Jarvis, 2006; Kirby, 2004; Kolb, 1984; Kyrö, 2005; Labaree, 2005; Löbler, 2006; Ollila & Williams-Middleton, 2011). To boost student entrepreneurs' creativity, other formats are needed, as shown in Figure 2.3.

While the new bases emerge as more established in research, a range of random, though sometimes innovative, ET methods predominate along most platforms for learners in entrepreneurship. These methods can be classified into conservative teaching methods and community outreach methods. The latter category aims to enable students and entrepreneurs to observe, engage, discover and gain expertise in strategies relevant to their ecosystem and local environment.

Conservative teaching methods:

- Lectures.
- Case studies.
- Group discussions.
- Role models or guest speakers.
- Business plan creation.
- Projects.
- Peer to peer

(Hegarty, 2006; Hindle, 2002; Verduyn, Delvaux, Van Coillie, Tuerlinckx, & Van Mechelen, 2009).

Community outreach methods:

- Incubators, accelerators and centers of entrepreneurship – entrepreneurs and students can meet with the local ecosystem and obtain technical and management assistance, as well as financial support.
- Internship opportunities in startups and small and medium-sized enterprises (SMEs) – gaining hands-on experience in the daily routines of startups.

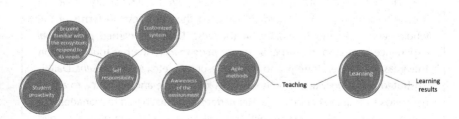

FIGURE 2.3 An innovative look at teaching methods

28 What Education Entails for Entrepreneurs

- Externships—the opportunity to gain insight and knowledge of a startup or any entrepreneurial endeavor, by experiencing the daily activities and responsibilities in entrepreneurship businesses first-hand.
- Apprenticeship – learning environments created by experts who transfer knowledge and reflect upon meaningful tasks for the students and entrepreneurs to accomplish; learners gain knowledge that is situated in the authentic activities of a particular discipline (Varghese et al., 2012). Research shows that the content dimension includes four components: domain knowledge, heuristic strategies, control strategies and learning strategies (Collins, Seely Brown, & Holum, 1991, p. 13)..
- Fellowship programs for entrepreneurs.
- Student consulting projects with local entrepreneurs

(Bennett, 2006; De Faoite, Henry, Johnston, & van der Sijde, 2003; Edwards & Muir, 2005; Fukugawa, 2005; Jesselyn Co & Mitchell, 2006; Kuratko, 2005; Robertson & Collins, 2003; Samwel Mwasalwiba, 2010; Hytti, 2002).

Kirby (2004) reviewed about 205 entrepreneurship programs and sorted them into three foci: orientation and awareness of entrepreneurship; acquisition of skills and competencies for starting a new venture; and scaling up small businesses. Bennett (2006) sorted the programs into two main categories: traditional, more 'passive' methods, and innovative, more active methods. In contrast to passive methods, active methods enable students' self-discovery, practical experience, and more accountability of the learners for their educational and entrepreneurial process and outcomes. The passive approach enables gaining knowledge and a deepening awareness of the discipline, research and theoretical knowledge, and being exposed to inspirational guest lecturers (Boyatzis, Stubbs, & Taylor, 2002; Forrest & Peterson, 2006; Huff & Jenkins, 2002; Schwandt, 2005).

AT-A-GLANCE

Dalit, the 29-year-old Israeli founder of a startup in the cybersecurity area, is looking for the best education in entrepreneurship to gain knowledge and scale up her startup. She and her friends completed their military service in a cybersecurity unit and immediately started their business. In terms of the whole-person pedagogy, looking at the *past*, Dalit has earned *professional* experience in areas a, b, and c; as to her *performance*, she has touched upon the areas of finance, strategy and human resources, etc.; in the *present*, Dalit is frustrated *emotionally* as she feels she lacks knowledge and resilience to adopt new ways to scale up her business. Her *performance* has shifted to management rather than technology, while, with respect to *potential*, she wishes to hire more people, and sharpen her social skills. The model enables both Dalit and the institution that she approaches to introduce an educational 'package' that will fit Dalit's dimensions, so that she can gain the most relevant knowledge and expertise that she is seeking, aligned with her accumulated experience.

Food for thought:

How is Dalit's experience related to the concepts of ET?

Teaching Entrepreneurially

A different perspective encapsulates EE as the development of entrepreneurial capabilities, mindsets and psychological competencies—key competencies that can be employed in any discipline. As such, engineering, computer sciences, or legal studies can be taught by strengthening a set of entrepreneurial capabilities, to be used for entrepreneurial-driven activities. The European Commission[3] has announced that key entrepreneurial competencies should be reinforced as they can enhance employability, social inclusion and active citizenship, as well as create value for others. Teaching entrepreneurially involves developing the capacity to generate value from simple to complex contexts, enabling anyone who wants to 'touch' entrepreneurship to embark upon this path, not necessarily as the founder of a new business (Bacigalupo et al., 2016;[4] Gibb, 2002; Harmeling & Sarasvathy, 2013; Neck & Greene, 2011). Teaching entrepreneurially entails:

- Introducing any content, not exclusively entrepreneurship-driven contents, entrepreneurially.
- Delivering the course through methods that align with entrepreneurial orientation, for example, using innovative, fun, challenging and team-based methods. This will maintain the learners' interest and engagement in the teaching process.
- Imparting 'meta-modeling'—the learning process requires entrepreneurial competencies, such as curiosity, proactivity, scouting, technological savvy.
- Offering an 'open-source' practice, providing any information and knowledge, the sources to gain that knowledge, and practices to interpret them in different approaches.
- Embedding entrepreneurial competencies for better performance in any job.
- Simulating real life, such as problem-based learning (PBL), project-based learning, collaborative learning.
- Implementing entrepreneurial rules in any discipline.

The value of teaching various curricula entrepreneurially has been recognized in research as a process enhanced by the use of a real-world project's challenges, through experiencing and developing the best solutions for the encountered situations. This pedagogical approach stems from the conceptual models on the key roles for EE proposed by Scott, Rosa, and Klandt (1998): (a) education about enterprise, (b) education through EE, and (c) education for enterprise. Accordingly, Jones and Matlay (2011) proposed a conceptual ET framework encompassing ten systems among students, educators and institutions, *inter alia*, which revealed the major impact of diversity in teaching entrepreneurially. For example, entrepreneurial pedagogical practices have been included in curricula for engineering, statistics, and mechanics, for example, which require entrepreneurial capabilities, and include entrepreneurship-based 'scenarios', such as involvement of the environment, alertness, curiosity, project-based learning (PBL), active and experiential learning, among others. The resulting effects revealed higher entrepreneurial mindsets, successful problem solving in the face of real-world complexities, and a higher engagement in the curriculum studies, that is, statistics, engineering, etc. As a consequence, the integration of entrepreneurial-oriented, innovative methods, extensive student practice of entrepreneurial skills, and the implementation of multifaceted themes into different disciplines' curricula seem indispensable (Liu, Mynderse, Gerhart, & Arslan, 2015; Neck, Greene, & Brush, 2014; Noyes & Brush, 2012; Vignola, London, Ayala, & Huang, 2017).

Entrepreneurship as a Career Choice

Entrepreneurship can be regarded as a career choice; hence, EE is expected to provide learners with the tools for proficiency in entrepreneurship. As such, in addition to academic content, EE encompasses extensive extracurricular offerings integrated into the traditional programs, so that learners can acquire the required tools to develop an entrepreneurial career. The value introduced by EE is in facilitating the transformation of entrepreneurial ideas into businesses in more effective ways, with more collaborators and through perceptions of higher self-efficacy and capability (Bae, Qian, Miao, & Fiet, 2014; Dickson, Solomon, & Weaver, 2008; Huber, Sloof, & Van Praag, 2014; Martin, Mcnally, & Kay, 2013; Peterman & Kennedy, 2003; Pittaway & Cope, 2007; Walter, Parboteeah, & Walter, 2013). Research has shown that exposure to entrepreneurship courses and programs improves learners' prospects in choosing entrepreneurship as their career path, though some show that entrepreneurship students are more passionate, and possess better entrepreneurial capabilities and agility than other students. Therefore, formal programs in entrepreneurship may seem futile to them (Athayde, 2009; Peterman & Kennedy, 2003; Sánchez, 2013; Walter & Dohse, 2012; Walter et al., 2013).

Summary

This chapter reviews the challenges and complexities faced by researchers, educators and student entrepreneurs in teaching entrepreneurship and entrepreneurially.

The main premise of EE lies in entrepreneurship rather than education, to promote lifelong capabilities that can be leveraged into any career, and will serve to enhance learners' future employability and further accomplishments, including, albeit not exclusively, setting up their entrepreneurial businesses.

The differences in the concepts and main terminology of EE, EL and ET, including an entrepreneurship vs. entrepreneurial focus, are introduced and discussed in this chapter, by proffering the contrasting approaches of more traditional, conservative education and a more progressive, individual-centered approach. These concepts are then transformed into guidelines for teaching and learning.

Entrepreneurial outreach methods are presented, such as learning in incubators, accelerators and centers of entrepreneurship; internship and externship opportunities; apprenticeship; fellowship programs for entrepreneurs; and student consulting projects with local entrepreneurs. Finally, entrepreneurship as a career choice is exposed, attesting to the crucial role of participating in EE programs to increase motivation to start an entrepreneurship career, as well as for prospective success as an entrepreneur, by attaining the capabilities and mindsets conveyed by EE programs.

Takeaways

For researchers:

- Elaborate research on each of the discussed segments—EE, EL, ET.
- Gain more data and findings on the role of EE in learners' future achievements.
- Provide new research-based models for entrepreneurship and EE and ET.
- Address EL academically to suggest a definition and concept delineation.

For educators and teaching developers:

- Determine the program's focus, and deliver it accordingly: individual-centered, business-centered, following content or processes, etc.
- 'Educate the market'—establish the terminology and employ it in the program's planning, structuring and implementation, by differentiating between EE, EL and ET.
- A top-down aspect—embrace a 'teaching the teachers' approach, and programs for educators, mentors and other entrepreneurship facilitators, to establish the meanings of education, teaching and learning.

For EE participants:

- Determine what you would like to gain from an entrepreneurial program.
- Your role is to *learn*, while as an entrepreneur, or future entrepreneur, you will focus on EL. As such, you may proactively promote EE and ET in the

class/program, by asking questions and exploring, rather than only absorbing the content. Disseminate these concepts to your colleagues and associates.
- Many entrepreneurs are resolute to learn 'from one point to the next' and feel that getting more insight and information, beyond their concrete next point, is a waste of time. However, research shows that the opposite is true. The more EL occurs, the more the entrepreneur gains. Embrace more knowledge, information and tools, even if they seem to be irrelevant for your immediate needs.

Case Study 2—An Entrepreneurial Look into EE, the Case of Art-preneurs

Kenneth Foster is the director of Arts Leadership at USC,[5] an innovative, artist-centric graduate degree program for artists, art administrators and cultural entrepreneurs who want a substantial career in the arts. In referring to artists, Foster says:

> I learned to admire and respect their ambition and their drive. In turn, the entrepreneurs I worked with learned to admire and respect not just the innovative spirit of the artist but the artists' drive to disrupt conventional ideas and thinking and to create an impact in the world. By integrating these impulses, as art entrepreneurs, there is no end to the great work that artists can do.

The characteristics of an artist-entrepreneur involve synergy between entrepreneurship and the arts, including thinking outside the box (or instrument case), a relentless passion for what they do, and their effort to create an impact. According to Foster: "Art entrepreneurship doesn't mean artists becoming businesspeople . . . it means applying the creative process that is at the heart of your art-making to the challenges you will face in making your artistic idea become a reality." According to Marc Zegans,[6] creative development advisor,

> School helped you develop discipline, take creative chances and learn from critical feedback, but it didn't give you a way of developing your creativity in the hurly burly of life outside the academy. If you approach this next phase with curiosity about how your creative identity needs to grow, then your possibilities begin to blossom.[7]

Vinitha Watson, the founder of Zoo Labs, the world's first music accelerator, opened Google's first office in India, was a fellow at the Institute for the Future, and sits on the boards of Nexleaf Analytics and California College of the Arts. Watson is the founder and Executive Director of Zoo Labs. In her TEDx talk on 'The messy process of fun',[8] she addresses the role of fueling our lives with creativity, and the necessity to weave fun and creativity and bridge career, creativity and the 'messy' parts of both to create a viable business option. Accordingly, Zoo Labs aims to empower artists by directing resources toward their ventures, as well as investing in and exploring the intersection between creativity, craft and commercial viability. Liam Nillson is a music-preneur, originally from Sweden, though he left home at the age of 14 and has wandered through different countries in Europe, Latin America and Africa ever since; today, at the age of 30, starting a business designed to guide musicians to 'struggle with the statistics' that, according, to Nillson, show that most of them will fail in their music career, he says:

Musicians are self-starters, they do not wait for things to happen, they make things happen. They are essentially entrepreneurs; even more than the leading known entrepreneurs, as entrepreneurship is implanted in their spirit. Yet, understanding the business basics can be extremely helpful to developing a business. Besides, musicians are lone wolves, and they need to trust others to make a living.

Nillson has never studied formally, yet, he has gained a lot of insight from people he considers to be mentors along the way. He says:

> Ira, my mentor in Russia, where I spent four years cleaning restaurants and bars in exchange for playing my music, encouraged me to trust other people, ask for their assistance, look for opportunities that can be attained through other people; and this was the turning point. I coupled with other musicians, we spent days and nights listening to music, and sharing, teaching each other; then through Ira, we joined a conductor who provided us with feedback on our music. Ira convinced us to spend time with the restaurants' and bars' guests to get their feedback and fine-tune our music, as well as build our playlist according to the audience's tastes. Out of these close relationships with the audience, we established a musician's network that has grown exponentially over the years. I have learned so much from these four years of informal, yet so experiential learning that it pushed me to start a business that provides business tools in creativity and experience for young musicians. I am looking for a home for entrepreneurs like me, to assist me in implementing my dreams and start a place for musician entrepreneurs.

Questions on the Case Study

1. Discuss the similarities and differences that you see between entrepreneurs and artists, based on the case study, and explain why education for both can be based on the same basics of EE, EL and ET.
2. List 3–4 components of 'teaching entrepreneurially' that you can identify from the accelerators' founders and the entrepreneurs' quotes.
3. Analyze the arguments illustrated in the case study to explain 'entrepreneurship as a career choice' with respect to the concepts introduced in the chapter.

34 What Education Entails for Entrepreneurs

4. Try to imagine a talk between Liam Nillson and either Vinitha Watson or Kenneth Foster on Nillson's wish to be part of an art accelerator. Write three questions that Nillson would ask, and three questions that the founders of those accelerators would ask Nillson. Explain your choice.
5. Search for the Art Thinking Lab (http://artthinkinglab.com/) which applies the art–business relationship from the direction opposite to that of the case study, because, according to the Wall Street Journal: "The arts are emerging as a role model for business and government organizations because the arts excel in areas where managers struggle the most: chaos, diversity, ambiguity, envisioning the future and the ability to dare to break molds." In your opinion, which of these directions, that is, artists gaining business skills, or entrepreneurs gaining artistic skills and mindsets, is more befitted to learning entrepreneurship versus learning entrepreneurially. Based on your conclusions, what model would you choose for an accelerator that you would develop? Explain.

Reflective Questions

1. Ask 3–5 different people around you to delineate the differences between EE and educating entrepreneurially. What are their main conclusions? What did you learn from their responses, and their alignment to the theory discussed in this chapter?
2. Search the internet for associations or organizations that emphasize, in their vision/purpose/goals: (a) teaching entrepreneurship; and others that focus on (b) educating entrepreneurially. Write down their names and website addresses. List 3–5 differences and similarities in the activities and programs that they offer. What are your conclusions based on your findings? Do you think that the practice is well associated with the theory and vice versa? Explain.
3. A global technology company decides to open a center aimed at both promoting its employees' creativity and proactivity, and research and development (R&D) of innovative projects. What are the 3–5 most crucial questions that you would ask them to gain more information on how to start such a center? How are these questions related to the concepts in this chapter?
4. Watch Cameron Herold's TEDxEdmonton talk: 'Let's raise kids to be entrepreneurs' (https://www.ted.com/talks/cameron_herold_let_s_raise_kids_to_be_entrepreneurs). List three different indicators related to EE, EL and ET (nine indicators overall). In your opinion, are Herold's suggestions relevant to any child and to any educational system? Explain your answer.
5. Search for Microsoft Teaching Innovation & Entrepreneurship around the World (https://www.microsoftinnovationcenters.com/). Ed Steidl runs Microsoft's Innovation Centers; here is a quote from an interview with Tina Seelig (https://medium.com/@tseelig/why-is-microsoft-teaching-innovation-entrepreneurship-around-the-world-7dd9a8c36b13):

Microsoft's mission is to help every person and every organization on the planet to achieve more. Developing an entrepreneurial mindset is perfectly aligned to this mission. As we race toward the Fourth Industrial Revolution, we want to empower people to solve local problems through technology, and innovation plays a key part in this journey.

Reflect on the concepts of this quote by addressing the main ideas of entrepreneurship as a career choice. In your opinion, what is Microsoft's motivation to educate entrepreneurship and entrepreneurially? Explain your responses.

Notes

1 See at: https://ec.europa.eu/growth/smes/promoting-entrepreneurship/support/education_en and https://ec.europa.eu/growth/smes/promoting-entrepreneurship/support/education/projects-studies_en
2 See at: www.oecd.org/cfe/leed/BGP_Entrepreneurship-in-Education.pdf
3 See at: https://ec.europa.eu/jrc/en/entrecomp ; https://ec.europa.eu/jrc/en/entrecomp/entrepreurship-competence-framework
4 European Commission. 2016. EntreComp: The Entrepreneurship Competence Framework https://ec.europa.eu/jrc/en/publication/eur-scientific-and-technical-research-reports/entrecomp-entrepreneurship-competence-framework
5 See at: https://music.usc.edu/departments/arts-leadership/
6 See at: http://mycreativedevelopment.com/
7 See at: https://mag.orangenius.com/marc-zegans-working-artist/
8 See at: www.youtube.com/watch?v=TwhC7svUbTg

References

Athayde, R. (2009). Measuring enterprise potential in young people. *Entrepreneurship Theory and Practice, 33*(2), 481–500. https://doi.org/10.1111/j.1540-6520.2009.00300.x

Bacigalupo, M., Kampylis, P., Punie, Y., & Van den Brande, L. (2016). EntreComp: The entrepreneurship competence framework. Publications Office of the European Union. https://doi.org/10.2791/593884

Bae, T. J., Qian, S., Miao, C., & Fiet, J. O. (2014). The relationship between entrepreneurship education and entrepreneurial intentions: A meta-analytic review. *Entrepreneurship Theory and Practice, 38*(2), 217–254. https://doi.org/10.1111/etap.12095

Baron, R. A. (2004). The cognitive perspective: a valuable tool for answering entrepreneurship's basic "why" questions. *Journal of Business Venturing, 19*(2), 221–239. https://doi.org/10.1016/S0883-9026(03)00008-9

Bennett, R. (2006). Business lecturers' perceptions of the nature of entrepreneurship. *International Journal of Entrepreneurial Behavior & Research, 12*(3), 165–188. https://doi.org/10.1108/13552550610667440

Boyatzis, R. E., Stubbs, E. C., & Taylor, S. N. (2002). Learning cognitive and emotional intelligence competencies through graduate management education. *Academy of Management Learning & Education, 1*(2), 150–162. https://doi.org/10.5465/amle.2002.8509345

Clarysse, B., & Moray, N. (2004). A process study of entrepreneurial team formation: The case of a research-based spin-off. *Journal of Business Venturing, 19*(1), 55–79.

Collins, A. (2006). Cognitive apprenticeship. In R. K. Sawyer (Ed.), *The Cambridge Handbook of the Learning Sciences* (pp. 47–60). Cambridge: Cambridge University Press. https://doi.org/10.1017/CBO9780511816833.005

Collins, A., Seely Brown, J., & Holum, A. (1991). Cognitive apprenticeship: Making thinking visible. *American Educator, 15*(3), 6–11.

Cope, J. (2003). Entrepreneurial learning and critical reflection. *Management Learning, 34*(4), 429–450. https://doi.org/10.1177/1350507603039067

Cope, J., & Watts, G. (2000). Learning by doing – An exploration of experience, critical incidents and reflection in entrepreneurial learning. *International Journal of Entrepreneurial Behavior & Research, 6*(3), 104–124. https://doi.org/10.1108/13552550010346208

Corbett, A. C., & Katz, J. A. (Eds.) (2012). *Entrepreneurial Action.* Bingley, UK: Emerald Group. https://doi.org/10.1108/S1074-7540(2012)14

Cuban, L. (2007). Hugging the middle: Teaching in an era of testing and accountability 1980–2005. *Education Policy Analysis Archives, 15,* 1–27.

De Faoite, D., Henry, C., Johnston, K., & van der Sijde, P. (2003). Education and training for entrepreneurs: |A consideration of initiatives in Ireland and the Netherlands. *Education + Training, 45*(8/9), 430–438. https://doi.org/10.1108/00400910310508829

Dickson, P. H., Solomon, G. T., & Weaver, K. M. (2008). Entrepreneurial selection and success: Does education matter? *Journal of Small Business and Enterprise Development, 15*(2), 239–258. https://doi.org/10.1108/14626000810871655

Edwards, L., & Muir, E. J. (2005). Promoting entrepreneurship at the University of Glamorgan through formal and informal learning. *Journal of Small Business and Enterprise Development, 12*(4), 613–626. https://doi.org/10.1108/14626000510628261

Erkkilä, K. (2000). *Entrepreneurial Education: Mapping the Debates in the United States, the United Kingdom and Finland.* New York: Garland.

Fleming, L., Yang, W., & Golden, J. (2010). Science and technology entrepreneurship for greater societal benefit: Ideas for curricular innovation. *Advances in the Study of Entrepreneurship, Innovation and Economic Growth, 21,* 165–182. https://doi.org/10.1108/S1048-4736(2010)0000021010

Forrest, S. P., & Peterson, T. O. (2006). It's called Andragogy. *Academy of Management Learning & Education, 5*(1), 113–122. https://doi.org/10.5465/amle.2006.20388390

Fukugawa, N. (2005). Characteristics of knowledge interactions between universities and small firms in Japan. *International Small Business Journal, 23*(4), 379–401. https://doi.org/10.1177/0266242605054052

Gartner, W. B. (2001). Is there an elephant in entrepreneurship? Blind assumptions in theory development. *Entrepreneurship Theory and Practice, 25*(4), 27–39. https://doi.org/10.1007/978-3-540-48543-8_11

Gibb, A. (2002). Creating conducive environments for learning and entrepreneurship. *Industry and Higher Education, 16*(3), 135–148. https://doi.org/10.5367/000000002101296234

Gruber, M. (2007). Uncovering the value of planning in new venture creation: A process and contingency perspective. *Journal of Business Venturing, 22*(6), 782–807. https://doi.org/10.1016/J.JBUSVENT.2006.07.001

Hannon, P. D. (2005). Philosophies of enterprise and entrepreneurship education and challenges for higher education in the UK. *International Journal of Entrepreneurship and Innovation, 6*(2), 105–114. https://doi.org/10.5367/0000000053966876

Hannon, P. D. (2006). Teaching pigeons to dance: Sense and meaning in entrepreneurship education. *Education + Training, 48*(5), 296–308. https://doi.org/10.1108/00400910610677018

Harmeling, S. S., & Sarasvathy, S. D. (2013). When contingency is a resource: Educating entrepreneurs in the Balkans, the Bronx, and beyond. *Entrepreneurship Theory and Practice*, *37*(4), 713–744. https://doi.org/10.1111/j.1540-6520.2011.00489.x

Heder, E., Ljubic, M., & Nola, L. (2011). *Entrepreneurial Learning - A Key Competence Approach*. Zagreb, Croatia: South East European Centre for Entrepreneurial Learning.

Hegarty, C. (2006). It's not an exact science: Teaching entrepreneurship in Northern Ireland. *Education + Training*, *48*(5), 322–335. https://doi.org/10.1108/00400910610677036

Heinonen, J., & Poikkijoki, S. (2006). An entrepreneurial-directed approach to entrepreneurship education: mission impossible? *Journal of Management Development*, *25*(1), 80–94. https://doi.org/10.1108/02621710610637981

Helle, L., Tynjälä, P., & Olkinuora, E. (2006). Project-based learning in post-secondary education – theory, practice and rubber sling shots. *Higher Education*, *51*(2), 287–314. https://doi.org/10.1007/s10734-004-6386-5

Hindle, K. (2002). A grounded theory for teaching entrepreneurship using simulation games. *Simulation & Gaming*, *33*(2), 236–241. https://doi.org/10.1177/1046878102332012

Hitt, M. A., Duane Ireland, R., Camp, S. M., & Sexton, D. L. (2001). Entrepreneurial strategies for wealth creation. *Strategic Management Journal*, *22*, 479–491. https://doi.org/10.1002/smj.196

Holcomb, T. R., Holmes Jr., R. M., & Connelly, B. L. (2009). Making the most of what you have: Managerial ability as a source of resource value creation. *Strategic Management Journal*, *30*(5), 457–485. https://doi.org/10.1002/smj.747

Honig, B., & Samuelsson, M. (2012). Planning and the entrepreneur: A longitudinal examination of nascent entrepreneurs in Sweden. *Journal of Small Business Management*, *50*(3), 365–388. https://doi.org/10.1111/j.1540-627X.2012.00357.x

Huber, L. R., Sloof, R., & Van Praag, M. (2014). The effect of early entrepreneurship education: Evidence from a field experiment. *European Economic Review*, *72*, 76–97. https://doi.org/10.1016/J.EUROECOREV.2014.09.002

Huff, A. S., & Jenkins, M. (2002). *Mapping Strategic Knowledge*. London: Sage.

Hytti, U. (2002). *State-of-art of Enterprise Education in Europe. Results from the ENREDU Project*. Turku, Finland: Small Business Institute, Turku School of Economics and Business Administration.

Izquierdo, E., Caicedo, G., & Chiluiza, K. (2007). Lessons learned from an innovative approach on an introductory entrepreneurship course: The case of ESPOL. Birmingham: National Council for Graduate Entrepreneurship Working Paper Series.

Jarvis, P. (Ed.) (2006). *The Theory and Practice of Teaching* (2nd ed.). London: Routledge.

Jesselyn Co, M., & Mitchell, B. (2006). Entrepreneurship education in South Africa: A nationwide survey. *Education + Training*, *48*(5), 348–359. https://doi.org/10.1108/00400910610677054

Jones, C., & Matlay, H. (2011). Understanding the heterogeneity of entrepreneurship education: Going beyond Gartner. *Education + Training*, *53*(8/9), 692–703. https://doi.org/10.1108/00400911111185026

Jones, O., & Lourenço, F. (2006). Developing entrepreneurship education: Comparing traditional and alternative teaching approaches. *International Journal of Entrepreneurship Education*, *4*, 111–140.

Karlsson, T., & Honig, B. (2007). Norms surrounding business plans and their effect on entrepreneurial behavior. *Frontiers of Entrepreneurship Research*, *27*(22), 1–11.

Katz, J. A. (2003). The chronology and intellectual trajectory of American entrepreneurship education: 1876–1999. *Journal of Business Venturing*, *18*(2), 283–300. https://doi.org/10.1016/S0883-9026(02)00098-8

King, K. P. (2002). Educational technology professional development as transformative learning opportunities. *Computers & Education*, *39*(3), 283–297. https://doi.org/10.1016/S0360-1315(02)00073-8

Kirby, D. A. (2004). Entrepreneurship education: Can business schools meet the challenge? *Education + Training*, *46*(8/9), 510–519. https://doi.org/10.1108/00400910410569632

Kolb, D. A. (1984). *Experiential Learning: Experience as the Source of Learning and Development*. Englewood Cliffs, NJ: Prentice-Hall.

Kuratko, D. F. (2005). The emergence of entrepreneurship education: development, trends, and challenges. *Entrepreneurship Theory and Practice*, *29*(5), 577–598. https://doi.org/10.1111/j.1540-6520.2005.00099.x

Kuratko, D. F., Ireland, R. D., & Hornsby, J. S. (2001). Improving firm performance through entrepreneurial actions: Acordia's corporate entrepreneurship strategy. *The Academy of Management Executive (1993–2005)*, *15*(4), 60–71. https://doi.org/10.2307/4165786

Kuratko, D. F., Ireland, R. D., Covin, J. G., & Hornsby, J. S. (2005). A model of middle-level managers' entrepreneurial behavior. *Entrepreneurship Theory and Practice*, *29*(6), 699–716. https://doi.org/10.1111/j.1540-6520.2005.00104.x

Kyrö, P. (2005). Entrepreneurial learning in a cross-cultural context challenges previous learning paradigms. In P. Kyrö and C. Carrier (Eds.), *The Dynamics of Learning Entrepreneurship in a Cross-Cultural University Context* (pp. 68–103). Hämeenlinna, Finland: University of Tampere Research Centre for Vocational and Professional Education.

Labaree, D. F. (2005). Progressivism, schools and schools of education: An American romance. *Paedagogica Historica*, *41*, 275–288. https://doi.org/10.1080/0030923042000335583

Lackéus, M. (2015). Entrepreneurship in education: What, why, when, how. Entrepreneurship360 background paper. Paris, France: OECD.

Lackéus, M., & Williams, K. M. (2011). Venture creation programs: Entrepreneurial education through real-life content. Paper presented to Babson College Entrepreneurship Research Conference, Syracuse, NY, June 8–11.

Leffler, E., & Falk-Lundqvist, Å. (2013). What about students' right to the "right" education? An entrepreneurial attitude to teaching and learning. In A. W. Wiseman (Ed.), *International Educational Innovation and Public Sector Entrepreneurship* (pp. 191–208). Umeå, Sweden: Emerald Group.

Liu, L., Mynderse, J. A., Gerhart, A. L., & Arslan, S. (2015). Fostering the entrepreneurial mindset in the junior and senior mechanical engineering curriculum with a multi-course problem-based learning experience. Paper presented to the *2015 IEEE Frontiers in Education Conference (FIE)* (pp. 1–5). IEEE. https://doi.org/10.1109/FIE.2015.7344040

Löbler, H. (2006). Learning entrepreneurship from a constructivist perspective. *Technology Analysis & Strategic Management*, *18*(1), 19–38. https://doi.org/10.1080/09537320500520460

Mahieu, R. (2006). *Agents of Change and Policies of Scale: A Policy Study of Entrepreneurship and Enterprise in Education*. Umeå, Sweden: Umeå University.

Martin, B., Mcnally, J. J., & Kay, M. (2013). Examining the formation of human capital in entrepreneurship: A meta-analysis of entrepreneurship education outcomes. *Journal of Business Venturing*, *28*(2), 211–224. https://doi.org/10.1016/j.jbusvent.2012.03.002

Meyer, M., Libaers, D., Thijs, B., Grant, K., Glänzel, W., & Debackere, K. (2014). Origin and emergence of entrepreneurship as a research field. *Scientometrics*, *98*(1), 473–485. https://doi.org/10.1007/s11192-013-1021-9

Mezirow, J. (1991). *Transformative Dimensions of Adult Learning*. San Francisco, CA: Jossey-Bass. https://doi.org/10.1177/074171369204200309

Mezirow, J. (2000). *Learning as Transformation: Critical Perspectives on a Theory in Progress*. San Francisco, CA: Jossey-Bass.

Miles, M. P., Munilla, L. S., & Covin, J. G. (2002). The constant gardener revisited: The effect of social blackmail on the marketing concept, innovation, and entrepreneurship. *Journal of Business Ethics*, 41(3), 287–295.

Minniti, M., & Bygrave, W. (2001). A dynamic model of entrepreneurial learning. *Entrepreneurship Theory and Practice*, 25(3), 5–16. https://doi.org/10.1177/104225870102500301

Mitchell, R. K., Busenitz, L. W., Bird, B., Marie Gaglio, C., McMullen, J. S., Morse, E. A., & Smith, J. B. (2007). The central question in entrepreneurial cognition research 2007. *Entrepreneurship Theory and Practice*, 31(1), 1–27. https://doi.org/10.1111/j.1540-6520.2007.00161.x

Morris, M. H., Kuratko, D. F., & Covin, J. G. (2010). *Corporate Entrepreneurship & Innovation* (3rd ed.). Mason, OH: South-Western Cengage Learning.

Neck, H. M., & Greene, P. G. (2011). Entrepreneurship education: known worlds and new frontiers. *Journal of Small Business Management*, 49(1), 55–70. https://doi.org/10.1111/j.1540-627X.2010.00314.x

Neck, H. M., Greene, P. G., & Brush, C. G. (2014). *Teaching Entrepreneurship: A Practice-based Approach*. Cheltenham, UK: Edward Elgar.

Noyes, E., & Brush, C. (2012). Teaching entrepreneurial action: Application of creative logic. In A. C. Corbett & J. A. Katz (Eds.), *Entrepreneurial Action (Advances in Entrepreneurship, Firm Emergence and Growth, Volume 14)* (pp. 253–280). Bingley, UK: Emerald Group. https://doi.org/10.1108/S1074-7540(2012)0000014011

Ollila, S., & Williams-Middleton, K. (2011). The venture creation approach: Integrating entrepreneurial education and incubation at the university. *International Journal of Entrepreneurship and Innovation Management*, 13(2), 161–178.

Peterman, N. E., & Kennedy, J. (2003). Enterprise education: Influencing students' perceptions of entrepreneurship. *Entrepreneurship Theory and Practice*, 28(2), 129–144. https://doi.org/10.1046/j.1540-6520.2003.00035.x

Pittaway, L., & Cope, J. (2007). Entrepreneurship education: A systematic review of the evidence. *International Small Business Journal*, 25(5), 479–510.

Politis, D. (2005). The process of entrepreneurial learning: a conceptual framework. *Entrepreneurship Theory and Practice*, 29(4), 399–424.

Rae, D. (2005). Entrepreneurial learning: a narrative-based conceptual model. *Journal of Small Business and Enterprise Development*, 12(3), 323–335. https://doi.org/10.1108/14626000510612259

Rasmussen, E. A., & Sørheim, R. (2006). Action-based entrepreneurship education. *Technovation*, 26(2), 185–194. https://doi.org/10.1016/J.TECHNOVATION.2005.06.012

Ravasi, D., & Turati, C. (2005). Exploring entrepreneurial learning: A comparative study of technology development projects. *Journal of Business Venturing*, 20(1), 137–164. https://doi.org/10.1016/j.jbusvent.2003.11.002

Robertson, M., & Collins, A. (2003). The video role model as an enterprise teaching aid. *Education + Training*, 45(6), 331–340. https://doi.org/10.1108/00400910310495987

Samwel Mwasalwiba, E. (2010). Entrepreneurship education: a review of its objectives, teaching methods, and impact indicators. *Education + Training*, 52(1), 20–47. https://doi.org/10.1108/00400911011017663

Sánchez, J. C. (2013). The impact of an entrepreneurship education program on entrepreneurial competencies and intention. *Journal of Small Business Management, 51*(3), 447–465. https://doi.org/10.1111/jsbm.12025

Schwandt, D. R. (2005). When managers become philosophers: Integrating learning with sensemaking. *Academy of Management Learning & Education, 4*(2), 176–192. https://doi.org/10.5465/amle.2005.17268565

Scott, M., Rosa, P., & Klandt, H. (1998). Educating entrepreneurs for wealth creation. In M. Scott, P. Rosa, & H. Klandt (Eds.), *Educating Entrepreneurs for Wealth Creation* (pp. 1–14). Aldershot, UK: Ashgate.

Seikkula-Leino, J., Ruskovaara, E., Ikavalko, M., Mattila, J., & Rytkola, T. (2010). Promoting entrepreneurship education: the role of the teacher? *Education + Training, 52*(2), 117–127. https://doi.org/10.1108/00400911011027716

Siegel, D. (2009). New developments in technology management education. *Academy of Management Learning & Education, 8*(3), 321–323. https://doi.org/10.5465/amle.8.3.zqr321

Smith, A. (2006). Embedding new entrepreneurship programmes in UK higher education institutions; challenges and considerations. *Education + Training, 48*(8/9), 555–567.

Taylor, E. W. (2007). An update of transformative learning theory: A critical review of the empirical research (1999–2005). *International Journal of Lifelong Education, 26*(2), 173–191. https://doi.org/10.1080/02601370701219475

Van Auken, H., Fry, F. L., & Stephens, P. (2006). The influence of role models on entrepreneurial intentions. *Journal of Developmental Entrepreneurship, 11*(02), 157–167. https://doi.org/10.1142/S1084946706000349

Varghese, M. E., Parker, L. C., Adedokun, O., Shively, M., Burgess, W., Childress, A., & Bessenbacher, A. (2012). Experiential internships: understanding the process of student learning in small business internships. *Industry and Higher Education, 26*(5), 357–367. https://doi.org/10.5367/ihe.2012.0114

Verduyn, K., Wakkee, I., & Kleijn, E. A. (2009). Filming entrepreneurship. *International Review of Entrepreneurship, 7*(3), 195–206.

Verduyn, P., Delvaux, E., Van Coillie, H., Tuerlinckx, F., & Van Mechelen, I. (2009). Predicting the duration of emotional experience: Two experience sampling studies. *Emotion, 9*(1), 83–91. https://doi.org/10.1037/a0014610

Verzat, C., Byrne, J., & Fayolle, A. (2009). Tangling with spaghetti: Pedagogical lessons from games. *Academy of Management Learning & Education, 8*(3), 356–369. https://doi.org/10.5465/amle.8.3.zqr356

Vignola, C., London, J., Ayala, R., & Huang, W. (2017). Cultivating an entrepreneurial mindset in an undergraduate engineering statistics course using project-based learning. Paper presented to the *2017 IEEE Frontiers in Education Conference (FIE)* (pp. 1–4). IEEE. https://doi.org/10.1109/FIE.2017.8190663

Walter, S. G., & Dohse, D. (2012). Why mode and regional context matter for entrepreneurship education. *Entrepreneurship & Regional Development, 24*(9–10), 807–835. https://doi.org/10.1080/08985626.2012.721009

Walter, S. G., Parboteeah, K. P., & Walter, A. (2013). University departments and self-employment intentions of business students: A cross-level analysis. *Entrepreneurship Theory and Practice, 37*(2), 175–200. https://doi.org/10.1111/j.1540-6520.2011.00460.x

Warren, L. (2004). Negotiating entrepreneurial identity: Communities of practice and changing discourses. *International Journal of Entrepreneurship and Innovation*, 5(1), 25–35.

Young, J. E., & Sexton, D. L. (2003). What makes entrepreneurs learn and how do they do it? *Journal of Entrepreneurship*, 12(2), 155–182. https://doi.org/10.1177/097135570301200201

Zahra, S. A., Kuratko, D. F., & Jennings, D. F. (1999). Entrepreneurship and the acquisition of dynamic organizational capabilities. *Entrepreneurship Theory and Practice*, 23(3), 5–10. https://doi.org/10.1177/104225879902300301

3
THE *WHAT, WHY* AND *HOW* OF ENTREPRENEURIAL EDUCATION

Any educational program designed for a particular discipline reflects that discipline's style: engineering and finance are taught systematically, law and accounting education is primarily based on rules and regulations, while music and painting are taught through experience. In the quest to craft the *what, why* and *how* of EE, it is imperative to demarcate entrepreneurship itself. Entrepreneurship involves the matrix concept of processes and outcomes, investigated through the individual and the business, surrounded by the environment and stakeholders. As such, EE should reflect these aspects, as shown in Table 3.1.

The process of EE primarily involves learning that derives from the individual, and combines the learner's existing experiences, knowledge and skills with the new, introduced knowledge and skills. The 'correct' *what, why* and *how* can come together in a comprehensive learning experience only by emerging from a particular layer of knowledge and skills. In entrepreneurship, this equivalence may appear confusing, as most entrepreneurial businesses start from scratch, that is, from non-existing knowledge. Hence, EE starts from an imagined knowledge, a vision, which is built upon unconventional knowledge springing from unconventional sources: invention, innovation, creation, intertwined with vision, passion and determination. Conventional systems, predominantly academic institutions, find it difficult to accept imaginary knowledge and tools as a substantive or reliable enough basis for education. EE is built upon the core essence of disruptive innovation.

To become familiar with the unconventional premises of EE, different segments of entrepreneurship have been developed, which we term a 'learning about' map, exhibited in Figure 3.1. This map presents the various areas of entrepreneurship in different boxes. For example, learning 'about oneself' (box a) draws on theoretical approaches to personality, human capital, personal characteristics,

Entrepreneurial Education: *What, Why* and *How* **43**

TABLE 3.1 Demarcating entrepreneurship for suitable education

	Process	*Outcome*
Individual	• Entrepreneurial-based capabilities, skills, and knowledge to start a business • Teamwork in an entrepreneurial ecosystem • Cognitive and emotional strategies for ideation and creation • Experience and hands-on work • Developing the mindset, the terminology and vibe • Meeting with the network	• Entrepreneurial capabilities, skills, and knowledge to be skilled for any job or company • Adaptation of a creative, proactive, inquiry-driven approach to society, economy, environment
Business	• Creating and evaluating the idea • Managing the business • Becoming acquainted with the entrepreneurial flow, stages of development • Becoming familiar with stakeholders • Managing competitors, partners, supporters, both locally and internationally	• Creating a business from scratch • Creating innovative projects within existing businesses • Managing the business stages properly • Managing the stakeholders properly • Gaining success and sustainability

environmental impact and cultural influences (Barbosa, Gerhardt, & Kickul, 2007; Baron, 2004; Barrick, 2005; Caliendo, Fossen, & Kritikos, 2014; Envick & Langford, 2000; Korunka, Frank, Lueger, & Mugler, 2003). Accordingly, learning about oneself from an entrepreneurial viewpoint, including experiencing one's own personal strengths and drawbacks and associating these to ideation, implementation of an idea or managing an entrepreneurial business, strongly promotes the learner. Learning areas related to the environment, the ecosystem, interested groups such as stakeholders and shareholders (box d) are founded on theories of the entrepreneurial ecosystem (network theories, strong ties and weak ties, and institutional theories), and contribute to a thorough awareness of the surroundings in which entrepreneurs act (Blackburn, De Clercq, & Heinonen, 2017; Cohen, 2006; Granovetter, 1973; Mack & Mayer, 2016; Mason & Brown, 2014; Spigel, 2015; Stam, 2015; Stam & Spigel, 2017).

Compatible models can then be established, aimed at teaching and facilitating each of these areas for the learner, as they appear along the arrow (Figure 3.1). These models can be specifically developed by merging different existing models, or used conventionally, but interpreted differently for the learner. For example, box c refers to understanding the purpose of crafting relevant and more feasible ideas to start a business; the teaching method is project/problem-based learning,

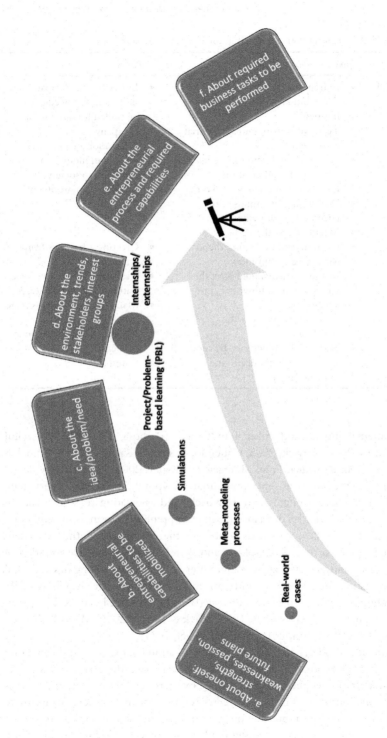

FIGURE 3.1 The 'learning about' map

and its application to entrepreneurship can be as follows: learners meet with a variety of leading figures [e.g., vice president of marketing, finance, research and development (R&D), innovation, production] from businesses representing different sectors, stages of development, and local/global success levels; they analyze the businesses' challenges and needs, and provide solutions. Up to this point, this is the usual PBL method. To apply it to entrepreneurship, the teacher would ask the learners to plan a business from the solution they have reached, or to integrate their solutions with those of others to create a new idea, for example. In this way, the PBL process resonates with the entrepreneurial process.

Modernizing the Prevailing Approach

The field of EE has led to increasing scholarly attention to, and interest in, three main foci: *why* is it valuable, *what* should be delivered, and *how* should it be delivered? These foci are then intertwined with concepts embedded in the entrepreneurship paradigm. Figure 3.2 introduces nine fundamentals of EE that should be part of EE, and present the three foci as they relate to EE.

- *What?* Modernizing conventional ideas, blending subject areas, inventing and innovating themes, being tolerant of innovative interpretations and implementation of existing knowledge; accepting non-academic knowledge
- *Why?* The real value of EE for the learner, the (potential) business, educators, investors, innovators, clients, academia, government
- *How?* Challenging the existing methods with digitized, customized, practical, relevant and 'fun' methods to match young entrepreneurs' learning styles, and attention capabilities.

Beyond the *what, why* and *how*, the following fundamentals should be considered when planning EE:

- Timing—entrepreneurs are typified as more energetic, dynamic and jumping constantly from one thing to the next; EE programs should be short, practical and exciting, to hold the learners' concentration and attention. Furthermore, some entrepreneurs are already engaged in setting up a business, thus programs might be more flexible in terms of hours spent in class, offering online sessions, teamwork (for better time utilization), a flexible schedule, etc.
- Goals—goals must be set and followed. Entrepreneurs choose programs based on the outcomes guaranteed by the program providers. Therefore, EE programs should determine and relay their goals, outcomes, success stories, and challenges. In addition, to ascertain that participants understand the declared goals, the methodology and settings used to achieve them should be transparent.

TAILOR-MADE LEARNING
Individualizing and customizing the missing parts to be taught

DISRUPTIVE INNOVATORS
Respecting the learner's new ideas and implementation of EE

EFFECTIVENESS
Evaluating the practicality and sustainability of the program's outcomes

FREE INTERPRETATIONS
Stimulating creative interpretations of the ecosystem's needs and solutions

Why?
The real value of education for different interest groups

How?
Challenging the existing methods with digitalized, customized, practical, relevant and 'fun' activities

What?
Modernizing conventional ideas, blending subject areas, inventing themes, tolerance to innovative implementation of existing knowledge

GEL
Global entrepreneurship learning

TIMING
Recognizing the learner's timing for EE

GOALS
Being consistent with agreed-upon EE goals

NETWORKING
Knowledge provided, shared and obtained by others; peer learning; mentors as knowledge backbones; networking skills

SUCCESS
Illustrating success, and measures to assess it

FIGURE 3.2 Diffusing EE foci

- Networking—while networking has not been traditionally regarded as a primary segment of EE, but a skill that must be developed mainly at the individual level and not necessarily through educational programs, today, this view has changed dramatically. Networking is now treated as a crucial skill for entrepreneurs. Moreover, as entrepreneurs are encouraged to set up their businesses in teams, networking is transformed into an educational mechanism, where sessions are assembled based on the premise of vibrant networking between the participants; peer sessions are fortified; participant sharing of the class or workshop contents is encouraged; and the establishment of communities, virtual and face to face, is invigorated—these are all crucial for the student entrepreneur's development. Such approaches break the traditional ones that advocate more closed and individual learning. A participative, shared and more communal approach to EE is important for entrepreneurs.
- Success—participants must understand what level of success they can reach through the program, and should be equipped with the measures to assess it. Such declarations and measures of success are valuable for everyone who is involved in the EE process: the learners, the program developers, heads and teachers, and researchers, among others. Many entrepreneurs expect to become the next Mike Krieger and Kevin Systrom—the founders of Instagram, or Brian Chesky, the founder of Airbnb, for example. However they, as well as other successful entrepreneurs, took risks and managed to disrupt and revolutionize the conventional approaches that were being used in different areas. These emphases should be transparent at the outset.
- Tailor-made learning—while entrepreneurs favor sharing knowledge and more participative learning, as independent individuals who are facing different challenges and sometimes have contrasting needs, tailor-made, customized learning is required. By providing the basics, and enabling an array of contents, experiences, mentors, networking and other learning methods, student entrepreneurs can construct their own programs to satisfy their specific needs and expectations.
- Disruptive innovators—entrepreneurs tend to think within unusual, alternative boundaries; this is not to say that they lack boundaries altogether, but they challenge and question the common wisdom, the known and the already established. This thinking style is often seen as rebellious and sometimes uncontrollable, and, therefore, hinders the EE teaching staff from pursuing the program's goals. By accepting that entrepreneurs are disruptive innovators, crafting programs that provide room for their thinking style, and directing them to observe the advantages but also the disadvantages of their innovation, learners will be encouraged to think openly and independently, and course instructors and developers may benefit from the learners' new and unexpected ideas. One interesting example is the Hult[1] International Business School in Cambridge, Massachusetts, which offers a Master's degree in Disruptive Innovation for entrepreneurs and other students who want to make a change and have an impact by harnessing technological advances.

- Effectiveness—knowledge and skills obtained from EE programs should be used by the participants long after the program is over. Effectiveness refers to the utility and practicability of the capabilities obtained, while accounting for their sustainability and dissemination to other people on the team, for example. Measures to assess effectiveness are important for both the learners and the program's head and teaching staff.
- Free interpretation—definitions of problems and solutions are in the eyes of the beholder, that is, a function of their interpretations. While education may dictate 'correct' and 'incorrect' (as reflected by learners' grades, for instance), entrepreneurial programs should strive to be non-judgmental by tolerating various interpretations of a particular situation. This is the way to stimulate innovative ideas and new solutions, as well as to construe the problems and needs in different ways.
- GEL (global entrepreneurship learning)—globalization means diversity, openness and innovation. A common situation for someone from Europe may seem unusual to someone from Asia, and so forth. Exposure to various contents, methods, models, and, above all, people from different cultures and countries is imperative for the student entrepreneur. GEL encompasses all of the previously introduced fundamentals, as the potential of disruptive innovation is developed in a participative way, and can be effective and sustainable in different areas and for different uses.

Reciprocal Relations between Exceptions and the Mainstream

In both academia and practice, EE programs denote the disruptive innovation process in teaching and education. The added value of EE is in tailoring the programs around unconventional standards, thus requiring a more agile and responsive approach to teaching. While most educational systems are established around thematic foundations, EE breaks the thematic rules by blending themes and disciplines. Furthermore, while knowledge acquisition is traditionally obtained by following developments in research and education, EE expands its methods by providing practical knowledge, offering a platform for experience as a learning method, and deeming lean models as acceptable teaching models. Lean models may seem, from a traditional point of view, to be a 'quick and dirty' approach to education that introduces approximate, rather than deep, fully formed and reliable knowledge; they may, therefore, be suspected of giving only a superficial outlook. However, this is not applicable in entrepreneurship, where testing and trying things out in the field—the 'quick and dirty' approach—are a matter of life and death for an idea or a newly invented innovation. The story of Daniel Ek, one of the founders of Spotify—the music streaming service that disrupted the music market, illustrates the drive for a lean and rapid test. In one of his interviews, Ek was quoted as saying:[2]

The way I looked at it was the problem that we had before was exactly that we tried to disrupt it without the industry's participation. I wanted to do something where in the end the artists, the labels, and everyone in the ecosystem was a part of the development. I didn't know much about licensing, but I thought that can't be too hard because there are all these illegal options out there. Surely they must be ready to embrace a legal option. It turned out that they were, but it took two and a half years to get them to that point . . .

EE strives to give the learner a tailored program that is personalized and responds to the learner's needs and expectations. It teaches the learner to take responsibility for the process and expected outcomes of EE. However, the planning and management of such a program is complex. Most systems are built on planned courses and activities, rather than on a 'buffet' system that provides a variety of options to choose from. Reluctance toward EE may originate from this complexity.

The *What*

Various content areas are encompassed in EE, spanning business to psychology, while crossing through specialty areas such as technology, medicine, food production, etc., all echoing the context, as well as national and educational foci. In addition, the *what* is strongly attached to learners' specific needs in obtaining knowledge in entrepreneurship and/or in entrepreneurial skills and tools. The learners might be corporate managers or professionals who are interested in better understanding their entrepreneur clients, such as lawyers or accountants; individuals who aspire to join entrepreneurial businesses as professionals, such as CEOs, CFOs, CTOs, etc; others who wish to consult for startups, as external advisors and mentors; and, obviously, individuals who are preparing themselves to start their own businesses. Expectations of the *what* by each of these types of learner stem from a wide range of motivations, interests, and gaps in knowledge or experience (Fiet, 2001a,b; Matlay, 2005; Neck & Greene, 2011; Piperopoulos & Dimov, 2015; Pittaway & Cope, 2007). According to the European Commission, there are several main clusters of areas that make up the *what* that is to be learnt:

- Academic and disciplinary knowledge through courses, workshops, activities, both separate and integrated. For example, entrepreneurs developing automobile-related endeavors should study content-based courses in strategy, finance and marketing to provide them with knowledge on how to start and manage their business; but also in car production, connectivity and car-related technology, to be able to control their product's development. Many programs, mainly in academia, consider disciplinary knowledge acquisition to be the key source for the *what* provision. However, this is no longer true or realistic, as new knowledge is required to create value, and compete with newly introduced ideas, products and individual capabilities. Such knowledge can be transmitted through the following approaches.

- Effectuation—identify a simple problem in real life that the learners would like to address. By interacting iteratively with the outside world, they can learn more about the problem, the people affected by it and how they can help. The book by Read, Saras, Dew, Wiltbank, and Ohlsson-Corboz (2011) provides ample practical advice on using the effectual approach.
- Business model canvas—outlined by Osterwalder and Pigneur (2010), this consists of nine basic building blocks to create value for external stakeholders. It can be viewed as a simple checklist that students can use when planning their value-creation attempts, where they need to provide answers to key value-creation questions.
- Lean startup—developed by Blank and Dorf (2012) for customer development and by Ries (2011), the lean startup focuses on the need for prompt validation of methods and tools which will help entrepreneurs act through experimentation with real-world stakeholders on how to create value and manage a value-creation process involving outside stakeholders.
- Appreciative inquiry—used to identify opportunities; a method suitable for generating new ideas that will trigger action. A unique contribution of this theory is its strong capacity to fortify inspiration and engagement in the teams that are working with it (Blenker, Korsgaard, Neergaard, & Thrane, 2011; Boekaerts, 2010).
- Design thinking—a creative search for what might be, rather than what is or should be, an action for the purpose of value creation; linking the creation of artifacts through problem-solving activities to ways of reasoning, reflecting and creating meaning. Design thinking consists of learners observing problems and opportunities; brainstorming around plausible ideas for concepts that can help people, and testing these ideas on users through prototypes (Boni, Weingart, & Evenson, 2009; Brown, 2008; Johansson-Sköldberg, Woodilla, & Çetinkaya, 2013).
- Service-learning—this *what* is located at the intersection of internships, practice and volunteerism, offering organized educational experiential knowledge that both meets the needs of the community and satisfies learning objectives, mainly in popular computer science, engineering, and teacher education and in business, nursing, and literacy learning. Its strength is in sharing theoretical roots with EE (Desplaces, Wergeles, & McGuigan, 2009; Giles Jr & Eyler, 1994; Litzky, Godshalk, & Walton-Bongers, 2010; McCulloch, 2009; Pepin, 2012).

The *Why*

"What's in it for me?" is the leading question of any participant in entrepreneurial programs. Since entrepreneurship is not a certified profession, and, concurrently, entrepreneurs are eager to advance their businesses, they may see the education process as time wasted, although the expected value of EE is of great importance. Forbes magazine published Murray Newlands' 2015 article: 'Is a degree in entrepreneurship worth it?'[3] where she writes:

> The answer is that it really depends on you. Today, you can get both an undergraduate and graduate degree in entrepreneurship from an accredited university. In fact, these types of specialized business programs are becoming more and more common, and there are even more specializations available within traditional MBA programs.

Taking this further, educational developers and teaching staff need to create programs where the value for each participant is noticeable, clear and prominent. This is a vital, albeit tricky, task, as entrepreneurs may attribute different values to their studies.

Entrepreneurs are independent innovators, business creators, and learners, and they should, therefore, be able to choose the program curriculum, content, and structure, as well as the expected value that they will consequently gain from the program. This value 'buffet' is a new and innovative idea in its approach to facilitation. Generally, programs endeavor to attract participants through the value they introduce; such value is relevant to some learners, but disappointing to others. Hence, by providing evidence that can be translated into value by the learners, the learners can build their own value package. From a business perspective, the individual return on investment (ROI) is pertinent for student entrepreneurs. The ROI measures the gain or loss generated on an investment relative to the amount of money invested; expanding the investment side to include more components, such as time spent in class and on assignments, energy used for class preparation, etc., provides a tool to assess the value assigned to participating in a program. Benjamin Franklin once said that: "An investment in knowledge pays the best interest." For entrepreneurs, not only knowledge, but also experience, the challenge, and mentors can be valuable; hence, the learner is provided with a 'buffet' of values, first, by demonstrating the richness and vibrancy of the program's evidential components—such as success stories (including those of entrepreneurs and companies), the ecosystem directly attached to the program, companies that support the program, the atmosphere and vibe, publications on the program and its alumni in the media, famous or popular mentors, instructors or faculty—and then by suggesting alternative values for each piece of evidence; thus, the learners can choose the values for their idea development and business advancement, as presented in Figure 3.3. This presents a more customized way of assessing the *why*, specifically for entrepreneurs, as it matches their unique characteristics, and takes into consideration their constant lack of time to engage in activities other than developing their ventures, such as learning, training or mentorship.

	Program's evidential facts	Value assigned	Your value
Mentors	• Leading figures from the local health industry • The founder of a successful company • The CEO of a global medical device company	• Deepen applied knowledge • Open doors to various figures • Obtain support from the mentor's company • Craft an advisory board	
Success stories	• Names and logos of companies that have been accelerated	• Inspiration and empowerment modeling • Obtain advice from these companies • Understand what the entrepreneurial process entails	
Supporters	• Partnership with a leading local university • Partnership with leading labs in the United States • Partnership in various applied research teams around the world	• Greatly expand exposure of the company/idea to the ecosystem • Potential partnerships • Valuable professional advice • Cutting-edge knowledge in the area	
Networking	• Faculty, researchers, research teams • Weekly guest lecturers • Office hours at the leading law and accounting firms	• Expand the relevant networks • Become acquainted with leading figures in a one-stop shop • Office hours with partners who can assist along the way	
Setting	• Pictures of the space	• Inspiring place • A cool place to work, brainstorm, interact	
Atmosphere	• Cool, vibrant, young • Show publications in media	• Feel part of a family, not alone • Pride in taking part in this accelerator • Leverage program participation in future activities and achievements	

FIGURE 3.3 The value 'buffet': example of a health and medicine accelerator program

In her book *Positivity*, Professor Barbara Fredrickson (2009) discusses the *critical positivity ratio*, which is also described in an interview[4] and introduced in the Positivity Self-Test.[5] Fredrickson stresses that experiencing positive emotions in a 3:1 ratio to negative emotions leads people to greater achievements that they once could only imagine (Fredrickson, 2009, 2013). This ratio seems to suit the value imagined by entrepreneurs as learners in EE programs. By espousing the critical positivity ratio, programs' leaders furnish the entrepreneur with the responsibility of forming their own positivity ratio of value gained from their studies in an EE program. For instance, participants who are unsatisfied with their businesses' progress upon completing an EE program would be regarded as being generally unhappy with the program. On the other hand, by delineating the positive emotions or experiences obtained from the program, for example, gaining new ideas for a new business, meeting with great mentors, and connecting with a relevant community of entrepreneurs—three positive aspects, the overall value of the program may be positive. This tool should be developed, according to Fredrickson's concepts, more thoroughly through research, while it could be used as a test case in active programs to assess their perceived value. Taken together, ensuring that the value 'buffet' reaches a 3:1 positivity ratio can create what will be deemed a successful learning experience.

The *How*

Entrepreneurship is taught and delivered in diverse ways, reflecting the indefinite way in which entrepreneurship is pursued, as well as the entrepreneurs' diverse learning styles. To gain value, entrepreneurs need to complete the curriculum through agile and customized methods. The *how* represents not only the way in which the course is delivered, but also a way of modeling what entrepreneurship entails. By preaching creativity but teaching conservatively, the message of entrepreneurship will not reach its learners and they will not adopt it; they may even come to distrust the program. To ascertain a *how* that is compatible with entrepreneurs' learning styles and expectations, the components that entrepreneurship entails should be mapped, and well-suited methods should be designed for each. For example, entrepreneurship entails 'pitching and convincing various stakeholders'; accordingly, a pitch workshop with leading gurus followed by a series of simulations in front of real people to get direct feedback can fit this element, rather than teaching the basics of an excellent pitch. Although the *how* can consist of existing, blended, co-created and newly invented methods, they should all be aligned with entrepreneurship components; for example:

- Iterative processes.
- Scenarios that trigger uncertainty, ambiguity and confusion.
- An applied teamwork approach, giving the students access to increased creative ability and more peer-learning opportunities.

- Time allowances for establishing fruitful relationships with external stakeholders.
- Educational assignments, triggered activities/events and developed entrepreneurial competencies.
- Learning by doing.

(Arievitch & Haenen, 2005; Egan, 2004; Kozulin, 2003; Kozulin & Presseisen, 1995; Miettinen, 2001; Vygotsky, 1991).

One of the initiators of an accelerator program in an insurance company in France stated, in an interview with me, that:

> as an accountant, I had neither ideas nor experience on how to accelerate these passionate entrepreneurs who are selected to our program. Our company is of a conservative nature, and, therefore, unconventional ways were outside the scope of our accelerator program. One of our managers implemented traditional, knowledge-based teaching methods for the startups. But they did not find it valuable, and complained. At this point, I jumped in and scanned our portfolio companies' needs. I was still idea-less on how to tackle them, so I decided to pursue a co-creation process. With a rise from five to ten portfolio companies in the past three years, all in insur-tech, reg-tech and fin-tech, we implement learning by doing, involving exceptional, external advisors and consultants. Our mentors provide us with scenarios from our company, and we pursue an iterative process, which is not only satisfactory for the incubated entrepreneurial businesses, but also for our company's clients. One of the startups is working on digitalizing insurance forms in a machine learning-based way, and one of our clients is negotiating a strategic collaboration with the startup.

Summary

Entrepreneurs are typified as practice-oriented and innovators, and, as such, are less prone to accept any curriculum *per se*, unless it is of value, interesting and can be promptly and successfully applied. In addition, most entrepreneurs who enroll in EE programs are busy developing their businesses, and are, therefore, very strict about the time they can devote to learning. These constraints place a deep responsibility on both the program heads and the student entrepreneurs. By mapping the constituents of entrepreneurship and developing the most compatible '*what*', '*why*' and '*how*', meaningful learning can be established. The responsibility of the program providers lies in building an agile curriculum, and methods and activities that can deliver the knowledge, skills and capabilities in various ways that will meet the entrepreneurs' expectations, learning styles and needs based on their businesses' development; the learners, on the other hand, need to ensure that they choose the best *what, why* and *how* to match the value that they foresee in enrolling in an EE. An ROI based on Frederickson's 3:1 positivity ratio is suggested as a means for learners to create their own learning 'package', chosen from a 'buffet' of contents, methods and values.

Takeaways

For educators and teaching developers:

- Entrepreneurship must be demarcated to develop well-suited processes and outcomes.
- A learning map should be developed that is relevant to the specific focus of the EE program, and the foundation of the program should be built on the basis of the map's elements, while giving different weights to the learning themes based on the program's focus.
- The participant entrepreneur's expected value from the program should be determined, and a matching pool of evidence created and translated into value so that the learner can choose a suitable program.
- A pool of *what, why* and *how* should be established and the participants encouraged to choose from, add to, and co-create with this pool

For EE participants:

- Take responsibility for your learning; decide what you are interested in learning in terms of content, and determine the value of that learning to you and to your business.
- Explore the different ways in which the curriculum is delivered; examine what is most applicable to you, and the most appropriate teaching mode.
- Use your entrepreneurial strengths in the learning process; if you are creative, or an innovator, engage those characteristics to leverage the curriculum that is taught; if you are proactive, look for mentors and networks that suit you; if you are a risk-taker, then try to study new areas to be implemented in your business, etc.

Case Study 3 – NOVUS, the Academic Accelerator

The NOVUS[6] Center of Entrepreneurship is an academia-driven center at the College of Management Academic Studies, the pioneering applied academic institution in Israel. As a private institution, the tuition is higher than at the public universities. NOVUS was established in 2014 by me to provide value to my students in the Business School. The motivation and inducement to initiate the center was twofold; first, while Israel is known to be a 'startup nation', there was a dearth of programs in entrepreneurship at the college, and students were looking for places to develop their ideas; some asked that a center be established on campus, while others enrolled in centers at different campuses. At the same time, I had been involved in different entrepreneurship centers around the world, had generated knowledge, had engendered data and facts, and was highly motivated to establish the center on campus. However, the journey to starting the center was difficult, both internally and externally: the campus management did not see the value or feasibility of such a center to its stakeholders, and their responsibility to their students, who paid a high tuition, was always at stake; on the other hand, academic centers for student entrepreneurs were beginning to be established elsewhere, and the competition was becoming more relevant. I had to craft a sustainable competitive advantage.

As with any startup, I had to convince the ecosystem to support my endeavor. I went from one disappointment to the next, with few people backing my idea and none who would offer assistance in developing the center. I decided to bring a competitive advantage by developing cutting-edge programs for entrepreneurs, as well as for anyone who wants to touch entrepreneurship. Being in academia, involved in research, and surrounded by international research teams, I was able to deepen the then unexploited advantage of R&D and test it with students. There were still few supporters for my endeavor, but the turning point came with a mentor who believed in my vision and supported my pursuit of it. I started a pilot incubation program that ended up being very successful, then received a World Entrepreneurship Forum award for the program. As I say,

> I had a dream... The establishment of NOVUS, the Center of Entrepreneurship, is the implementation of my personal dream. It exemplifies the startup process, and, as such, it may convey a model of the entrepreneurial process to our students, alumni and staff. The establishment of the center started with my 'dream' of creating a home for entrepreneurs. It then rapidly evolved into a platform that provides multiple tools, knowledge and networks, through the substantial support of our School of Business Administration at the campus in Israel and our stakeholders. The center has had its ups and downs, but the determination and full engagement of all of its stakeholders ultimately enabled its creation, development and growth. Our main endeavor has always been the establishment of a home for entrepreneurs and 'wanna-preneurs'. Anchored in research as well as in our cumulative entrepreneurial experience, we have founded a one-stop shop for anyone who is excited about entrepreneurship. Our home gives students, staff and alumni a boundless, non-judgmental place in which to dream. We bring our unique expertise to help those entrepreneurs translate their dreams into real, sustainable new businesses. We strive to add significant value for all of our stakeholders. Our accelerator process for implementation is conducted through our academic expertise, practical experience and vigorous ties with the business community and robust international collaborations. We are constantly creating new entrepreneurial teaching forms and are engaged in

teaching R&D, introducing cutting-edge know-how, and stimulating excellence. We are committed to creating an ethical and fair environment for our stakeholders. We are thrilled to play a part as our center's participants set out to 'change the world' . . .

NOVUS strives to introduce the most up-to-date programs in entrepreneurship to students, alumni and the public. It brings knowledge and content from various partners in academia and industry inside and outside of Israel. Its mentors are non-academic figures from the entrepreneurial landscape in Israel, and its experts, who provide office hours, come from global companies who support entrepreneurs, opening doors into their world for the participants. The center offers various programs, mainly thematically sorted, such as in fin-tech, sports-tech, property-tech, and social-tech, among others, with each gathering a relevant community around it. It is built on three main foundations: academia, industry relationships, and inspiration. To ensure that all of these foundations are introduced, the center has developed a R&D section that maps the participants' needs, the emerging global trends, and new research in the area, and develops programs, activities and projects, to echo these.

The mentors' voices: Anat, one of the mentors and a leading figure in the investment arena says,

> It is inspiring to watch the student entrepreneurs' progress on a weekly basis, to be part of such a change and contribution to the entrepreneurship landscape. In fact, like the students I mentor, I am constantly learning from them, and from the models and experiences used by NOVUS;

Erez, a renowned figure in the financial sector, adds, "

> I choose the projects very carefully; I want to achieve success. I have no tolerance for redundant learning. I do not define success only financially; rather, I can see the spark in the student entrepreneurs' eyes, I witness them implementing the ideas that we have discussed, reflecting on their experiences. I understand that at these points, learning happens;

finally, Karen shares her insights as a locally and globally renowned finance and marketing specialist:

> It's best understood as conducting an orchestra; many ideas seem reasonable and feasible, but then when they are 'played' together to produce beautiful music, things fall apart; no financial reasoning, no market strategies. Then, in NOVUS, they become committed to the process, and let go of the idea, and the 'music' improves, and, step by step, they absorb the meaning of entrepreneurship, they transform their mindset, they mature. Then the orchestra can play.

Questions on the Case Study

1. What is unique about NOVUS? Explain, using the chapter's main concepts.
2. In your opinion, what are the 3–4 major strengths of NOVUS, in the context of Israel, private colleges, and the competition?
3. Discuss 1–2 components of the *what, why* and *how* introduced by NOVUS. Explain your answer.
4. Search the internet for another academic center of entrepreneurship, and write down its name and website address. Discuss 2–3 main differences between NOVUS and that center, and try to explain them.
5. The management of NOVUS invites you to advise them on how to scale up the center's impact. Give 3–4 suggestions and explain them in light of the chapter's concepts.

Reflective Questions

1. Build a 'learning about' map for yourself, and fill in the boxes with content that fits your needs and expectations. For example, for box a. *About oneself: strengths, weaknesses, passion, future plans*—I am a nascent entrepreneur, I lack knowledge and know-how in business creation; I am not sure about my entrepreneurial capabilities and I am not sure about my motivation to become an entrepreneur. I wish to explore these.
2. You are invited to develop a tool for EE program participants that will assist them in exploiting the program's value. You have decided to adapt Professor Barbara Fredrickson's 3:1 positivity ratio for this purpose. Search for Frederickson's model, and suggest a tool accordingly.
3. Search for Stanford's Startup Garage Teaches Entrepreneurship at: www.gsb.stanford.edu/experience/learning/entrepreneurship/startup-garage and list 2–3 *why* and *how* aspects of the course for its student entrepreneurs. What is your conclusion on the garage concept and its implementation?
4. Station F in Paris (https://stationf.co) introduces a number of startup programs under the same roof. Choose three programs and investigate them thoroughly. Discuss the *what, why* and *how* from the student entrepreneurs' perspective and from that of Station F initiators.
5. A global company in gaming and entertainment technology has established a luxurious innovation center for the public and entrepreneurs, who can come freely to develop their ideas in the areas of gamification; however, it has been a resounding failure. Based on the chapter's concepts, list 5–6 diagnostic questions that you would ask the center's initiators to figure out why it was a failure. Explain your response.

Notes

1 See at: www.hult.edu/
2 See at: www.startups.co/articles/how-daniel-became-goliath

3 See at: www.forbes.com/sites/theyec/2015/04/20/is-a-degree-in-entrepreneurship-worth-it/#7d5da8b754e1
4 See at: www.youtube.com/watch?v=Ds_9Df6dK7c
5 See at: www.positivityratio.com/single.php
6 See at: http://english.colman.ac.il/research-and-learning-centers/novus-center-of-entrepreneurship/

References

Arievitch, I. M., & Haenen, J. P. P. (2005). Connecting sociocultural theory and educational practice: Galperin's approach. *Educational Psychologist, 40*(3), 155–165.

Barbosa, S. D., Gerhardt, M. W., & Kickul, J. R. (2007). The role of cognitive style and risk preference on entrepreneurial self-efficacy and entrepreneurial intentions. *Journal of Leadership & Organizational Studies, 13*(4), 86–104. https://doi.org/10.1177/10717 919070130041001

Baron, R. A. (2004). The cognitive perspective: A valuable tool for answering entrepreneurship's basic "why" questions. *Journal of Business Venturing, 19*(2), 221–239. https://doi.org/10.1016/S0883-9026(03)00008-9

Barrick, M. R. (2005). Yes, personality matters: Moving on to more important matters. *Human Performance, 18*(4), 359–372. https://doi.org/10.1207/s15327043hup1804_3

Blackburn, R. A., De Clercq, D., & Heinonen, J. (Eds.) (2017). *The SAGE Handbook of Small Business and Entrepreneurship.* London: Sage.

Blank, S., & Dorf, B. (2012). *The Startup Owner's Manual: The Step-By-Step Guide for Building a Great Company.* Pescadero, CA: K&S Ranch.

Blenker, P., Korsgaard, S., Neergaard, H., & Thrane, C. (2011). The questions we care about: paradigms and progression in entrepreneurship education. *Industry and Higher Education, 25*(6), 417–427.

Boekaerts, M. (2010). The crucial role of motivation and emotion in classroom learning. In *The Nature of Learning: Using Research to Inspire Practice* (pp. 91–111). Paris: OECD.

Boni, A. A., Weingart, L. R., & Evenson, S. (2009). Innovation in an academic setting: Designing and leading a business through market-focused, interdisciplinary teams. *Academy of Management Learning & Education, 8*(3), 407–417.

Brown, T. (2008). Design thinking. . *Harvard Business Review, 86*(6), 84.

Caliendo, M., Fossen, F., & Kritikos, A. S. (2014). Personality characteristics and the decisions to become and stay self-employed. *Small Business Economics, 42*(4), 787–814. https://doi.org/10.1007/s11187-013-9514-8

Cohen, B. (2006). Sustainable valley entrepreneurial ecosystems. *Business Strategy and the Environment, 15*(1), 1–14. https://doi.org/10.1002/bse.428

Desplaces, D. E., Wergeles, F., & McGuigan, P. (2009). Economic gardening through entrepreneurship education. *Industry and Higher Education, 23*(6), 473–484. https://doi.org/10.5367/000000009790156436

Egan, K. (2004). *Getting it Wrong from the Beginning: Our Progressivist Inheritance from Herbert Spencer, John Dewey, and Jean Piaget.* New Haven, CT: Yale University Press.

Envick, B. R., & Langford, M. (2000). The five-factor model of personality: Assessing entrepreneurs and managers. *Academy of Entrepreneurship Journal, 6*(1), 6–17.

Fiet, J. O. (2001a). The pedagogical side of entrepreneurship theory. *Journal of Business Venturing, 16*(2), 101–117. https://doi.org/10.1016/S0883-9026(99)00042-7

Fiet, J. O. (2001b). The theoretical side of teaching entrepreneurship. *Journal of Business Venturing, 16*(1), 1–24. https://doi.org/10.1016/S0883-9026(99)00041-5

Fredrickson, B. L. (2009). *Positivity.* New York: Three Rivers Press.

Fredrickson, B. L. (2013). Positive emotions broaden and build. In P. Devine & A. Plant (Eds.), *Advances in Experimental Social Psychology, Vol. 47* (pp. 1–53). San Diego, CA: Academic Press.

Giles Jr, D. E., & Eyler, J. (1994). The theoretical roots of service-learning in John Dewey: Toward a theory of service-learning. *Michigan Journal of Community Service Learning, 1*(1), 7.

Granovetter, M. S. (1973). The strength of weak ties. *American Journal of Sociology, 78*(6), 1360–1380.

Johansson-Sköldberg, U., Woodilla, J., & Çetinkaya, M. (2013). Design thinking: past, present and possible futures. *Creativity and Innovation Management, 22*(2), 121–146.

Korunka, C., Frank, H., Lueger, M., & Mugler, J. (2003). The entrepreneurial personality in the context of resources, environment, and the startup process—a configurational approach. *Entrepreneurship Theory and Practice, 28*(1), 23–42. https://doi.org/10.1111/1540-8520.00030

Kozulin, A. (2003). Psychological tools and mediated learning. In A. Kozulin, B. Gindis, V. S. Ageyev, & S. M. Miller (Eds.), *Vygotsky's Educational Theory in Cultural Context* (pp. 15–38). Cambridge, UK: Cambridge University Press.

Kozulin, A., & Presseisen, B. Z. (1995). Mediated learning experience and psychological tools: Vygotsky's and Feuerstein's perspectives in a study of student learning. *Educational Psychologist, 30*(2), 67–75.

Litzky, B. E., Godshalk, V. M., & Walton-Bongers, C. (2010). Social entrepreneurship and community leadership: A service-learning model for management education. *Journal of Management Education, 34*(1), 142–162.

Mack, E., & Mayer, H. (2016). The evolutionary dynamics of entrepreneurial ecosystems. *Urban Studies, 53*(10), 2118–2133. https://doi.org/10.1177/0042098015586547

Mason, C., & Brown, R. (2014). Entrepreneurial ecosystems and growth oriented entrepreneurship. *Paris, 30*(1), 77–102.

Matlay, H. (2005). Entrepreneurship education in UK business schools: Conceptual, contextual and policy considerations. *Journal of Small Business and Enterprise Development, 12*(4), 627–643.

McCulloch, G. (2009). The moral universe of Mr Chips: Veteran teachers in British literature and drama. *Teachers and Teaching: Theory and Practice, 15*(4), 409–420.

Miettinen, R. (2001). Artifact mediation in Dewey and in cultural–historical activity theory. *Mind, Culture, and Activity, 8*(4), 297–308.

Neck, H. M., & Greene, P. G. (2011). Entrepreneurship education: Known worlds and new frontiers. *Journal of Small Business Management, 49*(1), 55–70. https://doi.org/10.1111/j.1540-627X.2010.00314.x

Osterwalder, A., & Pigneur, Y. (2010). *Business Model Generation: A Handbook for Visionaries, Game Changers, and Challengers.* Hoboken, NJ: John Wiley.

Pepin, M. (2012). Enterprise education: A Deweyan perspective. *Education+ Training, 54*(8/9), 801–812.

Piperopoulos, P., & Dimov, D. (2015). Burst bubbles or build steam? Entrepreneurship education, entrepreneurial self-efficacy, and entrepreneurial intentions. *Journal of Small Business Management, 53*(4), 970–985. https://doi.org/10.1111/jsbm.12116

Pittaway, L., & Cope, J. (2007). Entrepreneurship education: A systematic review of the evidence. *International Small Business Journal: Researching Entrepreneurship, 25*(1). https://doi.org/10.1177/0266242607080656

Read, S., Saras, S., Dew, N., Wiltbank, R., & Ohlsson-Corboz, A.-V. (2011). *Effectual Entrepreneurship.* Abingdon, UK: Routledge.

Ries, E. (2011). *The Lean Startup: How Today's Entrepreneurs Use Continuous Innovation to Create Radically Successful Businesses*. New York: Crown Business.

Spigel, B. (2015). *Edinburgh's Entrepreneurial and Support Ecosystem*. Edinburgh: University of Edinburgh Press.

Stam, E. (2015). Entrepreneurial ecosystems and regional policy: A sympathetic critique. *European Planning Studies, 23*(9), 1759–1769. https://doi.org/10.1080/09654313.2015.1061484

Stam, E., & Spigel, B. (2017). Entrepreneurial ecosystems. In R. A. Blackburn, D. De Clercq, & J. Heinonen (Eds.), *The Sage Handbook of Small Business and Entrepreneurship* (pp. 407–421). London: Sage. https://doi.org/10.4135/9781473984080.n21

Vygotsky, L. S. (1991). Genesis of the higher mental functions. In P. Light, S. Sheldon, & M. Woodhead (Eds.), *Learning to Think, Vol. 2* (pp. 32–41). Florence, KY: Taylor & Frances/Routledge. [Reprinted from Leontyev, A., Luria, A., & Smirnoff, A. (Eds.) (1966) *Psychological Research in the USSR, Vol. 1*, Moscow: Progress].

4

THERE IS NO 'ONE SIZE FITS ALL'

New Concepts in Educating Entrepreneurs

The complexity in educating entrepreneurs is twofold: *the inflow entrepreneurial process*, consisting of the knowledge, ideas, skills, capabilities, mindsets, among others, that must be assembled and well delivered to trigger the entrepreneurial action; *the outflow process*, comprising the various influences, situations, opportunities, hurdles, etc., that have an exogenous impact on entrepreneurial activity. Acquisition of capabilities and knowledge allows entrepreneurs to manage the uncontrollable influences that they encounter. Hence, the entrepreneurial action can prosper by orchestrating these two opposing processes. The complexity is evident in the multiplicity of elements that must be considered in the educational planning, and the multifaceted roles and impact of each element on the whole educational process; for instance, the element of 'opportunity' (outflow process) requires specific 'capabilities' (inflow process) from one learner, but different capabilities from another. The matrix of these internal and external flows changes with the learner. There is no 'one size fits all' solution. A better understanding of how the relevant matrixes should be developed is needed so that entrepreneurs can benefit from the process.

Some well-established learning models that have been discussed in the research literature are illustrated in Figure 4.1, retrieving core concepts of the EE process, based on the guiding outline capturing EL ". . . create a high-involvement learning system, student co-producers can be provided with information, knowledge, power, and rewards that enable them to more effectively manage learning transformations" (Lengnick-Hall & Sanders, 1997=: 1339). The presented models expand the scope of the learning cycle to emphasize the role of key entrepreneurial skills, heuristics and knowledge, developed over time in response to endogenous and exogenous changes. While the models provide a deep look into learning styles, is it evident that simply 'learning' does not guarantee the integration of experience

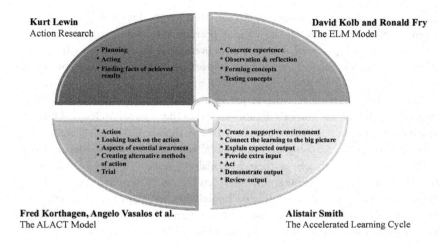

FIGURE 4.1 Leading models of learning cycles

across cognitive, emotional, and behavioral components (Deal, Leslie, Dalton, & Ernst, 2003; Javidan, Teagarden, & Bowen, 2010).

The Entrepreneurial Learning Cycles

Entrepreneurs require unique 'spaces' for free and independent study; their cognitive, emotional, social, processing and reflective 'spaces' are dynamic and agile, and blend different categories. Researchers and educators term these 'spaces' learning styles. In this book, 'spaces' represent the broader learning sphere, including learning styles, which are back-oriented, and the development of future unidentified and undisclosed learning needs, which represent the onward orientation.

Leading impactful researchers who have investigated dynamic learning styles advocate the experimental and experiential hands-on methods to achieve continual teaching effectiveness. Kolb's experiential learning cycle (Kolb & Kolb, 2009;Kolb, 1984), which drew on the earlier works of Piaget (1950) and Dewey (1963), introduced a dynamic, holistic approach driven by an active, experience-based learning process. Subsequent research introduced a wide range of new active-learning experiential approaches (e.g., real simulations, business plan competitions, gaining inspiration from entrepreneurs, and attending entrepreneurship forums) (Gibb, 2002; Jones & English, 2004; Piercy, 2013). These were followed by approaches to entrepreneurs' learning which postulated that intermittent experiences during the entrepreneurial process can stimulate distinct forms of higher-level learning, which contribute substantially to the stock of one's knowledge (Cope, 2003; Corbett, 2005; Deakins & Freel, 1998; Minniti & Bygrave, 2001; Politis, 2005). However, it is a mistake to assume that provision of experience is a sufficient condition for enhanced entrepreneurial activity or success. Experience, *per se*, does not ensure that the learner will further develop the various prerequisites, for example, cognitive, emotional, social, practical, etc., for entrepreneurial success; it may be a good harbinger, but experience needs to be 'leveraged' to achieve the specifically sought entrepreneurial practices to achieve success.

In the framework of EE, the acquisition of knowledge and skill is context-dependent, that is, the learner's demonstration of the curriculum learned through behavior is apt in a specific context, while it might not be well received in others. The general teaching of 'transferable' and 'generic' knowledge and skills is thus questionable in EE, as their potential applicability may be irrelevant to the business's specific context or, alternatively, as entrepreneurial conditions change and are unpredictable, generic knowledge and skills may not reflect the situational dynamics. Moreover, the student entrepreneur needs to process complex, erudite metacognition to apply the transferable knowledge and skills to the 'right' situation; yet, EE scarcely addresses the pairing of knowledge and skills to situations, resulting in an insufficient and volatile applied understanding of the use of generic skills. For example, the reflective practice, which is a do–learn–think process and behavior, is a crucial method for the bewildering, uncertain conditions in longer-term situations, but it can be an inhibitory method for competitive, prompt decision-making situations. Therefore, developing learners into reflective entrepreneurs to cater to transferable, generic capabilities would require another educational intervention that translates into how to grasp and synthesize these capabilities for different contexts (Bennett, Dunne, & Carré, 2000; Bennis & O'Toole, 2005; Bridges, 1993; Brockbank & McGill, 2007; Hinchliffe, 2002; Knight, P. & Yorke, 2004; Knight, P. T. & Yorke, 2002; Neck & Greene, 2011; Pfeffer & Fong, 2002; Pink, 2006).

Figure 4.2 gives a new view of EE based on, and adjusted from, the concepts and insights discussed in Neck, Greene, and Brush (2014). Their concepts bridged the need to deliver transferable knowledge and skills for entrepreneurs' effective interaction with their stakeholders, and the provision of a platform for free, specific and context-based learning 'spaces' for the prompt application of knowledge and skills. By playing, designing, reflecting, feeling, and sense-making, the flux between transferable and specific knowledge and skills can be more sound and compelling to EE.

The Blended-value Approach to Learning

EE requires a four-dimensional platform to enable learners to construct modified solutions for any contingency, and to provide them with an educational platform (cognitive, emotional, behavioral) from which they can create value from and to participants of the ecosystem. This is the blended-value approach. This blended-value framework was adopted from the field of social entrepreneurship with the proposition that 'value' balances economic and social benefits

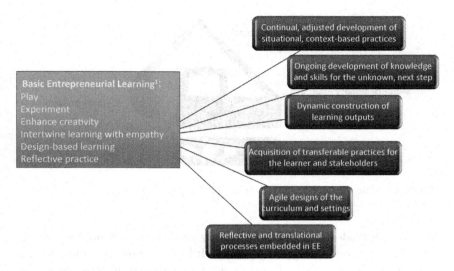

FIGURE 4.2 Agile view of entrepreneurial learning basics

(Emerson, 2003). Organizations that incorporate blended-value business models are actively seeking to maximize their value to society while simultaneously maximizing their financial efficiency, guaranteeing that all three components, that is, social, financial, and environmental, be integrated into any value assessment. The blended-value approach to entrepreneurial learning creates a richer and more enabling educational platform for entrepreneurs who wish to improve their entrepreneurial capacity-building toward creating solutions.

In the educational realm, a blended-value approach looks at the value gained by learners in experiencing hybrid teaching methods by balancing the value of each method and ensuring student control over time and place (Horn & Staker, 2011). Blended value has also been introduced in the context of impact investment to describe the effect of various categories of returns that the investor should be looking for (Rovai & Jordan, 2004). The entrepreneurial blended-value approach developed in this chapter includes four principles, as introduced in Figure 4.3.

Content-based building—The first principle addresses the building of richer and more diversified content for EE programs. The aim is to form a curriculum and practices that derive from various disciplines, which are directly or indirectly related to entrepreneurship, such as business, technology, communication, law, liberal arts, and psychology, some of which might not be intuitive choices for the EE framework. By being open to each discipline's contribution to the educational platform, creative educational outputs can arise, enriching the existing knowledge in this field and creating new insights and views. Such a multidisciplinary approach encourages disciplinary co-creation, where

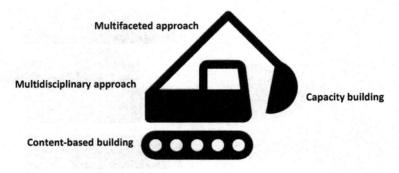

FIGURE 4.3 The blended-value approach—bridging the principles

each discipline adds its unique value to any curriculum without 'threatening' the validity or contribution of the others. It builds exponential value for any theme that is being learned. For example: exploration of the 'business model' using concepts from psychology, sociology and history can contribute not only to a richer business model, but also to synergetic solutions and the creation of new ones.

Multidisciplinary approach—The second principle involves a more investigative nature, complementary to the content-based building principle. It asserts that there are different, as yet unrevealed themes that are relevant to entrepreneurship, entrenched in disciplines that are considered to be less associated with entrepreneurship. The evolution of entrepreneurship from economy to areas such as computer sciences, technology or marketing has yielded many innovations, including current trends such as the Internet of Things (IoT), machine learning, bots, etc. Such evolution is the consequence of involving supposedly 'unrelated' disciplines in the core of entrepreneurship. Practicing a multidisciplinary approach constitutes a discovery process for the learners and other parties involved in the education process by adding models, mindsets and ways of thinking that are characteristic of these different disciplines to the entrepreneurship curriculum. An example might be visiting an art museum to understand the art of painting and adapting some of its principles to the entrepreneurial curriculum, such as skill development, broadening insights on entrepreneurship, exercising teamwork, etc.

Capacity building—The next principle aims to bridge the gap between theoretical education and implementation in the field, by forming a customized platform that can be managed by student entrepreneurs according to their own interests, pace and control. It focuses on the student entrepreneurs' ability to achieve their goals and create a long-term process that guarantees the goals' sustainability. This is a new, fresh look at gaining proficiency in entrepreneurship that can be formulated, transformed, and fused with other capabilities or knowledge in innovative, flexible ways. Specifically, capacity building is a tailored educational process that introduces teaching methods that are then fueled with content by the learners, and not by the educators or other stakeholders. As such, learners have the opportunity to 'exercise' control, decision making, management and other capabilities that they will ultimately need as entrepreneurs. Capacity building is most expedient in developing 'eccentric' capabilities, which are those that are rarely addressed in conventional EE; for example, developing an entrepreneurial mindset, or psychology-related capabilities, such as passion, enthusiasm and resilience. The capacity-building approach leads to the development of advanced educational infrastructures that can offer value to different players in the ecosystem. For example: a hackathon with learners and experts on constructing a program to develop traits relevant to entrepreneurship (e.g., resilience, thinking flexibility, passion) among the learners; in this case, the hackathon is the stimulus for forming entrepreneurial capabilities through learners' needs and expectations.

Multifaceted approach—The multifaceted view is meant to engage stakeholders in the educational process. Obtaining a broad value assessment of an EE program from learners and stakeholders is complex. It involves embedding opposite, yet harmonized approaches in EE development, implementation and sustainability processes: diversification and constant alterations, on the one hand, and a precise sense of the practicality, effectiveness and significance of EE to its stakeholders, on the other. For example: investigating an innovative idea for a new business by forming a think tank involving stakeholders to obtain holistic feedback on the idea, the implementers, the environment's suitability for such ideas, etc.

The blended-value edu-preneurial 'package' offers student entrepreneurs a solid, multifunctional backbone. It asserts that entrepreneurial proficiency will be achieved through an ongoing process based on co-creation. The knowledge and skills that are relevant to entrepreneurship are considered through multidisciplinary, multifaceted views that merge to create new concepts, which can then be implemented. Such an innovative educational approach necessitates the development and implementation of new methods by new participants and through various lenses, so that the blended value of the education process is introduced to the student entrepreneurs and their stakeholders. A deeper look into the methical development and implementation can be achieved through the personalized approach.

AT-A-GLANCE

An article published in Deloitte Insights in 2014 demonstrated the gaps in EE by proving that entrepreneurial action can be stimulated by non-entrepreneurial education. Christopher Strieter, co-founder of Senses Wines, a small-batch producer of West Sonoma Coast Pinot Noir and Chardonnay, describes

(continued)

(continued)

himself as always looking for a challenge, even enjoying difficult problems, as the wine business requires simultaneously solving the science of growing, the art of making, and the business of selling. He has been learning his whole life, including a major in Mathematical Economics and Physics at college, dreaming of traveling into space and making an impact. Characterizing learning, he says: "I've tried to pick each of my jobs based on an area of the business that I need to learn more about, and I learn by being immersed in it." Strieter says that he does not take any jobs that he cannot learn from. He says that his goal for each job includes continuing to meet more people from whom he can learn the business. His desire to start a wine business also drew from non-conventional learning: an unexpected relationship led to an internship and deep mentorship that stretched over several years and afforded him the opportunity to get more acquainted with the wine industry. The knowledge, energy, and passion of his mentor inspired him. Strieter decided not to follow the typical path of his classmates into tech or finance jobs; he went into a master's program to absorb more knowledge and inspiration and consider what it was that he was preparing himself for, then he took a 'harvest internship' working in a wine cellar.

Food for thought:

Are the learning models or the agile look at learning more pertinent to Strieter's journey?

The Personalized Approach

As discussed in the previous chapters, student entrepreneurs' engagement in the creation of their own education is crucial to their commitment to learning, and their consequent success. A personalized pedagogy adds to this in suggesting a personalized view, enabling each student to work at their own pace, through their individual and project-based needs, personal interests and passion. In view of entrepreneurs' intuitive, creative and innovative ways of thinking, the education program should allow them to use their preferred learning modalities, and receive frequent and timely feedback on their performance for a learning experience and performance that is of far higher quality. Recent teaching models are shifting from teacher-centered to learner-centered dynamics, with students being more actively involved in the learning process. Personalizing education calls for flexible pedagogies that put the student entrepreneurs' needs, interests, backgrounds and learning styles center stage, so that students are more empowered through having 'choice and voice' in their learning process (Keamy, Nicholas,

Mahar, & Herrick, 2007, p. 2). Such an approach fits the entrepreneurial spirit, and it can enable personalized learning by giving students greater variety and flexibility in their learning—hence personalized learning spaces, flexible delivery and more student choices (Brown & Green, 2015; Gordon, 2014; Johnson, Adams, & Cummins, 2012; Jones & McLean, 2012; Keamy et al., 2007; OECD, 2006; Ryan & Tilbury, 2013). sFBI[1] (small Factory Big Ideas), located in Israel, builds global ventures from unique human-centered ideas. The founder, Enon Landenberg,[2] said, in an interview with me:

> sFBI accompanies entrepreneurs throughout their journey, from ideation to exit strategy, prior to the decision to launch the startup, by looking at the people, their ideas and their passion. We offer expertise and technical know-how; knowledge and the need for the startups' success, but, as venture builders, we believe that it is only by focusing on the person, and implementing human-centered innovation, that we can deliver our promise to the startups.

The following components encompass the personalized approach embedded in blended value; they may function sequentially or reciprocally, as shown in Figure 4.4.

New entrepreneurial capabilities The underlying assumption in the developed model is that entrepreneurship is not limited to those possessing inborn entrepreneurial characteristics. Anyone who wants to touch entrepreneurship can get

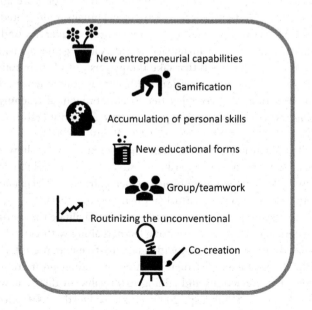

FIGURE 4.4 The personalized approach

involved in the process, by crafting their educational pursuit according to their capacity, enthusiasm, existing characteristics and experiences. The flow and flexibility introduced by the model allow individual choice in terms of the extent to which the learner is involved in the process of structuring his/her education (Drucker, 1985; Kuratko, 2005; Robinson, Stimpson, Huefner, & Hunt, 1991).

Gamification—Game-based learning (GBL) refers to active learning that allows students to develop entrepreneurial competencies in a friendly, modern and relatively safe zone. GBL aligns with serious games—interactive computer-based games connecting multiple players. All of these games aim to create reality-based situations that require actions and decisions; as such, they enable skill development and practice in 'real-life' situations through players' feedback in real time (Deterding, Dixon, Khaled, & Nacke, 2011; Hellevik, Settersten Jr, & Settersten, 2012; Padrós, Romero, & Usart, 2011; Popescu, Romero, Popescu, & Usart, 2013).

- Business simulations—serve as a realistic illustration of the real operations, processes, shortcomings and challenges encountered in entrepreneurship, in a virtual environment, and can be applied to the development of skills and capabilities.
- E-learning—makes use of information and communications technology by incorporating multiple methodologies using software, the internet, online learning and other online media (Moore & Kearsley, 2012). Such programs provide new content with high quality and agility that is not restricted in space or time; external changes can be rapidly embedded in the course.
- Video games—'play' and 'game' represent sources of pleasure and fun that motivate fantasy and curiosity, which are eventually represented (in video format) and felt as real. In addition, a game engages players around a mission, by immersing them in an imaginary world. Video games focus mainly on virtual interactive situations that take the players out of their comfort zone, by having to make serious decisions with serious consequences. Thus, they add a more serious and complex tier to entrepreneurial teaching by demonstrating the vision, rather than just the here and now (Fabricatore, 2000; Griffiths, D. 1999; Griffiths, M. D., 1996; Prensky, 2001).
- Game-allocated teams—massive multiplayer online games allow learners to experience different situations, make decisions, take responsibility for the outcomes and reflect on their resemblance to their entrepreneurial experiences—all with communities, teams or virtual (anonymous) members.
- MOOC (massive open online course)—aims to facilitate the sharing of text-based materials and knowledge among learners along with video lectures and forum-based interactions, often with a face-to-face expert guide. The learners are held accountable for their learning, including promoting the texts, advancing the interactions and adding extra value in different ways to the MOOC (Charney & Libecap, 2000; Finkle & Deeds, 2001; Honig, 2004; Kirby, 2004; Laukkanen, 2000).

Accumulation of personal skills—This requires exposure to, and engagement in, the complex stages of the entrepreneurial process's development. Building upon existing skills to develop new and more entrepreneurship-related ones, these are accumulated to form a personalized entrepreneurial archetype of skills that can be employed throughout the entrepreneurial process (Gibb, 2002; Jack & Anderson, 1999; Jones & English, 2004).

New educational forms—The entrepreneurial route requires a continual action orientation, an ongoing experimental approach, trial and error, problem-solving processes and peer evaluation; the teaching process should reflect these.

> Entrepreneurial skills are learned in a variety of ways and methods. Some entrepreneurial skills are best learnt by doing and observing others. Whilst lecture based education has its place in the curriculum, the training of future entrepreneurs should also include interactive and action orientated methods. (Zahra & Welter, 2008, p. 188)

EE should introduce new forms, by adding, reconstructing or adjusting recurring methods. New EE forms must include real-life experiences, creative problem-solving scenarios and action-centered methods intertwined with higher sensibility to entrepreneurs' learning styles and constantly changing needs, based on changes in their business' development and their unique view regarding the role of EE (Arvanites, Glasgow, Klingler, & Stumpf, 2006; Bevan & Kipka, 2012; Jones & Iredale, 2010; Kientz et al., 2008).

Group work—The personalized approach entails working within groups to form learning missions that are flexible, relevant and result in potential employability while creating a team-based learning experience. Such a cooperative learning experience can enhance the learner's satisfaction rate, motivation and engagement in the learning process through sharing, being more deeply involved in cooperative learning, supporting, refining a sense of accountability, and having a more enjoyable, fun experience (Ormrod, 2008; Patel, 2003; Tsay & Brady, 2012). The entrepreneurial process frequently matures in teams; therefore, constructing the teaching mission in teams can serve as a metabehavioral playground, a 'beta site' to obtain training in team-related situations and challenges.

Routinizing unconventional processes—The personalized approach encourages the embracing of unconventional processes, tools and mindsets in the educational endeavor. The idea is to test the innovative process, assess its relevance to the learners, adjust wherever needed, and gain feedback from other interest groups—such as companies that support entrepreneurship and innovation, consultants and researchers—to develop the broadest, most all-encompassing process. Such innovative discoveries are then routinized to become the rule rather than the exception. As an example, take virtual learning: this started back in the 1960s and was developed in the 1970s with the pioneering work of Murray Turoff and Roxanne Hiltz at the New Jersey Institute of Technology; they developed a networked collaborative learning approach that they called computer-mediated communication (CMC), which they used as a blended learning model that predated the internet (Hiltz & Turoff, 1978). This approach was routinized such that today, every educational program includes online, virtual and hybrid methods of EE.

Co-creation—According to the personalized approach, this refers to a joining of forces between learners and their stakeholders, for example, program developers, educators, and members of the industry, community and government, to produce an educational process that brings value to all of those who are involved in the process and reinforces each side's central role and responsibility in reaching the 'right' process and outcomes. The value of co-creation in EE is manifold: (a) *tailoring the most relevant, meaningful content and methods*, strongly associated with the students' needs; (b) *developing a metacognitive awareness of what is being done*, developing self-authorship, by intently analyzing what constitutes learning for one's own needs; (c) *positioning student entrepreneurs as active agents* in analyzing, revising, and pivoting the program; (d) *enabling a metabehavioral experience*: during the course of their entrepreneurial activity, entrepreneurs will eventually practice the skills and capabilities required for co-creating their own learning (e.g., generating data from the environment, working in teams, persuading their peers of their ideas, managing conflicts, monitoring, etc.); (e) *employability*: the learners' voice provides a unique perspective on teaching and learning and their relevance to the market and business arena; (f) *creating a more democratic intellectual community*, by introducing values such as more authentic co-inquiry, diversity, and the elimination of allocation between students and educators or other stakeholders (Cook-Sather, 2006; Davis & Sumara, 2002; Delpish et al., 2010; Dreier, 2003; Hutchings & Huber, 2010; Kuh, Kinzie, Schuh, & Whitt, 2010; Magolda, 2009; McCulloch, 2009; Rudduck, 2007).

Table 4.1 demonstrates an additional way to plan and implement an EE program by planning the steps and involving the participants throughout development and operation, through the provision of effective feedback and the determination of each step's value. 'Additional' refers to the learners' standpoint, where they indicate components of the blended-value approach (e.g., content building, multidisciplinary approach, multifaceted approach, capacity building) and the personalized approach (e.g., co-creation, teamwork, customization) that are substantial to their learning.

The overall idea is to create a reciprocal, dynamic structure that involves the blended-value and personalized approaches to build a platform for edu-preneurial learning, as illustrated in Figure 4.5. Each component of the blended-value approach can be developed into an applied program or process, which is then implemented through the personalized approach, while the feedback gained on these processes from the personalized approach helps adjust the ideas encompassed in the blended-value approach.

TABLE 4.1 Planning and pre-routinizing steps to programs reflecting the edu-preneurship approach

Steps	Involved participants	Value	To be completed by the learner		
			Value: blended approach	Personalized approach
Exploring the environment, trends, changes, emerging themes	Learners Educators Different stakeholders	Relating the content to current situations		
Investigating teaching methods	Learners Educators Program developers Think-tank teams of different stakeholders	Providing a large scope of teaching techniques in a customized way		
Deciding on content and methods (including goals, deadlines, expected outcomes, etc.)	Learners Researchers Mentors Stakeholders Focus groups of potential clients	Prioritizing the content to be delivered Offering a multidisciplinary view		
Constructing the process: activity, session, course, program, etc.	Learners EE program heads Program developers Educators Mentors	Focusing on the required and outcome-driven processes first		

(continued)

TABLE 4.1 (continued)

Steps	Involved participants	Value	To be completed by the learner	
			Value: blended approach	Personalized approach
Implementation in different forms: multiple choices on how, when, why, which program and where to learn	Educators Mentors Stakeholders Potential Student entrepreneurs	Hands-on processes: introducing platform to real experience		
Echo and feedback from the environment	Educators Mentors	Adjusting and pivoting		
Escorting the learners	EE program heads Mentors Virtual mentors Members of global companies	Enabling being continually informed to solve the problem, assess, and develop accordingly		
'Turning' the learners into mentors and education producers	EE program heads Mentors	Gaining the learners' approach to EE to develop adequate new programs; empowering the learners		

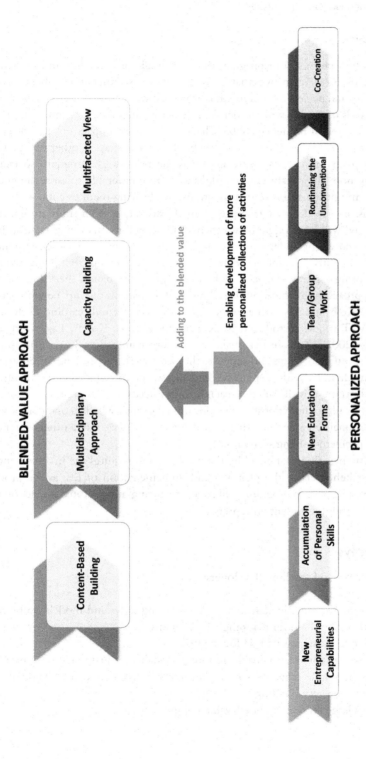

FIGURE 4.5 Relations between the blended-value approach and personalized approach in edu-preneurial learning

Summary

There is no one model or program that can fit all entrepreneurs and their ventures' needs. Research proves that EE is essentially based on complexities deriving from *inflow* and *outflow* entrepreneurial processes; while some are controllable and in the hands of the learners, academia, instructors, mentors, etc. (inflow), others consist of external influences, which have a significant impact on the entrepreneurial activity of the entrepreneurs themselves, as well as on other competitors and groups in the ecosystem. Hence, it is the role of EE programs to enable capturing both the capabilities and skills that are transferable to assist the entrepreneurs in unexpected, external situations, by allowing them to cope with such situations, escape them or leverage them. However, as such skills are generic, 'everybody' will be equipped with them, and, therefore, managing relationships with the ecosystem under external situations will not provide the entrepreneur with a competitive advantage. Thus, an edu-preneurial approach is introduced, encompassing a more advanced look at education that blends the values of different approaches to education, based on the foundations of Kurt Lewin's action research, Kolb and Fry's ELM model, Smith's accelerated learning cycle, and the ALACT model introduced by Korthagen, Kessels, Koster, Lagerwerf, and Wubbels (2001). A more personalized structure is introduced as a platform to develop specific programs and activities that will enable the student entrepreneurs to become familiar with, experience and adjust, the introduced components, so that the learning is well-suited to each learner's needs. For example, some entrepreneurs would rather choose 'new educational forms', which is one component of the personalized approach, that is, real-life experiences, while others favor the creative problem-solving scenarios.

Entrepreneurship is affected by the outflow, and requires the involvement of various stakeholders in the planning and implementation of EE, as the process and the results of such programs will have a recurring, reciprocated impact on the ecosystem and the student entrepreneurs.

Takeaways

For educators and teaching developers:

- Become thoroughly acquainted with learning styles and models, to be able to prioritize them for planning EE programs.
- Accept a more passive role for the instructor.
- Become facilitators to enable a more personalized edu-preneurial approach.
- Use the whole scope of ways to develop EE, from content building all the way to capacity building.
- Use a large array of blended-value components.

For EE participants:

- Become familiar with the learning styles, and reflect upon their fit to your learning style.
- Be tolerant of inconsistencies in learning: learning is not 'one size fits all'. Sometimes, the same curriculum will be understood differently by different individuals.
- Allocate time to non-learning: play, reflect, test.
- Add emotions to learning, to gain more holistic insights from the process.

Case Study 4 – Venture Building: A New Blended-value Type of Education to Assist Entrepreneurs

Xiabo Zhōngháng[3] from Hangzhou, Zhejiang, China was a highly talented accountant in a local, yet most successful, construction company, aimed at conquering global markets. Zhōngháng obtained her academic degrees with the support of governmental grants in Canada and returned to her native country as per undisputable family tradition. She met with various small local companies that had introduced innovative ideas to advance the construction field, and whose founders had the entrepreneurial and go-global zeal; yet, she felt that they were all lacking the basics of the go-to-market. During one of her work visits to a potential customer's company in Canada, she came across the accelerator system, and was determined to start it in China as a complementary service for the company where she would work. As an accountant, and having roots in Canada, she succeeded in securing some seed money from Pierre Leblanc, a Canadian angel investor, who was involved in businesses in China; together they opened an accelerator within the construction company, in a small but cozy renovated hall, for small businesses in the field of construction that had innovative ideas. But the concept was still immature, an unknown in China, and niche-based; thus, it did not reach the expected outcomes. The construction company's management, therefore, decided to close down the accelerator's activity. Leblanc and Zhōngháng began looking for alternative models to empower and enable small businesses in the construction field to start, manage and scale up their businesses. They started a company based on the 'venture builders' approach, aimed at systematically producing new companies, which they helped grow and succeed by identifying business ideas, building teams, finding capital, helping manage the ventures, and providing shared services, while employing a methodology of entrepreneurship, and providing talent to the ventures. Zhōngháng quit her job and dedicated her time to developing this business.

Venture-building companies develop various business models simultaneously, then build separate companies around the most promising ones by assigning operational resources and capital to those portfolio companies. Following this strategy, Zhōngháng contacted the Canadian university where she had studied and signed an agreement for a collaborative research project whose outcomes would help businesses in the construction field explore different ideas and prototype concepts, and create the most accurate future models to build companies.

One common form of a venture-building company is a holding company that owns equity in the various corporate entities it has helped create. The most successful venture builders are, however, much more operational and hands-on than holding companies: they raise capital, staff resources, host internal coding sessions, design business models, work with legal teams, build minimum viable products (MVPs), hire business development managers, and run very effective marketing campaigns during their ventures' pre- and post-launch phases. Leblanc contacted some companies that he had previously worked with to acquire funds for the companies built in this new endeavor, and they facilitated access to capital for around a third of the construction startups developed by the venture-building company. The competitive advantages introduced by Zhōngháng and Leblanc to the Chinese market manifested themselves in several aspects: like all venture-building companies, they continuously produced new ventures, whereas accelerators or incubators provide mentoring and shared services for a limited period of time. Zhōngháng and Leblanc insisted on developing all ideas in-house, and teams were built from the ground up; they established long-term, deeply engaged relationships between their venture builder and the companies. Moreover, Leblanc was deeply involved in the daily management of the operation for each company that they built.

The idea behind venture builders is that they pull business ideas from within their own network of resources and assign internal teams to develop them. In the case of Zhōngháng and Leblanc, they assembled their ideas based on Zhōngháng's contacts with construction companies in China; there she hoped to develop as many companies as possible with as many of the existing companies' teams as possible. However, their venture-building company also did not reach its expected outputs; many small business founders with great ideas refrained from engaging with Zhōngháng and Leblanc's program. They, therefore, pivoted the idea and relocated to Canada, to start a venture-building company for a larger array of entrepreneurs.

Questions on the Case Study

1. What is unique about the venture-building program that Zhōngháng and Leblanc started, with respect to the *agile view of entrepreneurial learning basics* discussed in the chapter? Choose three components and analyze them according to the detailed case study. What are your insights?
2. In your opinion, is there a connection between Zhōngháng's experience in her previous corporate accelerator and the construction of the venture builder? Explain by discussing the blended-value approach in this context.

3. In what way does the venture builder created by Zhōngháng and Leblanc mirror the personalized approach discussed in this chapter? Give three examples. What are your conclusions?
4. Search the internet and gain more insights on venture builders; write down the name and website address of one of them. Choose two components of the personalized approach that you can identify in this venture-building company and compare them to the components of Zhōngháng and Leblanc's company. Describe your findings.
5. In your opinion, what differences can Zhōngháng and Leblanc expect by opening a venture builder in Canada, compared to the activity and (low) success rate of their program in China? Explain your response by referring to this chapter's concepts.

Reflective Questions

1. Search the internet for a MOOC; write down the name and website address. Briefly describe its main essence. Discuss how the MOOC represents the 'personalized approach' to learning discussed in this chapter.
2. Search the internet for a program/business for educational games/gamification; write down the name and website address. Briefly describe its main products and services. Discuss how it offers agile learning, based on the components presented in the chapter. Explain.
3. Imagine Coursera https://www.coursera.org/browse/business/entrepreneurship invites you to contribute a one-day course for entrepreneurs depicting the entrepreneurial process from the founder's perspective. They ask you to format a personalized course. List five questions that you will ask Coursera in order to plan your course.
4. Read 'How can incubators, accelerators and co-working spaces in India help innovation?', by Muthu Singaram, founder of VibaZone (Canada, India and Malaysia) and CEO of HTIC-MedTech Incubator, IIT Madras (https://www.entrepreneur.com/article/304225), on India's numerous governmental programs for startups and their benefits and disadvantages for the startup. Based on the article, discuss the blended-value components of these programs; which would you recommend for nascent entrepreneurs? Explain your answer.
5. Watch Matt Goldman's TED talk on 'The search for "aha!" moments' at https://www.ted.com/talks/matt_goldman_the_search_for_aha_moments.

    In 1988, Matt Goldman co-founded *Blue Man Group*, an off-Broadway production that became a sensation, known for its humor, blue body paint and wild stunts. The show works on the premise that certain conditions can create 'aha' moments—moments of surprise, learning and exuberance—frequently and intentionally rather than randomly and occasionally. Now Goldman is working to apply the lessons learned from *Blue Man Group* to education, creating Blue School, a school that balances academic mastery, creative thinking and self and social intelligence. "We need to cultivate safe and conducive conditions for new and innovative ideas to evolve and thrive," Goldman says.

Discuss Goldman's ideas with respect to the premise of the chapter that there is no 'one size fits all' learning experience and how Goldman provides new views to solve this.

Notes

1 See at: www.s-fbi.com/
2 Enon Landenberg, founder, dreamer and doer at sFBI, is serving in various companies, including President of Infinity Augmented Reality; he was the co-founder and managing partner of E-Dologic, Israel's first interactive advertising agency; he is also the Chief Commercial Marketing Officer for SpaceIL's project to land an Israeli spacecraft on the moon. He has mentored startups at NOVUS, the College of Management Academic Studies, Rishon Lezion, Israel.
3 The names have been changed as per the interviewee's request; most of the other details are well matched to the interviewee's story, apart from details that could breach confidentiality.

References

Arvanites, D. A., Glasgow, J. M., Klingler, J. W., & Stumpf, S. A. (2006). Innovation in entrepreneurship education. *Journal of Entrepreneurship Education*, *9*, 29–43.

Bennett, N., Dunne, E., & Carré, C. (2000). Skills Development in Higher Education and Employment. Buckingham, UK: Society for Research into Higher Education & Open University Press.

Bennis, W. G., & O'Toole, J. (2005). How business schools lost their way. *Harvard Business Review*, *83*(5), 96–104.

Bevan, D., & Kipka, C. (2012). Experiential learning and management education. *Journal of Management Development*, *31*(3), 193–197.

Bridges, D. (1993). Transferable skills: a philosophical perspective. *Studies in Higher Education*, *18*(1), 43–51.

Brockbank, A., & McGill, I. (2007). *Facilitating Reflective Learning in Higher Education* (2nd ed.). Maidenhead, UK: Society for Research into Higher Education & Open University Press.

Brown, A., & Green, T. (2015). Issues and trends in instructional technology: maximizing budgets and minimizing costs in order to provide personalized learning opportunities. In M. Orey & R. M. Branch (Eds.), *Educational Media and Technology Yearbook. Vol. 39* (pp. 11–24). New York: Springer.

Charney, A., & Libecap, G. D. (2000). *The Impact of Entrepreneurship Education: An Evaluation of the Berger Entrepreneurship Program at the University of Arizona, 1985–1999.* Kansas City, MO: Kauffman Center for Entrepreneurial Leadership.

Cook-Sather, A. (2006). 'Change based on what students say': Preparing teachers for a paradoxical model of leadership. *International Journal of Leadership in Education*, *9*(4), 345–358.

Cope, J. (2003). Entrepreneurial learning and critical reflection. *Management Learning*, *34*(4), 429–450. https://doi.org/10.1177/1350507603039067

Corbett, A. C. (2005). Experiential learning within the process of opportunity identification and exploitation. *Entrepreneurship Theory and Practice*, *29*(4), 473–491.

Davis, B., & Sumara, D. (2002). Constructivist discourses and the field of education: Problems and possibilities. *Educational Theory*, *52*(4), 409–428.

Deakins, D., & Freel, M. (1998). Entrepreneurial learning and the growth process in SMEs. *The Learning Organization, 5*(3), 144–155.
Deal, J. J., Leslie, J., Dalton, M., & Ernst, C. (2003). Cultural adaptability and leading across cultures. *Advances in Global Leadership, 3*, 149–166. https://doi.org/10.1016/S1535-1203(02)03008-3
Delpish, A., Holmes, A., Knight-McKenna, M., Mihans, R., Darby, A., King, K., & Felten, P. (2010). Equalizing voices: Student–faculty partnership in course design. *Engaging Student Voices in the Study of Teaching and Learning*, 96–114.
Deterding, S., Dixon, D., Khaled, R., & Nacke, L. (2011). From game design elements to gamefulness. In *Proceedings of the 15th International Academic MindTrek Conference on Envisioning Future Media Environments – MindTrek '11* (p. 9). New York: ACM Press. https://doi.org/10.1145/2181037.2181040
Dewey, J. (1963). *Liberalism and Social Action, Vol. 74*. New York: Capricorn Books.
Dreier, O. (2003). Learning in personal trajectories of participation. In N. Stephenson, H. L. Radtke, R. Jorna, & H. J. Stam (Eds.), *Theoretical Psychology: Critical Contributions* (pp. 20–29). Ontario, Canada: Captus Press.
Drucker, P. F. (1985). The discipline of innovation. *Harvard Business Review, 63*(3), 67–72.
Emerson, J. (2003). The blended value proposition: Integrating social and financial returns. *California Management Review, 45*(4), 35–51.
Fabricatore, C. (2000). Learning and videogames: An unexploited synergy. 1–17. www.learndev.org/dl/FabricatoreAECT2000.pdf
Finkle, T., & Deeds, D. (2001). Trends in the market for entrepreneurship faculty, 1989–1998. *Journal of Business Venturing, 16*, 613–630.
Gibb, A. (2002). Creating conducive environments for learning and entrepreneurship. *Industry and Higher Education, 16*(3), 135–148. https://doi.org/10.5367/000000002101296234
Gordon, N. (2014). *Flexible Pedagogies: Technology-enhanced Learning*. York, UK: Higher Education Academy.
Griffiths, D. (1999). Presentation skills. In C. K. Chris & L. S. Walsh (Eds.), *The Experience of Managing: A Skills Guide* (pp. 193–203). London, UK: Palgrave Macmillan. https://doi.org/10.1007/978-1-349-27328-7_1
Griffiths, M. D. (1996). Computer game playing in children and adolescents: A review of the literature. In T. Gill (Ed.), *Electronic Children: How Children Are Responding to the Information Revolution* (pp. 41–58). London, UK: National Children's Bureau
Hellevik, T., Settersten Jr, R. A., & Settersten, R. A. (2012). Life planning among young adults in 23 European countries: The effects of individual and country security. *European Sociological Review, 29*(5), 923–938. https://doi.org/10.1093/esr/jcs069
Hiltz, S. R., & Turoff, M. (1978). *The Network Nation: Human Communication via Computer*. Cambridge, MA: MIT Press.
Hinchliffe, G. (2002). Situating skills. *Journal of Philosophy of Education, 36*(2), 187–205.
Honig, B. (2004). Entrepreneurship education: Toward a model of contingency-based business planning. *Academy of Management Learning & Education, 3*(3), 258–273.
Horn, M. B., & Staker, H. (2011). *The Rise of K–12 Blended Learning*. Lexington, MA: Innosight Institute.
Hutchings, P., & Huber, M. T. (2010). *Citizenship across the Curriculum*. Bloomington, IN: Indiana University Press.
Jack, S. L., & Anderson, A. R. (1999). Entrepreneurship education within the enterprise culture: Producing reflective practitioners. *International Journal of Entrepreneurial Behavior & Research, 5*(3), 110–125.
Javidan, M., Teagarden, M., & Bowen, D. (2010). Making it overseas. *Harvard Business Review, 88*(4), 109–113.

Johnson, L., Adams, S., & Cummins, M. (2012). *Technology Outlook for Australian Tertiary Education 2012–2017: An NMC Horizon Report Regional Analysis*. Austin, TX: The New Media Consortium.

Jones, B., & Iredale, N. (2010). Enterprise education as pedagogy. *Education+ Training*, 52(1), 7–19.

Jones, C., & English, J. (2004). A contemporary approach to entrepreneurship education. *Education + Training*, 46(8/9), 416–423. https://doi.org/10.1108/00400910410569533

Jones, M. M., & McLean, K. J. (2012). Personalising learning in teacher education through the use of technology. *Australian Journal of Teacher Education*, 37(1), 75–92.

Keamy, R. L., Nicholas, H. R., Mahar, S., & Herrick, C. (2007). Personalising education: from research to policy and practice.

Kientz, J. A., Patel, S. N., Jones, B., Price, E., Mynatt, E. D., & Abowd, G. D. (2008). The Georgia Tech aware home. In *Proceeding of the Twenty-Sixth Annual CHI Conference Extended Abstracts on Human Factors in Computing Systems –CHI '08* (pp. 3675–3680). New York: ACM Press. https://doi.org/10.1145/1358628.1358911

Kirby, D. A. (2004). Entrepreneurship education: Can business schools meet the challenge? *Education + Training*, 46(8/9), 510–519. https://doi.org/10.1108/00400910410569632

Knight, P., & Yorke, M. (2004). *Learning, Curriculum and Employability in Higher Education*. London: RoutledgeFalmer.

Knight, P. T., & Yorke, M. (2002). Employability through the curriculum. *Tertiary Education and Management*, 8(4), 261–276.

Kolb, A. Y., & Kolb, D. A. (2009). Experiential learning theory: A dynamic, holistic approach to management learning, education and development. In S. J. Armstrong & C. V. Fukami (Eds.), *The SAGE Handbook of Management Learning, Education and Development* (pp. 42–68). London: Sage

Kolb, D. A. (1984). *Experiential Learning: Experience as the Source of Learning and Development*. Englewood Cliffs, NJ: Prentice-Hall.

Korthagen, F. A., Kessels, J., Koster, B., Lagerwerf, B., & Wubbels, T. (2001) *Linking Practice and Theory: The Pedagogy of Realistic Teacher Education*. Mahwah, NJ: Lawrence Erlbaum.

Kuh, G. D., Kinzie, J., Schuh, J. H., & Whitt, E. J. (2010). *Student Success in College: Creating Conditions that Matter*. San Francisco CA: Jossey-Bass.

Kuratko, D. F. (2005). The emergence of entrepreneurship education: Development, trends, and challenges. *Entrepreneurship Theory and Practice*, 29(5), 577–598. https://doi.org/10.1111/j.1540-6520.2005.00099.x

Laukkanen, M. (2000). Exploring alternative approaches in high-level entrepreneurship education: Creating micromechanisms for endogenous regional growth. *Entrepreneurship & Regional Development*, 12(1), 25–47. https://doi.org/10.1080/089856200283072

Lengnick-Hall, C. A., & Sanders, M. M. (1997). Designing effective learning systems for management education: Student roles, requisite variety, and practicing what we teach. *Academy of Management Journal*, 40(6), 1334–1368. https://doi.org/10.2307/257036

Magolda, M. B. B. (2009). The activity of meaning making: A holistic perspective on college student development. *Journal of College Student Development*, 50(6), 621–639.

McCulloch, G. (2009). The moral universe of Mr Chips: Veteran teachers in British literature and drama. *Teachers and Teaching: Theory and Practice*, 15(4), 409–420.

Minniti, M., & Bygrave, W. (2001). A dynamic model of entrepreneurial learning. *Entrepreneurship Theory and Practice*, 25(3), 5–16. https://doi.org/10.1177/104225870102500301

Moore, M. G., & Kearsley, G. (2012). *Distance Education: A Systems View of Online Learning* (3rd ed.). Belmont CA: Wadsworth Cengage Learning.

Neck, H. M., & Greene, P. G. (2011). Entrepreneurship education: Known worlds and new frontiers. *Journal of Small Business Management, 49*(1), 55–70. https://doi.org/10.1111/j.1540-627X.2010.00314.x

Neck, H. M., Greene, P. G., & Brush, C. G. (2014). *Teaching Entrepreneurship: A Practice-based Approach*. Cheltenham, UK: Edward Elgar.

OECD (2006). *Schooling for Tomorrow: Personalising Education*. Paris, France: OECD.

Ormrod, J. E. (2008). *Human Learning*. Upper Saddle River, NJ: MerrillPrentice Hall.

Padrós, A., Romero, M., & Usart, M. (2011). Developing serious games: From face-to-face to a computer-based modality. *ELearning Papers, 25*, 1–12.

Patel, N. V. (2003). A holistic approach to learning and teaching interaction: Factors in the development of critical learners. *International Journal of Educational Management, 17*(6), 272–284. https://doi.org/10.1108/09513540310487604

Pfeffer, J., & Fong, C. T. (2002). The end of business schools? Less success than meets the eye. *Academy of Management Learning & Education, 1*(1), 78–95.

Piaget, J. (1950). Explanation in sociology. *Sociological Studies*, 30–96.

Piercy, N. (2013). Evaluating experiential learning in the business context: Contributions to group-based and cross-functional working. *Innovations in Education and Teaching International, 50*(2), 202–213.

Pink, D. H. (2006). *A Whole New Mind: Why Right-brainers Will Rule the Future*. New York: Riverhead Books.

Politis, D. (2005). The process of entrepreneurial learning: a conceptual framework. *Entrepreneurship Theory and Practice, 29*(4), 399–424.

Popescu, M., Romero, M., Popescu, M. M., & Usart, M. (2013). Serious games for serious learning using SG for business, management and defense education. *International Journal of Computer Science Research and Application, 03*, 5–15.

Prensky, M. (2001). Digital natives, digital immigrants Part 1: Do they really think differently? *On the Horizon, 9*(5), 1–6.

Robinson, P. B., Stimpson, D. V., Huefner, J. C., & Hunt, H. K. (1991). An attitude approach to the prediction of entrepreneurship. *Entrepreneurship Theory and Practice, 15*(4), 13–32.

Rovai, A. P., & Jordan, H. (2004). Blended learning and sense of community: A comparative analysis with traditional and fully online graduate courses. *The International Review of Research in Open and Distributed Learning, 5*(2).

Rudduck, J. (2007). Student voice, student engagement, and school reform. In D. Thiessen & A. Cook-Sather (Eds.), *International Handbook of Student Experience in Elementary and Secondary School* (pp. 587–610). Dordrecht, the Netherlands: Springer.

Ryan, A., & Tilbury, D. (2013). Uncharted waters: Voyages for Education for Sustainable Development in the higher education curriculum.. *Curriculum Journal, 24*(2), 272–294.

Tsay, M., & Brady, M. (2012). A case study of cooperative learning and communication pedagogy: Does working in teams make a difference? *Journal of the Scholarship of Teaching and Learning, 10*(2), 78–89.

Zahra, S. A., & Welter, F. (2008). Entrepreneurship education for central, eastern and southeastern Europe. In J. Potter (Ed.), *Entrepreneurship and Higher Education*, 165–189. Paris, France: OECD.

5
THE ENTREPRENEUR'S PERSPECTIVE

Why Do Entrepreneurs Enroll in Entrepreneurship Programs?

Bringing an idea to fruition is ambiguous and risky and requires a substantial amount of personal sacrifice along the way, with failure as a potential option. Entrepreneurship programs provide a safety net by imparting knowledge, skills, and networks that, even if they are general, are valuable in providing a space for the emotional part of the journey. This chapter focuses on the individual's perspective, the cognitive, affective and motivational aspects of entrepreneurship and education. In particular, it discusses the knowledge, skills, and ability (KSA) required in EE programs, which are relevant to the specific personality traits typifying entrepreneurs—creativity, innovation, proactivity, curiosity, passion, inventiveness and a propensity for risk, among others. These entrepreneurial traits include the following aspects:

- Cognitive—the intuitive, creative, innovative and rebellious ways in which entrepreneurs tackle situations. Inventions start from such outside-the-box, counter to the mainstream, original interpretations of situations; opportunity exploitation ensues by identifying things that others do not naturally see, and pitching investors on ideas that could work with the help of improvised thinking.
- Attitudes—intent to become an entrepreneur; orientation to personal, career or business growth, personal or team's perceptions about the pace and directions of business development, approaches to the ecosystem's role in the business, ideation, pivots, etc.; personal interpretation of support systems (these systems have exclusive interests which do not perfectly match the entrepreneur's interests; they are useful only for the first stages of the business, etc.). These, among others, are the backbone of the learning process.

- Emotional—self-efficacy, self-confidence, and personal maturity (versus a naïve, immature nature) are important factors bridging the entrepreneur's emotional orientation to his/her business's success and entrepreneurial skill development through EE; in other words, even the best curriculum will not transform a learner into a successful entrepreneur, unless the learner perceives such skills and resources as essential to becoming successful.
- Motivation—why do learners join EE programs, what is their motivation to become entrepreneurs? Are they looking to become more entrepreneurial, or considering entrepreneurship as a career choice?
- Social support—team building and development, engaging partners to offer genuine support in locating clients, providing referrals, opening doors to investors, among others.
- Behavioral aspects—skill acquisition, know-how enrichment, learning the right terminology, improving capabilities such as making pitches, negotiating with stakeholders, financial skills, marketing-related skills

Each of these aspects leads to the development of different programs, in terms of goals, structure, implementation, and KSA delivery. For example, a program focused on offering tools based on the entrepreneur's typical cognitive traits should provide intuitive and creative activities, encourage its instructors to be tolerant of creative interpretations, and, if the program includes assessments and grades, theses should harmonize with the program's principles and be more flexible in their assessments as well.

Research largely discusses the following as reasons that entrepreneurs enroll in EE programs:

- Deepen knowledge.
- Acquire relevant tools.
- Identify personal capabilities.
- Develop self-confidence and self-efficacy.
- Develop relevant networking skills.
- Understand the ecosystem.
- Be part of a community.
- Deepen creativity, innovation in an existing business/job.
- Improve communication with entrepreneurs (for professionals, such as customers, suppliers, stakeholders).
- Find partners, investors, interested parties.
- Identify and enhance relevant personality traits.
- Career development or change.
- Become inspired; meet role models in the form of leading figures (e.g., mentors, guest lecturers).
- Curiosity, interest in the subject area.

On the other hand, research also shows that the satisfaction and value gained from these programs are more associated with:

The experience:

- Meeting with the finest leading figures in the entrepreneurial scene.
- Developing the relevant network with other participants, academic staff, instructors.
- Enjoying an awesome atmosphere in the venue (accelerator, incubator, co-working place).
- Interesting activities, projects, hackathons.
- Professional staff to learn and gain inspiration from.
- Being part of the 'coolest' scene.

The deliveries:

- Acquiring business tools that learners can use.
- Acquiring knowledge that learners can use.
- Connecting to investors and funding partners.
- Establishing partnerships.
- Becoming a business (including legal, operational and technical aspects).

These reasons can be categorized as push and pull reasons to join EE programs: the push orientation refers to perceiving the program as a resource for escaping problems and challenges that have been encountered previous to, and along, the entrepreneurial journey; the pull orientation refers to perceiving education as the best vehicle to pursue competitive advantages, even when past and present situations have been/are successful and promising.

Educational programs should build their KSA delivery according to potential participants' push and pull expectations. Table 5.1 provides a blueprint for program managers and developers who are planning to establish new programs as a support system, and for entrepreneurs in their process of choosing a program. Examples are presented in the push/pull cells. Interviews of entrepreneurs and potential entrepreneurs participating in EE programs can clarify their blend of reasons, motivations and expectations with respect to EE programs.

AT-A-GLANCE: STARTUPBOOTCAMP—THE STARTUPS' VIEW

Startupbootcamp is a global startup accelerator located in Berlin that provides mentorship, a global network, potential corporate partners and investors, funding, and co-working space. Two startups in the health field that participated in this program for three months considered its main competitive advantages to lie in the mentors' and experts' network.* The links that they gained through their participation in the program expanded from academic institutions, labs and researchers that elevated their projects to higher levels, to serial entrepreneurs and experts in digitalization and health innovations who elevated their businesses to a higher level. One of the founders was keen to penetrate the European market; she searched various programs and decided to apply to the Startupbootcamp program due to its global networking, covering more than 40 countries. She made use of the global connections daily and assessed her startup's progress through these connections. The other founder applied to the program as he needed to engage more talented people on his team; yet, he had developed a niche project that required specific qualifications and knowledge. He was looking for a co-working space with opportunities to meet with people in his area—a specialized place that was focused on the field of his business expertise. Both valued the relatively reasonable cost and the optimal location of the venue, along with the customized mentorship, as a life experience that boosted their startups' progress. The postgraduate support given by Startupbootcamp is regarded as a substantive advantage in their areas.

Food for thought:

Where is the line between a specialized and too narrowly specialized accelerator? What is recommended? Does one size fit all?

* From a face-to-face interview of the founders conducted by me.

Psychological Perspectives in EE: The Meeting Point of Psychology–Entrepreneurship–Education

Research shows varying views on the psychological aspect of EE while stressing that a reciprocal relationship exists between EE programs and the entrepreneurs' psychological traits. EE programs intervene in the learners' psychological traits, and may make them better suited to entrepreneurial-oriented processes, while, apparently, entrepreneurs possessing specific entrepreneurial traits enroll in EE programs.

Studies investigating these reciprocal relationships address entrepreneurship mainly as a career choice; therefore, individuals need to be well equipped with the skills, capabilities and mindsets, and to be able to absorb the drivers for their entrepreneurial success. This aspect is mainly debated through the theory of planned behavior (Ajzen, 1991) while focusing on who can become an entrepreneur. EE programs are the facilitating vehicle to becoming an entrepreneur for anyone who has an innovative idea; EE programs are, thus, regarded as responsible for shaping their learners' mindsets, attitudes and behavior toward becoming

TABLE 5.1 Reasons to join entrepreneurial programs: a push/pull perspective

Reasons	Push: *encountering a problem*	Pull: *creating a competitive advantage*
Deepen knowledge	Due to a problem in marketing the product	Founder expert in technology wishes to know how the financial aspects of the business work
Acquire relevant tools		Founder expert in finance wishes to experience some marketing tools
Identify personal capabilities	Due to difficulty recovering from an investor's refusal	Startup team leaders interested in elevating the team's capabilities
Develop self-confidence and self-efficacy		"Now things are going well, I should prepare myself for the next stage"
Develop relevant networking skills	When the prototype is completed and it needs to be introduced to the market, but so far, there is no interest	Expanding the networking to the next stage's needs
Understand the ecosystem		Acquiring tools to predict the ecosystem's needs
Be part of a community		Establishing the business' reputation
Deepen creativity, innovation in an existing business/job	Experiencing burnout at an existing job	Even when things are progressing satisfactorily, it is important to understand how to innovate for the next phase
Improve communication with entrepreneurs (for professionals such as customers, suppliers, stakeholders)	In situations where the professional (accountant, lawyer, advisor) finds it difficult to communicate with the entrepreneur	Planning for the next niche of customers
Find partners, investors, interested parties	At 'money time', when funding and support are needed but there is no luck	Forecasting the needs of the business by starting to build trusting relationships with investors
Identify and enhance relevant personality traits	Difficulties deciding on the career, and on suitability to the job	Delineating one's strengths and weaknesses to make the most accurate decisions in the future
Career development or change		
Get inspired; meet role models in the form of leading figures (e.g., mentors, guest lecturers)		Looking for ideas and future alternatives through inspiration by role models
Curiosity, interest in the subject area		

more successful as entrepreneurs. Theories and models that are employed for this perspective include the big personality traits: self-efficacy, achievement, motivation, proactivity, and the 'dark' traits of narcissism and psychopathology. While EE programs do not directly claim that it is their responsibility to intervene in such psychological aspects, their participants expect to feel the program's impact in these spheres. As an example, the term 'geek' used to describe technological entrepreneurs, which implied mainly bizarre, non-social individuals who were obsessed with their technological pursuit, has become a term that reflects a source of pride, indicating that the approaches to psychological traits change, and that EE programs must track these changes to remain relevant.

Psychology influences EE through studies on cognition and abilities, such as entrepreneurs' cognitive style and practical intelligence. These studies contribute greatly to the understanding of the content to be delivered and the way in which it should be delivered to entrepreneurs with different cognitive styles. Cognitive styles are affected by more dynamic psychological aspects, such as motivation and self-efficacy, as well as by prior experiences; hence, these should be taken into consideration when developing programs for entrepreneurs. More specifically, there are proven relations between cognitive and motivational dynamics and specific entrepreneurial behaviors, including active information seeking, opportunity identification, risk-taking, and financial decision leadership. Thus, a meticulous construction of the matrix can link the three elements: EE methods with specific cognition or motivational factors and specific entrepreneurship performance, to produce a more accurate process (Armstrong & Hird, 2009; Baum, Bird, & Singh, 2011; Blonk, Brenninkmeijer, Lagerveld, & Houtman, 2006; Frese & Gielnik, 2014; Harms & Spain, 2015; Hodzic, Ripoll, Lira, & Zenasni, 2015; Schröder & Schmitt-Rodermund, 2006; Schyns, 2015).

Entrepreneurs' emotional and affectual perspectives, such as well-being, optimism, resilience and passion, are also related to components of entrepreneurial performance, including creativity, innovation, teamwork and leadership, and, thus, should be tackled in EE programs.

Professor Oren Kaplan[1] considers psychological traits to be critical components in the entrepreneurial process, and, as such, should be incorporated into EE and training. As an expert in positive psychology who has not only worked with many organizational and entrepreneurial teams, but also leads the entrepreneurship-pioneering College of Management Academic Studies in Israel, he distinguishes two main perspectives intertwining psychological traits and EE: (a) the founding team's view—founders and their entrepreneurial teams continually encounter a large assortment of unexpected, dynamic and chaotic situations, critical to their businesses' progression. Such situations result in stress, be it *destructive* or *constructive*. The former type of stress can decrease the capacity for creativity, and greatly reduce energy as well as cognitive resources; thus, stressed entrepreneurs experience depressed ideation and creativity processes, and difficulties in decision making. Outcomes of this type of stress, even in physiological aspects, inhibit thinking processes, and are, thus, risk-averse and lead the stressed individual to seek the known, and his/her comfort zone. Constructive stress demands a facilitating, trusting and nurturing environment, and, thus, requires the entrepreneurial founding teams to orchestrate their capacities. In this case, the stress becomes a challenge, like a riddle to be solved; it promotes curiosity and creativity to directly resolve the stressful condition, along with positive affection for, and constructive engagement of, the team, strengthening their relationship; (b) the stakeholders' view—investors, strategic corporate partners, and members of the startup's board are risk-averse. They expect sustainable, robust business development, and are, therefore, intolerant to the team's conflicts and disputes in the long run. Due to the substantial importance of each team member in a startup, holding a specific expertise as well as the business's most furtive developments, the option of repeatedly changing the team's composition is unrealistic. The team needs to create capacities to regulate and harmonize their activities, in order to build resilience and enable openness, well-being, and flow. According to Kaplan, these psychological traits must be included in EE by introducing the content and knowledge, and establishing that the main tool possessed by the founders is their personality, and their teams. By expanding their understanding in these areas, including practical knowledge, accelerators will more effectively nurture sustainable teams. At the same time, training is required for 'feeling and sensing'. Mentoring and coaching entrepreneurs toward team dynamics, personal development and mental resource processes will allow the founders to obtain these tools for use along the startup business's process. Finally, academic institutions should develop programs to 'train the trainers', that is, to teach mentors and coaches of entrepreneurs the positive psychology processes.

Entrepreneurship is the result of individuals' perceptions of their available alternatives to start a business and respond to challenges encountered along the way, dependent on their levels of self-efficacy, motivation, and knowledge. Adding to the debate, recent studies have expanded on the role of knowledge in fine-tuning the perceived feasibility into more realistic scenarios; for example, a highly motivated entrepreneur who is proficient in coding may perceive his/her odds of becoming an entrepreneur as high, but prior knowledge of what is required to start a business, the basics of finance and marketing or successful entrepreneurs' challenges may enable him/her to reassess the resources and expertise needed to start a business, thus minimizing mistakes. An awareness of education's role in contributing through knowledge to the individual's realistic perceptions is also important, and can enhance the perceived value from EE. In addition, EE exposes learners to various people and groups associated with entrepreneurship (e.g., mentors, guest lecturers, visits to startups, coaches), thus broadening the learners' relationships with the entrepreneurial landscape; this may affect the individuals' perceived desire to become entrepreneurs.

The relations between attitudes toward, and awareness and knowledge of, EE can take different forms: entrepreneurs join EE programs because they feel unsure about their abilities to start or scale up their business; they are enthused (perceived desirability) to become entrepreneurs but do not feel confident about the innovation or feasibility of their idea; they are confident in the relevance of their personal traits for entrepreneurship, yet need more knowledge; they have been exposed to startup education in the past, stimulating their curiosity and eagerness toward entrepreneurship; they would like to explore whether they are suited to entrepreneurship, among other forms that connect attitudes to EE.

At the same time, the impact of EE on attitudes rebounds: a positive educational experience can enhance individuals' awareness of education, their knowledge and intentions; moreover, business success that occurred during, or very close in time to participation in the program can also be perceived by learners as a direct contribution of the EE program, thereby promoting self-efficacy, desirability, or intentions related to both entrepreneurship and education as a valuable vehicle to acquire the needed knowledge and skills. Taken together, EE is simultaneously affected by, and affects, the entrepreneur's personal identity by enabling the formation of relevant traits, while, accordingly, constantly adjusting the program to be able to touch as many components of the entrepreneurial identity as possible. Success in entrepreneurship through EE depends on the learners' attitudes toward the usefulness and value of their learning (Ahmad & Seymour, 2008; Ajzen, 2001, 2002; De Faoite, Henry, Johnston, & Van Der Sijde, 2003; Kolvereid, 1996; Komarkova, Gagliardi, Conrads, & Collado, 2015; Liñán, Ceresia, & Bernal, 2018; Sarasvathy & Venkataraman, 2011). Figure 5.1 shows the reciprocal relations of EE and attitudes.

A Process-driven View

Although entrepreneurs seem to be more outcome-driven, and expect immediate improvement from EE programs in their entrepreneurial skills and knowledge, as well as visible progress in their idea and business, they are also influenced by the educational process. In fact, experiencing progress as the outcome of a program while the experience of the educational process was disappointing would be experienced as overall inconsequential educational learning.

The educational process should develop rigorously around the individual components of all aspects, that is, cognitive, emotional, social, etc., to give the learners a multilayered practice that involves the individuals' various facets. The tenet in establishing such a rich process lies in enabling learners to experience the learning journey to its fullest, thereby allowing them to exercise the components of the different aspects, that is, cognitive, emotional, attitudes, etc., rather than focusing on a single area. One such example is the idea-thon, which comprises brainstorming events in which participants throw out their ideas, in order to get feedback on what they should be working on or how they should be going about it. As such, the idea-thon's focus on oneself, including who can help in implementing the idea (social support), what are one's strengths

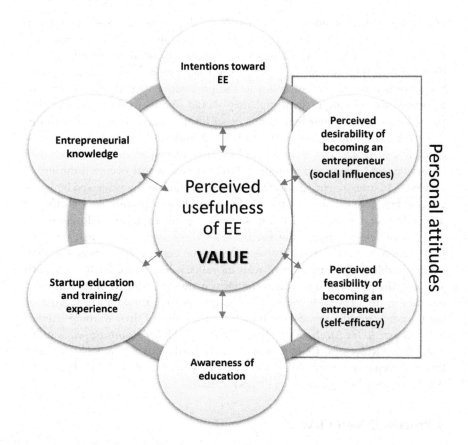

FIGURE 5.1 Reciprocal relations of EE and attitudes

Adjusted and altered from Liñán (2004), modeled on: differing effects of entrepreneurship education courses; and Liñán, Ceresia, and Bernal (2018). Model of path diagram for the hypothesized structural equation model

that propelled the development of this idea (emotional), what are the skills and know-how required to generate the resources for developing the idea (behavioral aspects), among others, is valuable for sustaining and retaining the learning process, so that it can be replicated in other situations. More conservative activities would teach how to ideate by exclusively emphasizing the ideas' practical features, for example, feasibility, innovation, costs of implementation, etc.

An additional aspect of the process regards objective indicators: the length of the program, the level of the participants' businesses' development, as well as of the participants themselves, that is, bachelor, graduate or postgraduate. These have been found to affect the individual level. Of the objective process-based indicators, the following influence the learners' satisfaction level and the perceived development of their businesses:

- Length of the program.
- Number of activities, encounters with investors, inspirational figures.
- Program's affiliations (university, private or governmental corporation, municipality, association).
- Program quality, innovativeness, 'coolness', high branding.
- Program's focus: nascent entrepreneurs, early stage, or scaleup accelerator.
- Pedagogical methods.
- Thematic focus: fin-tech, sports-tech, health-tech, etc.

(Lange, Marram, Jawahar, Yong, & Bygrave, 2014; Mentoor & Friedrich, 2007; Miguel Calado Dominguinhos & Margarida Cagica Carvalho, 2009; Ohland, Frillman, Zhang, Brawner, & Miller, 2004; Packham, Jones, Miller, Pickernell, & Thomas, 2010; Pei-Lee & Chen-Chen, 2008; Petridou & Sarri, 2011; Piperopoulos & Dimov, 2015; Pittaway & Cope, 2007; Souitaris et al., 2007).

Teamwork—An additional perspective of the individual view regarding teamwork, as entrepreneurship evolves in teams. In the individual's view, the responsibility to create an effective team lies with the entrepreneur, to promote teamwork for the effectiveness of both the educational process in class and the entrepreneurial process inside and outside the classroom. According to an article in *Fortune* magazine,[2] one of the most important parts of scaling up a company is building the right team; yet, this can be a hurdle for founders who are used to doing everything on their own. Giving control to someone else is difficult, but crucial to scaling up and growing faster in the long run. Trust, communication and alignment are the essential centerpieces of successful team building in the entrepreneurial realm. Obviously, the teams comprise members who possess the unique entrepreneurial traits described earlier in the chapter; hence, they are more apt to encounter difficulties in managing themselves and, thus, may develop internal conflicts and overall hampered business activity. Ingraining the individuals' aspects, that is, cognitive, emotional, behavioral, social, etc., in EE can simplify the teams' functional development. Many EE programs offer team activities, simulations and workshops to practice team dynamics, as well as to experience entrepreneurial practices within teams. By focusing on the individual, learners can improve their own team-related performance, and strengthen their skills in managing and leading entrepreneurial teams, co-founders, colleagues and partnering teams, by recognizing their strengths and blind spots, building emotional intelligence to communicate effectively, influencing others by earning trust and building long-term relationships, developing their management style and handling complex situations. An individual perspective fosters the learners' understanding of their colleagues' and competitors' motivations, so that they can convey their insights and recommendations more effectively. Moonshot Horizon[3] is a Chicago-based innovation services company for digital products and services, aimed at creating and servicing the innovative digital products that businesses will need to transform entire industries. Tackling an outcome approach to assisting businesses achieve results in the immediate future and facilitating their pursuit of hypergrowth and efficiency, Moonshot Horizon accentuates the process approach through the Innovation Outpost as a Service (IOaaS) model, and Design Thinking workshops; these are used to generate ideas to solve complex digital and physical interactions pertaining to digital ecosystems, such as validation with customer feedback, and implementation of the digital product using techniques from lean innovation and agile methodology.

An Outcome Outlook

Entrepreneurs are in a constant restless, aroused state, due to both the turbulent external competitive conditions surrounding them and their distinct psychological disposition. Their external surroundings involve hectic workloads, deadlines, parallel assignments, and a relentless lack of resources, that is, funds, expertise, human resources, machinery. Entrepreneurs are often portrayed as 'living on the edge'. They are, therefore, very careful about the time and money spent on any activities that are not directly related to their daily work with the business. As to their internal disposition, they are frequently bored, looking for the practical sides of learning and expecting the change to be immediate, and precisely aligned to their expectations, even if unrealistic, and non-sustainable. These are hard to guarantee. Therefore, EE programs should concurrently monitor and sort the types of impact that programs have on the student entrepreneurs and their businesses, as well as the impact of the outcomes on the ecosystem in terms of development, innovation and employment, for example. Alongside this, the people involved in the EE programs should educate entrepreneurs to adjust their expectations, and synchronize them with reality.

The other aspect of the outcome perspective regards the impact of EE programs on the learners and stakeholders. EE's impact on the individual level includes:

- Personal change in skills and knowledge.
- Enhancement of entrepreneurial intention: to become entrepreneurs, to maintain an entrepreneurial career.
- Change in attitudes and perceived personal development, growth, feasibility.
- Emotional change, such as in subjective norms, optimism, uncertainty, ambiguity, tolerance.
- Deepening the psychological aspect of entrepreneurial inclination, such as a sense of psychological ownership, social engagement, multiple sense of responsibility, independent thinking, and connecting to one's own and others' needs; entrepreneurial passion.
- Satisfaction with the EE program; emotional or related approaches to assessing EE's impact; positive link through a dynamic process of internal self-reflection; inspiration as the most important benefit of EE, implying a 'change of heart'.

(Bernhofer & Han, 2014; Boukamcha, 2015; Burrows & Wragg, 2013; Chang, Benamraoui, & Rieple, 2014; Crane, 2014; Donnellon, Ollila, & Middleton, 2014; Fayolle, Gailly, & Lassas-Clerc, 2006; Joensuu, Viljamaa, Varamäki, & Tornikoski, 2013; Lackéus, 2014; Packham et al., 2010; Piperopoulos & Dimov, 2015; Premand, Brodmann, Almeida, Grun, & Barouni, 2016; Rauch & Hulsink, 2015; Shinnar, Hsu, & Powell, 2014; Turker & Sonmez Selçuk, 2009; Vorley & Williams, 2016; Wang & Verzat, 2011).

The Individual and the Stakeholders

Entrepreneurs join educational programs to better penetrate the market, exploit opportunities more quickly and more accurately, establish a competitive advantage—all of which have to do with the perceptions and attitudes of their surrounding environment with regard to the capabilities, skills and knowledge gained from the program. Many student entrepreneurs will seek the environment's feedback on their EE-related changes, and will estimate their value gained from a program based on such feedback. This feedback might be directly communicated to them, or indirectly expressed through their performance; for instance, an improvement in understanding market needs may be expressed to the learner by the co-founder, or be revealed by feedback on the actual preparation of an accurate marketing plan.

One way to tackle this is the user–client relationship. The users of the EE programs are mainly the entrepreneurs, while the clients may be big corporations, the government or consumers. The relationships between those parties are demonstrated in Figure 5.2.

Many groups that are interested and involved in EE are affected by the outcome 'packages', with the student entrepreneurs at their center. The impact can take various forms, as shown in Table 5.2.

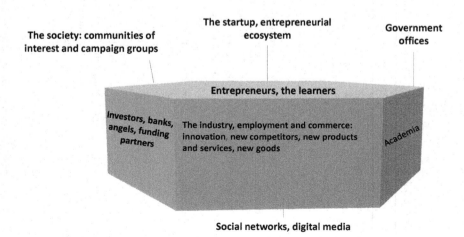

FIGURE 5.2 The EE user–client relationships

TABLE 5.2 Interested groups, how they are affected by, and affect, EE

	How they are *affected by* EE	How they can *affect* EE
Investors, banks	➤ More deal flows, investments, loans, debts ➤ More startups to support and fund ➤ Development of expertise to be nurtured and supported (aerospace-tech; bio-tech, etc.) ➤ More innovation that can be related to finance, to be incorporated into their activities	• More interest in supporting EE programs • Opening doors for startups to more partnerships and more business activity • Dialogue with interest groups, corporate social responsibility (CSR)
The industry and commerce	➤ More products and services for private customers and businesses ➤ More competition for big, medium and small businesses ➤ More potential expert entrepreneurial labor	• More potential proficient and entrepreneurial employees for the industry • More healthy, vibrant affluence of products and services • More expertise, innovation • Higher dynamics in the market
Governmental offices	➤ Employment and labor ➤ Education ➤ Professional offices for which startups produce innovation (e.g., ed-tech for the Education Office; regulation-tech for the Finance Office; health-tech for the Health Office, etc.) ➤ Gaining knowledge and innovation from the startup products and services, as well as processes and human resources	• Contributing to EE programs with knowledge, skills, training • Accumulating activities in a one-stop shop (education and health, for example) • Partnerships with startups • Supporting EE programs • Developing internal or affiliated EE programs to promote employees' innovation

The startup ecosystem	▲ Intensified competition for clients, investors, funds ▲ Boosted potential partnerships and collaborations ▲ Opening of opportunities ▲ More products, knowledge and skills can affect other startups in the ecosystem ▲ Vibrant and dynamic market	• Partnering, merger and acquisitions (M&As) • Potential closure of existing startups due to competition • Promoting with founders as mentors in EE programs
The society, interest groups	▲ Mobilizing resources ▲ Enhancing subjects of interest, especially for thematic EE programs (crypto, environment-related issues, health-related issues, etc.)	• Shared values, accelerators and incubators mobilize the ecosystem's action, hence enable a vibrant debate among interest groups on mutual subjects
Social networks and digital media	▲ Exposure of startups and EE programs ▲ Dissemination of activities, projects, entrepreneurial processes, products ▲ Project sustainability ▲ Engagement of the most interested groups in startups, by thematic blog, Facebook and LinkedIn groups of interest, for example	• Intensified exposure and sustainability of the interest groups • Higher sustainability of the corporate companies, such as Facebook, LinkedIn, Instagram, Snapchat, etc.
Academia	▲ Concurrent, cutting-edge and empirical knowledge ▲ Research into various processes, outcomes, fit between student satisfaction and program quality, etc. ▲ Interns ▲ Research skills to be delivered to student entrepreneurs ▲ Teaching courses, workshops, academic hackathons	• Innovation in the world of academia, which suffers from a conservative approach/perception • Collaboration with the industry to enrich the curriculum for regular programs • Familiarization with the stakeholders for potential support, donations, etc.

Summary

The individual is the main user and client of EE programs, although the role of the environment and ecosystem in the learning process and outcomes is substantial. Thus, EE develops and delivers KSA that are relevant to the user's expectations and needs. However, entrepreneurs as learners are unique in terms of specific personality traits and learning styles. Moreover, unlike the 'normative' scenario of learners who are driven by the desire for knowledge or expertise, entrepreneurs have a variety of motives for joining EE programs, which are even more complex when considered with their demographic and business characteristics. As such, the expectations of nascent student entrepreneurs for scaling up a business are completely different from those of an entrepreneurial team that has already raised money in a seed round.

The entrepreneurial personality traits that are relevant to EE include: cognitive (e.g., the intuitive, creative, innovative and rebellious ways in which entrepreneurs tackle situations); attitudes (i.e., intention to become an entrepreneur, personal, career or business growth orientation); emotional (e.g., self-efficacy, self-confidence, personal maturity); motivation (i.e., why learners wish to join EE programs); social support (such as team building and development, engaging partners); behavioral aspects (e.g., skill acquisition, know-how enrichment, learning the right terminology). These are relevant to team building and development and to mastering leadership skills in managing entrepreneurial teams. The area of personality traits should be embedded in EE to gain a higher quality of learning, which better suits the entrepreneurial learning styles and can raise higher levels of perceived value and satisfaction from the EE process.

The two main views of EE are the process and outcome perspectives; the process needs to develop around the individual's components to enable a multilayered practice that involves the individual's various facets. This requires an investigation of how process-based characteristics, such as length of the program, number of activities, program affiliations, quality of the program, innovativeness, and pedagogical methods, among others, reflect the individual's aspects and provide appropriate trajectories for valuable EE in the individual's eyes. The outcome perspective focuses on the impact of EE and consists of changes in skills and knowledge, enhancement of entrepreneurial intentions, perceived development and growth, and changes in emotional characteristics such as optimism, tolerance of uncertainty and ambiguity, as well as in psychological ownership, such as social engagement, and satisfaction with, and value perceptions of the EE.

The individual level cannot be investigated in isolation, as the expected changes from EE mirror the individuals' thoughts about how they are perceived in their environment, to generate a competitive advantage by introducing a better fit to stakeholders, clients, investors, interest groups, and the media. Each of these groups can contribute greatly to EE, while expecting to gain from the reciprocal relationships between the various pairs: stakeholder groups and startups and entrepreneurial businesses; stakeholder groups and different EE programs; different EE programs and startups and entrepreneurial businesses, as well as their combinations.

Takeaways

For EE participants:

- When considering EE, be open to the individual level in addition to the practical and professional aspects.
- Team building is a crucial component in creating and scaling up a business; to master it, you should self-reflect on your attitudes, motivations, strengths and weaknesses. This will enable you to both understand your team members more effectively, and determine how to develop and lead the team.
- The process (rather than just the outcome) is extremely important along the educational journey. Rigorously inspect the components, such as length of the program, innovativeness, exposure to leading figures, and doors opened through the program.
- The outcomes are obviously the main trigger for entrepreneurs to enroll in EE programs. But outcomes are diverse and can be revealed with different timing, i.e., during, right after, or a long time after completing the program. Nevertheless, you should set realistic expectations regarding the outcomes; discuss others' experiences and achievements, experts' suggestions, etc.

For stakeholder groups:

- Get acquainted with local EE programs to become involved in one of many possible activities, such as mentoring, hosting entrepreneurial events, coaching, providing a place for internships, providing a place for a beta site, etc.
- Look for opportunities to be affiliated with EE activities or programs, to both support startups and gain exposure for the business.
- Blend with other sectors to create value for your networks; if you are part of the industry, partner with academia; if you are an academic institution, partner with government offices, etc., as a 'package' that introduces a high-level complementary capacity, making your contribution to EE and startups through networks more substantial.
- Initiate your own program to support entrepreneurs under your company's umbrella, to provide another stream of support to the entrepreneurial community as well as expose your teams and employees to innovative, vibrant approaches and entrepreneurial vibes. You may invite your employees to become facilitators of practices offered in EE to empower them.

Case Study 5 – "Living in a Nursing Home to Get Closer to my Customers": Insights from the Y Combinator Accelerator Experience

Dr. Tim Peck, MD, is the co-founder and CEO of Call9, a company based in Brooklyn, New York that has developed a mobile technology platform for patients to connect to physicians in emergency situations. Its products include a technology platform that connects emergency physicians to on-site clinical care specialists who are with patients in nursing homes to deliver bedside emergency care.

Call9 has raised more than $30 million in venture capital financing from half a dozen investment firms and angels, including 23andMe's Anne Wojcicki, Sam Altman of the Y Combinator (YC), and Ashton Kutcher. The company expanded to its second market in the fall of 2018, is adding new nursing homes on a monthly basis, and has more than half a dozen contracts with major national insurance payers. Peck attributes much of the company's success, and his approach to entrepreneurship, to his time at the startup accelerator YC.

Peck joined the YC program in 2015, after two unsuccessful attempts: "the selection process at YC is extremely difficult; one of the most difficult situations in my life," says Peck (who attended NYU, one of the top medical schools in the US, and was a resident at Beth Israel Deaconess, one of the most sought-after residencies);

> for the application process, I prepared myself for three months by interviewing YC alumni on the selection process; I simulated interviews with many people whom I asked to provide me with feedback, ask me harsh questions and help me construct my idea and my story in a convincing form.

Today, from a time perspective, Peck attests to the value of this preparation for the selection process, not only in facilitating the fulfilment of YC's requirement, that is, to accumulate a client base while still interning in the program, but also in mirroring the reality faced by startup founders on a regular basis.

> In real life, as an entrepreneur, you have to follow what your clients say very closely, then constantly refine your idea to adjust it to your clients' needs; this is the way to convince your customers, investors and strategic collaborators;

these are parallel processes.

As part of the terms of participation in the YC program, Peck had to resign from his positions as physician at the hospital and as faculty at Harvard, and fully engage in the program. In this intensive, three-month program, the YC fosters building the startup by 'walking around'. Peck explains that the idea is to reach out for customers while you are a tenet of the program, asking them about their hassles, understanding their problems and expectations, and continually honing your product, pitch and selling methods, until you develop a value proposition that you can then monetize.

The YC's statement proclaims that a thorough understanding of the customers' needs can create a value proposition. Peck felt the impact of this focus on customers' needs at various decision points while developing his company:

> Being alert to [customers'] needs enabled exploiting opportunities. For example, starting Call9 under the ideal timing; for about five years, regulators had been penalizing nursing homes for sending patients back to the hospital within 30 days. The opportunity only revealed itself when I decided to move from Silicon Valley to Long Island to live in the conference room of a nursing home. This allowed me to understand the staff's needs, which proved to be invaluable knowledge to get my startup, Call9, off the ground. My only request was to fly back to California every week or two to attend the YC events.

At the end of the YC accelerator program, on demo day, startups pitch to leading investors, angels, and representatives from venture capital companies. To prove their relevance and value to their targeted market, the startups are asked to generate letters of interest (LOI) from companies, signifying the market's readiness to buy or use the startup's products. The YC states that by a proven business-to-business outcome, that is, equipped with LOI contracts, as well as with an extended network and mentors' guidance, the tenet startups can more easily approach investors to raise funds. One of the YC's strongest statements is that investors will invest when they are confident that the startup's products and team are robust and trustworthy. Peck says, from his experience,

> scouting for the companies that might be potential customers, being alert to their needs and expectations by delving into what they really want, and identifying the problems on an ongoing basis, working day and night to adjust the product, the business models, the solutions to provide them with real value—while you are still in the development stage, this is difficult. Nevertheless, it is a valuable routine that I have applied to Call9 along the way. In fact, one of the main pivots in my company's strategic market, from nursing homes to insurance companies, drew from identifying a new market niche that was interested in our products. This would not have been possible if I had not been taught to listen carefully to my customers. I have a personal connection with my clients, even though I have digitized my interactions with them; nothing can replace the reciprocal impact of a face-to-face interaction.

As companies do not easily sign contracts with nascent startups, Peck says,

> I lived in Central Island Healthcare to capture the needs of the nursing home's staff; in return for the lodging, I treated the sick residents. It was only after this experience that I was able to build a rapport with the nursing home's residents and staff, and to see potential opportunities for patients to get the care they need without an expensive emergency room visit.

An article on Peck's life in the nursing home was published by CNBC.[4]

The YC embeds an agile culture in its portfolio startups, as demonstrated by its relatively unstructured program. Its message is that its role as an accelerator is to facilitate the startup's journey by providing the best mentors, networks, space to develop connections, and seed money to develop a proof of concept. However, the entrepreneurial action itself should not be imposed on the startup participants but exposed to them; they must choose the YC resources that they find useful for the startup's growth. Another application of the YC's statement is "its queries to quicken your job"; their mission is to teach the startups to raise money on their own, by making customers believe in their product, rapidly and effectively. "While there are many accelerators that favor teaching how to develop a startup through business planning and implementation, YC insists on the proof" says Peck. In fact, this was Peck's main motivation to enroll in the YC program: as a physician, he recognized his weaknesses as an entrepreneur and looked for the best place to gain more focus from experts on the product and the technology; in addition to fulfilling this expectation, he gained a long-term expert community and very valuable hands-on practice, primarily as a starting point with business-to-business contracts through the LOIs.

While the program did not follow any specific structure or formula, Peck and his team, supported by the two mentors matched to them by the YC—Paul Buccheit, the creator of Gmail, and Dalton Caldwell, CEO of Mix MediaLabs, worked day and night on the business. "It was intensive, hectic work in a short period of time, in which every company that we approached to assemble the contracts required ample pre- and post-work to customize our products to its needs," says Peck. While startups participating in the YC are not required to be physically present at the incubator on a daily basis, their engagement is complete: they meet many renowned figures from the industry, mentors and experts, investors and venture capitalists with whom they strive to talk, get advice and share experiences; this massive and intensive interaction allows the participants to enjoy the richness of the YC's network. "YC's networking is powerful; it is a community of knowledge, advice and assistance. Whenever I face any business concerns, in hiring people, raising money, or any other related issues, I turn to the YC community," testifies Peck. The community is also active and helpful in the startups' investment rounds, both during and after their participation in the YC program. Many mentors from the network guide and escort the startups at the conclusion of the program; in Peck's case, the connection during the YC program with his mentor, Buccheit, developed into a fertile relationship; "he guides me, he advises me in any finance-related aspects and fund raising, thanks to his experience, expertise and substantial knowledge," says Peck.

Peck confirms that Call9 would never have reached its achievements promptly and effectively without the experience at the YC accelerator. He concludes,

The impact of YC on me personally, my team and Call9 is reflected in almost every process that we activate. As to my mindset, YC unleashed my conception that we must succeed. I accept failures, in fact I believe that these are a learning experience that we have to go through to be more alert, creative and feel what is entailed. We grow from failures. We also have many signs in our venue in Brooklyn testifying to this belief.

Questions on the Case Study

1. Search the web for the YC accelerator program, and list the objective indicators offered in the program. Then, choose two out of the six entrepreneurial traits discussed in this chapter (cognitive, attitudes, emotional, motivation, etc.). Discuss how YC develops the entrepreneurial traits you have selected and what is innovative in the YC model with respect to these traits.
2. In your view, what are the main reasons Peck joined the YC accelerator? Discuss 2–3 push and pull reasons, based on the points raised in this chapter. What is your main conclusion?
3. Read thoroughly Professor Kaplan's psychological view on the role of accelerators for the individual. Explain this view with regard to Peck's experience with the YC program. Explain your answer.
4. Discuss the perceived value Peck gained from the YC for Call9 through the model presented in this chapter of reciprocal relations of EE and attitudes (5.1). What are your main conclusions?
5. Search for Call9 on the web; based on the outcome outlook discussed in this chapter. Which main innovative constituents in Call9, including Peck's managerial conduct, the team, the pivot, development, growth, etc., would you ascribe to Peck's participation in the YC accelerator? Explain your response.

Reflective Questions

1. Locate five entrepreneurs (either among friends and family or through the social media) that have gone through acceleration, incubation or any other educational process. Interview them about this process. What are your conclusions with regard to the changes made by EE to their KSA? Explain.
2. Search the internet for three programs for entrepreneurs; inquire about their vision and/or goals, and list the emotional elements that they use (for example, 'the program will enhance your self-confidence', 'through the program

you will be inspired . . .'; 'you will be empowered through our mentoring system', etc.). What is your conclusion about including psychological aspects in the programs?
3. A non-profit organization asks for your assistance in opening a three-month program for entrepreneurial individuals with simple disabilities, where the psychological aspect is crucial. Which elements would you suggest including in such a program? Give an example for each element.
4. Read the following stories. Suppose the founders decide to scale up through an accelerator. What suggestions would you recommend that they consider, and for which goals? Base your answer on the chapter's main arguments.

A. Empower Orphans—Neha Gupta[5]

From an early age, Neha Gupta has participated in her family's tradition of celebrating birthdays by traveling to India and bringing food and gifts to orphans in their hometown. In 2005, at the age of nine, she decided she wanted to do more, to make a real difference in these children's lives. She began selling wind chimes door-to-door and at community events to raise money for orphans' schoolbooks and other educational expenses. This effort led her to create Empower Orphans, a registered non-profit organization. Empower Orphans has conducted more than 27 projects and raised more than $1.6 million, and Gupta recently received the International Children's Peace Prize.

B. Nay Games—Robert Nay[6]

In 2010, a new mobile game app called "Bubble Ball" was launched in the Apple app store. In its first two weeks it received more than one million downloads, surpassing "Angry Birds" as the most downloaded free game from Apple. Robert Nay, a 14-year-old with no previous coding experience, created this game. According to CNN, Nay learned everything he needed to know through research at the public library, and produced 4,000 lines of code for his physics-based puzzle game in just one month. Nay Games now offers games to help students learn sight words and spelling, Bubble Ball Pro, and Bubble Ball: Curiosity Edition, in addition to the original Bubble Ball.

5. Watch Raphael Arar's TED talk, 'How we can teach computers to make sense of our emotions' (2018) at: www.ted.com/talks/raphael_arar_how_we_can_teach_computers_to_make_sense_of_our_emotions

Arar suggests that we start by making art. He shares interactive projects that help artificial intelligence (AI) explore complex ideas like nostalgia, intuition and conversation—all working toward the goal of making our future technology as much human as it is artificial.

Reflect on the main ideas presented in Arar's talk, and try to adjust them to EE. Give examples. What are your conclusions?

Notes

1 Professor Kaplan is a clinical psychologist and economist. He is a professor of cognitive psychology; founder and director of the Business Psychology MBA program at the College of Management Academic Studies, Israel, and President of the College of Management Academic Studies, Israel. Professor Kaplan was interviewed in person by me.
2 See *How Employee Turnover Can Be Good for Business*, Dale Chang, June 16, 2016 at: http://fortune.com/2016/06/16/team-building-entrepreneurs-business/
3 See at: https://www.moonshot-io.com/about/
4 See at: www.cnbc.com/2018/02/15/tim-peck-call9-telemedicine-founder-lived-in-nursing-home.html
5 See at: www.businessnewsdaily.com/5051-young-entrepreneurs.html
6 See at: www.businessnewsdaily.com/5051-young-entrepreneurs.html

References

Ahmad, N., & Seymour, R. G. (2008). Defining entrepreneurial activity: Definitions supporting frameworks for data collection. OECD Statistics Working Paper. https://doi.org/10/1787/18152031

Ajzen, I. (1991). The theory of planned behavior. *Organizational Behavior and Human Decision Processes*, 50(2), 179–211.

Ajzen, I. (2001). Nature and operation of attitudes. *Annual Review of Psychology*, 52(1), 27–58.

Ajzen, I. (2002). Perceived behavioral control, self-efficacy, locus of control, and the theory of planned behavior 1. *Journal of Applied Social Psychology*, 32(4), 665–683.

Armstrong, S. J., & Hird, A. (2009). Cognitive style and entrepreneurial drive of new and mature business owner-managers. *Journal of Business and Psychology*, 24(4), 419–430.

Baum, J. R., Bird, B. J., & Singh, S. (2011). The practical intelligence of entrepreneurs: Antecedents and a link with new venture growth. *Personnel Psychology*, 64(2), 397–425.

Bernhofer, L., & Han, Z. (2014). Contextual factors and their effects on future entrepreneurs in China: A comparative study of entrepreneurial intentions. *International Journal of Technology Management*, 65(1–4), 125–150.

Blonk, R. W. B., Brenninkmeijer, V., Lagerveld, S. E., & Houtman, I. L. D. (2006). Return to work: A comparison of two cognitive behavioural interventions in cases of work-related psychological complaints among the self-employed. *Work & Stress*, 20(2), 129–144. https://doi.org/10.1080/02678370600856615

Boukamcha, F. (2015). Impact of training on entrepreneurial intention: An interactive cognitive perspective. *European Business Review*, 27(6), 593–616.

Burrows, K., & Wragg, N. (2013). Introducing enterprise—research into the practical aspects of introducing innovative enterprise schemes as extra curricula activities in higher education. *Higher Education, Skills and Work-Based Learning*, 3(3), 168–179.

Chang, J., Benamraoui, A., & Rieple, A. (2014). Learning-by-doing as an approach to teaching social entrepreneurship. *Innovations in Education and Teaching International*, 51(5), 459–471.

Crane, F. G. (2014). Measuring and enhancing dispositional optimism and entrepreneurial intent in the entrepreneurial classroom: A Bahamian study. *Journal of the Academy of Business Education*, 15.

De Faoite, D., Henry, C., Johnston, K., & Van Der Sijde, P. (2003). Education and training for entrepreneurs: A consideration of initiatives in Ireland and the Netherlands. *Education + Training*, 45(8/9), 430–438. https://doi.org/10.1108/00400910310508829

Donnellon, A., Ollila, S., & Middleton, K. W. (2014). Constructing entrepreneurial identity in entrepreneurship education. *International Journal of Management Education, 12*(3), 490–499.

Fayolle, A., Gailly, B., & Lassas-Clerc, N. (2006). Effect and counter-effect of entrepreneurship education and social context on student's intentions. *Estudios de Economía Aplicada, 24*(2), 509–524.

Frese, M., & Gielnik, M. M. (2014). The psychology of entrepreneurship. *Annual Review of Organizational Psychology and Organizational Behavior, 1*(1), 413–438.

Harms, P. D., & Spain, S. M. (2015). Beyond the bright side: Dark personality at work. *Applied Psychology, 64*(1), 15–24.

Hodzic, S., Ripoll, P., Lira, E., & Zenasni, F. (2015). Can intervention in emotional competences increase employability prospects of unemployed adults? *Journal of Vocational Behavior, 88*, 28–37.

Joensuu, S., Viljamaa, A., Varamäki, E., & Tornikoski, E. (2013). Development of entrepreneurial intention in higher education and the effect of gender—a latent growth curve analysis. *Education+ Training, 55*(8/9), 781–803.

Kolvereid, L. (1996). Prediction of employment status choice intentions. *Entrepreneurship Theory and Practice, 21*(1), 47–58.

Komarkova, I., Gagliardi, D., Conrads, J., & Collado, A. (2015). *Entrepreneurship Competence: An Overview of Existing Concepts, Policies and Initiatives:Final Report*. Seville, Spain: European Commission, Institute for Prospective Technological Studies Joint Research Centre.

Lackéus, M. (2014). An emotion based approach to assessing entrepreneurial education. *International Journal of Management Education, 12*(3), 374–396.

Lange, J., Marram, E., Jawahar, A., Yong, W., & Bygrave, W. (2014). Does an entrepreneurship education have lasting value? A study of careers of 3,775 alumni. *Frontiers of Entrepreneurship Research, 31*, 210–225.

Liñán, F. (2004). Intention-based models of entrepreneurship education. *Piccola Impresa/Small Business, 3*(1), 11–35.

Liñán, F., Ceresia, F., & Bernal, A. (2018). Who intends to enroll in entrepreneurship education? Entrepreneurial self-identity as a precursor. *Entrepreneurship Education and Pedagogy, 1*(3), 222–242. https://doi.org/10.1177/2515127418780491

Mentoor, E. R., & Friedrich, C. (2007). Is entrepreneurial education at South African universities successful? An empirical example. *Industry and Higher Education, 21*(3), 221–232.

Miguel Calado Dominguinhos, P., & Margarida Cagica Carvalho, L. (2009). Promoting business creation through real world experience: Projecto Começar. *Education+ Training, 51*(2), 150–169.

Ohland, M. W., Frillman, S. A., Zhang, G., Brawner, C. E., & Miller, T. K. (2004). The effect of an entrepreneurship program on GPA and retention. *Journal of Engineering Education, 93*(4), 293–301. https://doi.org/10.1002/j.2168-9830.2004.tb00818.x

Packham, G., Jones, P., Miller, C., Pickernell, D., & Thomas, B. (2010). Attitudes towards entrepreneurship education: A comparative analysis. *Education + Training, 52*(8/9), 568–586. https://doi.org/10.1108/00400911011088926

Pei-Lee, T., & Chen-Chen, Y. (2008). Multimedia University's experience in fostering and supporting undergraduate student technopreneurship programs in a triple helix model. *Journal of Technology Management in China, 3*(1), 94–108. https://doi.org/10.1108/17468770810851520

Petridou, E., & Sarri, K. (2011). Developing "potential entrepreneurs" in higher education institutes. *Journal of Enterprising Culture*, *19*(01), 79–99. https://doi.org/10.1142/S0218495811000647

Piperopoulos, P., & Dimov, D. (2015). Burst bubbles or build steam? Entrepreneurship education, entrepreneurial self-efficacy, and entrepreneurial intentions. *Journal of Small Business Management*, *53*(4), 970–985. https://doi.org/10.1111/jsbm.12116

Pittaway, L., & Cope, J. (2007). Entrepreneurship education: A systematic review of the evidence. *International Small Business Journal*, *25*(5), 479–510.

Premand, P., Brodmann, S., Almeida, R., Grun, R., & Barouni, M. (2016). Entrepreneurship education and entry into self-employment among university graduates. *World Development*, *77*, 311–327.

Rauch, A., & Hulsink, W. (2015). Putting entrepreneurship education where the intention to act lies: An investigation into the impact of entrepreneurship education on entrepreneurial behavior. *Academy of Management Learning & Education*, *14*(2), 187–204.

Sarasvathy, S. D., & Venkataraman, S. (2011). Entrepreneurship as method: Open questions for an entrepreneurial future. *Entrepreneurship Theory and Practice*, *35*(1), 113–135.

Schröder, E., & Schmitt-Rodermund, E. (2006). Crystallizing enterprising interests among adolescents through a career development program: The role of personality and family background. *Journal of Vocational Behavior*, *69*(3), 494–509.

Schyns, B. (2015). Dark Personality in the Workplace: Introduction to the Special Issue. *Applied Psychology*, *64*(1), 1–14.

Shinnar, R. S., Hsu, D. K., & Powell, B. C. (2014). Self-efficacy, entrepreneurial intentions, and gender: Assessing the impact of entrepreneurship education longitudinally. *International Journal of Management Education*, *12*(3), 561–570.

Souitaris, V., Zerbinati, S., Al-Laham, A., Souitarisa, V., Zerbinatib, S., & Al-Laham, A. (2007). Do entrepreneurship programmes raise entrepreneurial intention of science and engineering students? The effect of learning, inspiration and resources. *Journal of Business Venturing*, *22*(4), 566–591.

Turker, D., & Sonmez Selçuk, S. (2009). Which factors affect entrepreneurial intention of university students? *Journal of European Industrial Training*, *33*(2), 142–159.

Vorley, T., & Williams, N. (2016). Between petty corruption and criminal extortion: How entrepreneurs in Bulgaria and Romania operate within a devil's circle. *International Small Business Journal*, *34*(6), 797–817.

Wang, Y., & Verzat, C. (2011). Generalist or specific studies for engineering entrepreneurs? Comparison of French engineering students' trajectories in two different curricula. *Journal of Small Business and Enterprise Development*, *18*(2), 366–383.

6
THE SHARING ECONOMY AND SHARED ENTREPRENEURIAL SPACES NEXUS

The Sharing Economy in the Entrepreneurial Context

The shared-platform economy is emerging so fast that entire platform-based markets and ecosystems have been created and are operational. People around the world have become hooked to big data and cloud computing, and have gotten so used to machine learning and IoT functions for leisure, business, banking, education and social activities that they probably could no longer bear a world without these facilities. However, despite their diverse functions and structures, these are all platforms that introduced 'disruptive innovation', provoking basic business concepts and, consequently, forcing deep changes in a variety of incumbent views about entrepreneurship, success factors and the meaning of value. The sharing economy enables free, open and friendly searches and social media, an open source of technological infrastructures on which other platforms can be developed to introduce new technologies, processes and products. Information flows much more smoothly through the internet and, as a consequence, acquisition of information on fundraising, investors and strategic collaborators is simpler to obtain and more accurate, thus expanding entrepreneurs' scope of funding opportunities and successful outcomes. Thus, entrepreneurs of this era are termed 'digital entrepreneurs'. While giants such as Google, Amazon, Facebook, AirBnB, Salesforce, and Uber are more and more dependent on their businesses' online structures for customer use, the entrepreneurial businesses in a sharing economy are placed in an even position with their stakeholders, as they all depend on the same platforms and can generate the same information and knowledge. The sharing economy has triggered developments that have changed the perceptions about value creation and actual profit accumulation, through the perspectives of both the entrepreneurs and the ecosystem. For example, in their first phases, today's startups are more active in accumulating 'traction' rather than 'unripe' money, termed 'dumb money'; they strive to be more visible and acknowledged in the social media and to become more attractive to investors; startups now seek funding at a later stage of their business's development, as the R&D and technological developments are easily drawn from existing technological platforms that are open-source and user-friendly, and these, as well as self-learning, do not require money at these early stages of development.

Moreover, the digital platforms, the information technology (IT) transformation of services, and the cloud have changed both the format of personal interactions and the need to memorize and retain human knowledge, which has all been transformed into virtual applications. In addition, the meanings of distance, time and globalization have changed. Consequently, the breadth of support systems for entrepreneurs has greatly expanded; entrepreneurs can participate in virtual incubators and hackathons, study online for free with top instructors from the world's best universities and best programs, receive mentoring from leading figures around the world, among others. Technology deployment in different countries and regions, and across industries and sectors, affects entrepreneurial emergence, development, attractiveness, and, in the larger reach, it is the main incentive for economic growth and the deluge of a more global and more disruptive entrepreneurship.

Education, support processes, and programs for entrepreneurs should match their development to that of the sharing economy. The challenges revolve around adding 'something' that is of value for entrepreneurs, mainly as they can easily and freely generate knowledge, resources and networks from the existing shared, technological platforms. Moreover, as data, information, and knowledge are stored and well preserved on the web, education should endeavor to enable unleashing 'something' new, and ensure that entrepreneurship, innovation and creativity are not just a replication of that which is already known on the web.

The shared platforms induced by the sharing economy have been transformed into shared entrepreneurship. Nevertheless, the entrepreneurs' approach to sharing is multifaceted, and this should be taken into consideration when developing EE. A shared platform can be perceived by entrepreneurs through the aspects delineated in Table 6.1.

EE must therefore meet the challenges of a sharing economy (Table 6.2).

Digital entrepreneurs depend on three core dimensions of the sharing economy:

- Access to community-shared assets—maximizing their use.
- Community-based economy—interactions that bring potential or actual value, without any contract or guarantee, including with renowned figures.
- Platform economy—any type of exchange of money, goods, knowledge or advice among peers through digital platforms.

TABLE 6.1 Opportunities and hurdles

Opportunities	Hurdles
Accumulation of knowledge and information is powerful; entrepreneurs are no longer in an inferior position *vis à vis* their strategic collaborators	Entrepreneurs tend to be more suspicious, skeptical and defensive of their ideas; hence, digital entrepreneurs may be less involved in both sharing information and appreciating feedback or reflections regarding their ideas
Sharing platforms facilitate the entire entrepreneurial process, by enabling the easy acquisition of tools, best practices and relevant knowledge freely or inexpensively	The web stimulates the surge of new ideas; even by reading about innovations on social media. For digital entrepreneurs, such public exposure can be seen as intensifying competition, and they may therefore be unwilling to share their innovations
FOMO![1] Everybody wants to be 'in the loop'; being visible brings traction, attractiveness and exposure	Misuse of other people/bodies of published (unprotected) information on digital entrepreneurs and their businesses, which can give a competitive advantage to other players; for example, such information can be duplicated by others, 'possessed' by others (such as using the design of one company in another company and taking the credit for that design)
Entrepreneurs can better control value creation and funding acquisition, which are also made easier (although this does not guarantee higher success rates in funding generation)	Putting intellectual property (IP) on technology, design, production, innovative financial models, etc., at risk
Distribution, circulation and reformatting of digitalized content is easy and makes integration effortless	Sharing can be costly and is not always fair (once I use more, then you use more), and entrepreneurs should pursue business models that meet their needs, with clear agreements, while protecting them from misuse
Maximizing (and therefore reducing costs) the sharing of utilized assets for either monetary or non-monetary benefit	The means become the goal: innovation in business model process and design is more significant in business development than innovation in products or services

These dimensions are materialized through:

- *Digital content*—peer-to-peer models, such as social media, networks, file-sharing, mobile clouds, online platforms, blogs and other forms enable users to create, share and distribute content.

TABLE 6.2 The challenges of a sharing economy

Value	Bring 'something' that will be perceived as generating value for entrepreneurs and for the ecosystem
Progress	Use the sharing economy's concepts and the shared platforms' functions to advance entrepreneurial businesses
Diversity and modification	See the shared platforms as a means to expand and modify EE content; enable learners to use the boundless shared platforms (i.e., removing time and distance boundaries) for customized and personalized learning
Connections	Connect with academic institutions, industry, and entrepreneurs to contribute to the sharing economy by disseminating and sustaining the learning deliveries
Unleash creativity	Unleash creativity and innovation rather than forming a 'copy–paste' society

- *Sharing physical goods, infrastructures and space*—a business model that capitalizes on physical spaces, infrastructures and the ownership of goods, and getting the most from them.
- *Crowdfunding*—an online platform for raising capital by individuals who attract a crowd to participate in small- to medium-sized investments in startups' ideas and businesses, while rewarding the crowd with either monetary benefits or shares in the business offerings. Thus, crowdfunding contributes to active participation in entrepreneurship in obtaining financial support in feasible ways, compared to the difficulties associated with traditional investments.

These dimensions should be catered to in EE development and implementation. As such, value delivery should be reformed, co-creation should lead the strategic models, and critical sets of personal and team skills should be developed, as demonstrated in Figure 6.1 (Belk, 2014; Gold, 2004; Katz, Lucani,

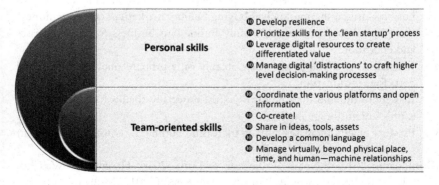

FIGURE 6.1 The digital entrepreneur—need for a changing skill set

Fitzek, & Seeling, 2014; Kempf, 2013; Kenney & Zysman, 2016; Mishra, 2017; Möhlmann, 2015; Richter, Kraus, Brem, Durst, & Giselbrecht, 2017; Sahm, Belleflamme, Lambert, & Schwienbacher, 2014; Sultan & van de Bunt-Kokhuis, 2012; Sundararajan, 2016).

Digital Content

Digital content, a main factor in the development of a sharing economy, emerged with the growing surge of the social web, social networks, blogs, platforms, and online media, which proved that "everything that can be digitized" (Shapiro & Varian, 1998, p. 3). Today, tangible and intangible content: products, for example, books, software, music or film; services, such as buying and selling, money transfer, or acquiring an education; and information items, such as databases, talks, and lectures, can be transferred from anyone to anyone else anywhere, bypassing physical channels. The growing spread of the media for mobile internet use, especially smartphones, is regarded as a catalyst for this development.

These trends have pivoted entrepreneurs' conduct, their businesses' development and their interactions with their stakeholders; for example, digital content enables entrepreneurs to develop their tangible and intangible products and services with minimal outside financial or technological assistance, as knowledge exists on the web; their interactions with investors change, as funding is sought only in the advanced stages of the business, when its valuation is higher, and thus advantageous for the entrepreneurs.

These changes in entrepreneurial dynamics are associated with the following digital content characteristics:

- It is free to use, or entails only a nominal charge.
- It is developed in user-friendly, intuitive ways.
- It can be easily and continually customized to consumers' needs.
- There is almost no capacity limit for digital content.
- Online interactions diffuse from personal-driven sharing, such as of selfies of personal experiences with products or services, or links to texts; to business-driven sharing, such as buying, selling, marketing, charging money; and general-driven content, mainly business-to-business for news releases and education.
- It entails low development costs, mainly only primary ones, then marginal costs for reproduction.
- It is more durable than physical goods, especially thanks to the cloud and sophisticated storage methods.
- Product quality increases with an increasing number of consumers (traction)

(Brinkmann, 2012; Etemad, Wilkinson, & Dana, 2010; Hargittai & Walejko, 2008; Katz, Roberts, Strom, & Freilich, 2014; Kempf, 2013; Mullan, 2011).

These developments should be reflected in EE, though simply uploading EE materials online is not enough, and might even be damaging for learning, as it will create an unhealthy 'storage dependency' in the learner on the digital content. Rather, EE strives to construct customized tools that can circulate through the vast digitized content that is relevant to EE and its learners, in ways that can trigger the student entrepreneurs' thoughts, reflections and insights and empower them so that their motivation for entrepreneurship will deepen by enabling them to search for, and discover, the relevant content, integrate it, prepare it, and apply it to their needs.

The abundance of shared content lies in duplications of original content (redundancies), inconsistencies, replications with additions or deletions, non-disclosure of sources, unsuitable modifications, and poor maintenance, resulting in lack of updates. Therefore, EE should teach entrepreneurs to scout for knowledge through different digitalized sources, criticize the existing material, and prioritize the discovered knowledge according to its relevance to the entrepreneurs' needs.

Moreover, as EE digital content is not subject to place or time, KSA involving interdisciplinary discourses, collaboration with other people and engagement in complex problem solving that involves a higher level of awareness inside the ecosystem's needs should be the focus of EE, as demonstrated in Figure 6.2.

Digital content for EE is offered in programs such as Coursera,[2] Udacity,[3] Udemy,[4] and specifically for entrepreneurs, the Digital Business Academy;[5] these are a few examples of the use of digital content availability to create academic and practical contents for entrepreneurs to facilitate their learning process. The challenge is to change the programs' content to educate entrepreneurs on how to leverage the digital content and make full use of it for their needs as learners and as entrepreneurs. This change can be taught virtually or in a classroom; it addresses competencies that align with the digital content and the digital-driven generation of entrepreneurs.

The role of experts—The role of experts, expertise and specialization in the entrepreneurial realm is increasing, but also changing. Expertise can be valued when its representations are multifaceted and it encompasses various disciplines, various approaches and innovative, unexpected thinking—all gathered into one solution. As such, expertise is a solution that can bring, concurrently, deep and still cutting-edge proficiency in a specific field, and innovative thinking accumulated in other, related fields; for example, expertise in 'planning an autonomous car' would be valued if it included deep specialization in the field of autonomous vehicles along with an in-depth understanding of drivers' psychology, leisure time activity (for the driver, while the car is driving autonomously), and ergonomics, for example. This expertise package is totally different from the conventional one required a decade ago.

Moreover, the sharing economy has split the experts' role into two opposing modes: the first refers to the more generic expertise, general knowledge that can be easily found on the web, including that from 'unreachable' experts; the second

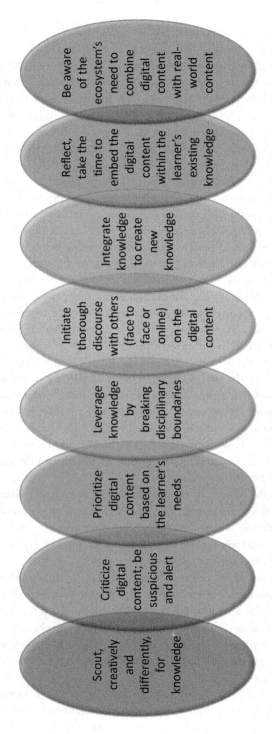

FIGURE 6.2 New EE skills to be developed to leverage the digital content trend

is customized expertise, where the tailoring is exclusive to a specific business; it is rare, expensive and most valuable. Due to its rarity and distinctiveness, it protects the business from duplication (Johri & Pal, 2012; Kahle & Hansen, 2009; Peters, Besley, Araya, & Peters, 2014; Schmitt, 2015; Short, Bohn, & Baru, 2011; Signer, 2010; Thille, 2010).

Shared Spaces

The sharing economy has created a novel concept for entrepreneurship, the new-generation 'workplace', that is, the shared, or co-working, spaces. Shared spaces were initially an urban phenomenon designed to stimulate creativity through casual networking, yet with great potential in a synergetic, dynamic, and inspiring space. Entrepreneurs, the main users, gain from the built-in interactions, as participants spend time together in the same location; this can then develop into collaborative work and meaningful networking. The latter is one of the main powers of shared spaces, due to acquaintance not only with other tenants of the co-working space, or the venue's management, but also with stakeholders surrounding those tenants and management teams, creating a large, continuously expanding networking circle.

This phenomenon represents the new generation of EE from both the tenants' side and that of the entrepreneurship ecosystem. Guy Franklin, the manager of SOSA in New York City, attests to the notion that shared spaces serve as 'shop windows' for anyone from the ecosystem who wishes to be more hands-on in innovations. Research stresses that entrepreneurial performance improves through the learning processes gained in co-working spaces as it coincides with the young generation's expectations from EE; that is, flexibility, independence, sharing through meaningful interactions and a 'cool' place to work.

Co-working spaces enable a blended-learning practice, based on the formal activities introduced into those spaces: formal events, meetings, office hours, etc., as well as the informal interactions that occur naturally within the space, formal mentoring as well as informally obtaining advice from peers, being inspired by other tenants, or formally exploiting opportunities that arise in guest lectures, or by informal connections and referrals that can appear "just by talking to another tenant."

Shared-space businesses can attract entrepreneurs with various backgrounds, or with a common interest; both models allow their occupants to create communities that serve as an internal marketplace; each user becomes a service provider for other users, thus expanding the businesses' clientele. These experiences, gained through trial and error, albeit in a contained, collaborative environment, are an important feature in the EE learning journey.

An online survey of more than 70 tenants of shared spaces around the world,[6] followed up with online interviews, revealed their insights, demonstrated in Table 6.3.

TABLE 6.3 Insights from shared-space tenants

Shared-space features	Testimonials	Educational insights: *What about co-working spaces can be applied to the EE process?*
Mitigating the loneliness that comes with entrepreneurship	Maor Cohen, applications developer working with startup teams, Israel: "I had to constantly prove my skills and achievements; so rather than doing what I am best at, and introducing the technological skills that are sought by all startups, I found myself searching for clients. I wanted to concentrate on my strengths: technological solutions. By renting the desk at this co-working space, I am getting clients easily; I am no longer by myself; we are all a big family that helps each other"	➢ Teach the meaning of loneliness as well as its positive aspects to acquire resilience, reflecting on strengths ➢ Encouraging 'learning by sharing'
Being in the loop; reduces the FOMO effect; being in the coolest place for entrepreneurs	Wyatt Tong, IT developer, Taiwan: "When I arrived in the US, I wanted to swallow up everything; I was already an entrepreneur and stayed in the country for my last bachelor year. I wanted to make the most of it for my business back home. Luckily, my apartment was so bad that I had to find a place to work on my business. This co-working place suited my financial capacity. But the most important thing is that I was well informed, I got information on the coolest things before anyone else knew; I met with the others who rented desks daily. The collaboration was amazing. Back home, I decided to strengthen the co-working space concept in my home town"	➢ Teaching smart ways to scout for information ➢ Encouraging 'learning by meeting & talking' ➢ Explaining the meaning of FOMO and how to manage it
Low-cost, and cost-effective, location: shared facilities, infrastructure	Luis Martinez, a lawyer providing counsel to startups, Mexico: "I graduated from my studies and started my business by consulting for startups. I enjoyed it greatly, but financially it was very discouraging; the startups are	➢ Training to develop interaction and communication skills ➢ Preparing unique 'pitch' presentations for the different stakeholders that entrepreneurs meet

Meeting with many individuals	limited in money and it takes time until they pay. In this co-working space, I have reduced my costs. Moreover, I get many more referrals from the participants, as well as from their colleagues" Diantha Nagai, a lawyer providing counsel to entrepreneurial businesses and promoter of a female entrepreneurship concept, Turkey: "I studied in the UK, then returned to my home town and started to work on the female entrepreneurship concept. I joined an incubator in a co-working space. Since then, I have been overbooked with meetings with leading figures who can contribute to my business"	⋀ Sharpening the concept of value; when meeting with many people, it is important to decipher what they see as value. By furnishing the value as a first impression, the communica-tion is more productive ⋀ Collaborating with networking associations and experts to teach and train entrepreneurs
Easy creation of your own community, as the tenants share common interests	Ives Gardinier, a music entrepreneur, France: "I tried to form so many communities in music-tech, through the social media and meetups, but they did not last, even when the start was promising. Here at the co-working space, we meet each other every day, all day long, for a period of time. Communities are created more naturally, and most importantly, they add value to the members. They are dynamic, business-oriented. I see the difference: this one will endure for a long time"	⋀ Building the new job of community developer; it is still a bottom-up, unestablished, yet most needed job ⋀ Developing expertise in community creation among entrepreneurs ⋀ Involving community creators and managers in EE
A self-learning process	Tej Agarwal, an entrepreneur in the IT sector, India: "You have to initiate the contact with the other tenants and be alert when they meet their partners outside of the co-working space to expand your opportunities and create an open environment. You should also be attentive, kind and responsive to the others, this is the only way to gain their collaboration. I had to learn how to do this the hard way. Now, I have already recruited my desk neighbor as our marketing advisor"	⋀ Encouraging use of the shared space as a beta site, to build, test, adjust and implement the related, entrepreneur-ial KSA, mainly in the areas of communica-tion and opportunity exploitation ⋀ Enhancing self-reflective, learning processes ⋀ Facilitators are needed to discuss the learning process

These interviews showed that entrepreneurs more easily procure best practices, knowledge, and valuable information by talking, sharing, and brainstorming with other occupants of shared spaces and their stakeholders; they enjoy easier access to communities and social networks; and they take part in or create cohort-based communities. Research shows that these shared-space communities provide entrepreneurs with collective meaning, professional identity, and emotional support.

The proliferation of shared spaces has resulted in upgrading the technologically advanced venues, including the required facilities for entrepreneurs—attractive and stimulating, and most suitable for effective, creativity-driven EE. Mukul Pasricha, founder of Spring House Coworking,[7] has been quoted as saying:

> With incubation being on the rise, certain themed co-working spaces host young startups, train them, mentor them and make them market-ready. They provide additional corporate shared services to all of their residents and scout particular startups that would eventually be backed by various investors/stakeholders. These are all effective business strategies that help such spaces stay afloat in this ambitious market.

According to Pasricha,

> Apart from the influx of knowledge and productivity that one improves by meeting like-minded people, it is the creation of new opportunities that come your way when you collaborate with others. Many times you will get stuck on projects that are too challenging or demanding, and it is the help of these co-working peers from various professional backgrounds that will enable salvaging the situation.

At the same time, leaders of the co-working concept, We Work,[8] declare the mission as follows:

> Make a life, not just a living.

> WeWork is a global network of workspaces where companies and people grow together. We transform buildings into dynamic environments for creativity, focus, and connection. More than just the best place to work, though, this is a movement toward humanizing work. We believe that CEOs can help each other, offices can use the comforts of home, and we can all look forward to Monday if we find real meaning in what we do.

Further on:

> Space as an Experience
> The nature of work is changing. Recruitment, retention, innovation, and productivity now require not just coffee, but also yoga, not just

printers, but also art installations. WeWork offers companies of all sizes the opportunity to reimagine employees' days through refreshing design, engaging community, and benefits for all.

In this era of thriving shared spaces for entrepreneurs, EE should follow the trend, which is to enable and encourage flexibility and sharing by:

- Changing the mindset toward sharing; treating it as an educational means.
- Using shared spaces for learning, developing, planning, monitoring; sitting together provides the occasion to reflect, co-create, and form new knowledge sets.
- Shifting responsibility from the instructor, expert or teacher to both the learner and the community.
- Focusing on 'translating' the vast knowledge surrounding entrepreneurs in shared spaces; for example, meetings with the co-working space stakeholders could be operationalized to learning outcomes, by discussing those meetings' meaning, value and potential impact on the entrepreneur, the business, future plans, etc.

Shared spaces combine other shared activities to emphasize the relevance and impact of the sharing economy; some innovative examples are: Edspace,[9] where entrepreneurs and innovators share the same vertical EE (EDtech), and create a unique community; Tahoe Mountain Lab[10] in South Lake Tahoe, where collaborative outdoor activities are offered, such as paddle boarding, hiking, wakeboarding, mountain biking, etc., along with co-working space offerings, considering the collaborativity as a booster for creativity productivity; Mokrin House[11] in the north of Serbia is a co-working and co-living space for entrepreneurs that offers accommodation and food, along with workshops, educational seminars, cooking classes, and other activities, with the shared-living facilities serving as a component to engage more deeply in ideation, brainstorming and reflection to improve the business venture-creation process; KantoorKaravaan,[12] a space in a caravan for entrepreneurs that are mobile and need to travel in the countryside. The community of KantoorKaravaan offers brainstorming sessions, workshops and related activities. These examples confirm that the phenomenon is growing, becoming more complex, and is able to provide more shared activities for EE (Balakrishnan, Muthaly, & Leenders, 2016; Bouncken & Reuschl, 2016; Fuzi, 2015; Huwart, Dichter, & Vanrie, 2012; Parrino, 2015; Spinuzzi, 2012; Weijs-Perrée, van de Koevering, Appel-Meulenbroek, & Arentze, 2018).

Crowdfunding

Crowdfunding is not a typical component of EE, but it has a strong link to entrepreneurship and it encompasses vast potential for spurring innovation, creating jobs, and stimulating the economy. A recent World Bank statement called for greater access to collective financing through crowdfunding platforms and strengthening the role of crowdfunding in the entrepreneurial realm. As such, even though it does not represent a typical program, it is a major topic that should be comprehensively addressed by EE.

As a response to the needs of entrepreneurs who were unable to raise money to start their businesses in the aftermath of the 2008 recession, and capitalizing on the new, internet-enabled communications tools that have allowed entrepreneurs to start their businesses, crowdfunding introduced a 'many-to-many' form of communication. Largely, crowdfunding platforms enable various campaigns to raise money from the crowd through four main models: donations, rewards, lending, and equity; however, innovations are constantly being introduced for more fundraising options.

Research in this field is still embryonic, and the processes and reciprocal impact of crowdfunding on entrepreneurship and, therefore, on EE, are still relatively unexplored. The financial aspects of crowdfunding and its four models are taught in business schools and sought after for implementation by managers of accelerators and incubators, but a more inclusive perspective in EE is lacking. A more advanced EE view of crowdfunding as a larger field than just a financial concept is needed, as suggested in Figure 6.3.

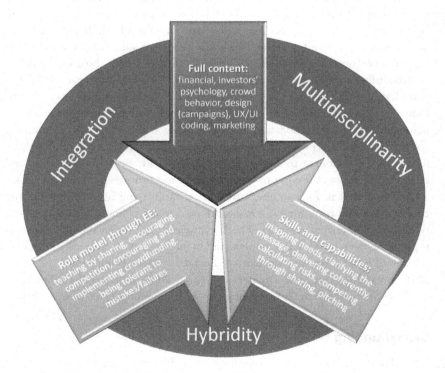

FIGURE 6.3 Crowdfunding in the context of EE

Crowdfunding is a compound concept involving areas such as psychology and behavioral science to delve into the crowd and investors' decision-making processes and behaviors, ecosystem models, marketing and sales, coding the user experience (UX) and user interface (UI), and designs for campaigns, among others. Skill deliveries should refer to this platform's 'requirements', to be aligned with the new generation's entrepreneurship modes, and include training/mentoring in clarifying and simplifying the message, composing it so that anyone, regardless of language, cultural or educational differences, will understand it; pitching, convincing, etc., and modeling the use of crowdfunding as a teaching technique to strengthen its practicality, including boosting the learners to use, even as a test, crowdfunding campaigns, or initiate such campaigns for other startups (Belleflamme, Lambert, & Schwienbacher, 2013; Bruton, Khavul, Siegel, & Wright, 2015; Harrison, 2013; Mollick, 2014; The World Bank, 2013).

Summary

The sharing economy has contributed to a major transformation in various fields that affect EE. In a world where everything is shared, free of charge (or inexpensive and affordable), collaborative, and 'on the web', adding new value to EE becomes a challenge. Shared content, shared spaces and crowdfunding have shifted entrepreneurs' needs from absorbing knowledge—mainly at the academic level—from formal, structured programs to free-shared-content methods that can be obtained from the most renowned experts in their fields, and from the best academic institutions (by taking digital courses or attending virtual talks, such as TED), or by random people contributing to the same blog or post, or sharing the same co-working space. Informal gatherings have also become a substantial means of sharing and gaining knowledge through inspiring discussions, feedback and insights. The sharing economy has also changed the relationship between entrepreneurs and their stakeholders, which is reflected in EE through knowledge delivery. Experts are still very relevant to the sharing-generation entrepreneurs, yet their contribution has been transformed into either generic and easy to obtain, or customized and, therefore, trustworthy, rare and expensive.

EE is taking on new forms, knowledge is being given new meanings, and the educational challenges are turning to facilitation by delivering the meaning of the changes brought on by the sharing economy and, therefore, improving communication skills and emotional competencies such as resilience and trust, refining the digital search, and acquiring the mindset and capabilities to prioritize, ask questions, search deeper and self-customize the obtained knowledge, spotlighting opportunities from the vast and unfiltered information flow, working collectively, sharing, and keeping an open mind while specializing in specific fields.

Takeaways

For educators and teaching developers:

- Embrace *sharing* in EE contents, delivered skills and modeling.
- Invite experts from different disciplines, mindsets, sectors, etc. to be part of the EE curriculum and delivery, to gain more EE diversity and richness.
- Web-sharing and economy-related functions are enabling the development of multiple EE platforms, projects and programs; these can be easily 'tested' to decode the differential impacts on different types of entrepreneurs (for example, virtual incubators provide value to more mature entrepreneurs; coding delivered peer-to-peer is more substantial for women entrepreneurs, etc.).
- Create shared-program development with the learners, using sharing-economy concepts, while allowing the learners to map and prioritize their needs, and offer their own solutions.
- Shared spaces can be the venue to deliver EE and the 'factory' to test and develop it further; they are usually free, they do not consist of structured programs, and they may be the best place to introduce new R&D factories, while testing them on the tenants, and gaining their feedback.

For EE participants:

- Awareness: the sharing economy is one of the main enablers for you, the entrepreneur. However, it is overwhelming and confusing, due to the plenitude of information and knowledge that it brings, both physically and virtually. Acknowledge your need for means to prioritize, select, question and exploit this for the benefit of your business.
- A shared, collaborative, and free environment can boost your progress; to ascertain this, spot the *what, how* and with *whom* of the existing facilities that can really advance the business; for example, using a co-working space with only those specializing in your startup field, coding by yourself, then asking a designer to provide feedback, or using crowdfunding, but only for a specific component of the business.
- Like the EE developers, you must change your mindset on EE delivery and value gained; many of you are still used to attending courses to 'really gain knowledge', yet, in this era of shared content, any knowledge should be considered valuable, and, therefore, tested and evaluated.
- Proactively assemble content, methods and tools with the support of the ecosystem's players, to construct the most fitting EE.
- Since the sharing economy is free, open and collaborative, take advantage of this by trying out, examining and assessing many tools or platforms; the risk is lower, the examination process can be insightful, and it has the potential to provide the needed support and assistance.

Case Study 6—The Nexus of a Co-working Space: Diversity and Multisectoriality, the Canadian Experience of entrePrism, Montreal, Canada

entrePrism[13] is a multisectorial incubation program aimed at supporting entrepreneurs from all backgrounds, with a particular focus on immigrants to support their involvement in the Quebec business ecosystem. entrePrism's mission is to underpin budding entrepreneurs, to help them turn their ideas into business projects with the support of established entrepreneurs, professionals and professors.

According to Professor Luis Cisneros,[14] co-founder and scientific director[15] of entrePrism,

> HEC Montréal business school attracts students with different backgrounds. We wanted to leverage our position in the educational sector to attract more entrepreneurial students, and we were confident that we had succeeded. However, we observed that in some of the undergraduate and graduate programs in entrepreneurship, only ten out of 30–40 students complete the program, even if we use a fully comprehensive process for selection (e.g., with interviews) for mentoring, including cutting-edge teaching models. It was obvious that entrepreneurs will be entrepreneurs 'with us or without us'; so we changed our mindset and consequently, our method. We learned thoroughly the real drivers and motivations of the student entrepreneurs and decided to enroll 60[16] into the program in entrepreneurship; our challenge was to support them in completing their academic track by offering, among other things, incubation and accelerator programs.

Cisneros and his team are aware of the value of diversity in creating value in all strata of the ecosystem. He himself is originally from Mexico, and the team comprises members from five different countries. Cisneros considers this program to be an innovative model for supporting entrepreneurs, particularly those from cultural communities, in starting up new businesses and growing existing ones. According to Manaf Bouchentouf, co-founder and executive director of entrePrism:

> This program offers personalized support as well as training sessions, seminars, webinars, conferences and one-on-one coaching sessions. entrePrism also invites speakers from various sectors, assists in funding opportunities, including teaching how to seek funding and connect with potential investors and donors, provides access to a loan of honor program (up to $10,000 per entrepreneur) and to competitions, networking activities and personalized support, among others.

The entrePrism team sees their mission as professionally enabling immigrant entrepreneurs to acquire the knowledge, skills, capabilities, network and funding to successfully start a business and to have a positive impact on the economy, as well as society.

entrePrism is situated in a modern co-working space. According to Cisneros,

> This is not only a physical place and this is not a business model *per se*, it has to be an enabler, a facilitator. Student entrepreneurs are continuously sharing the co-working space during the whole process of business creation with professionals, team members, partners and alumni. We can, thus, follow their progression, oversee their entrepreneurial process and intervene through a facilitation process. They meet other entrepreneurs who give them advice, emotional support and help them expand their business network. The co-working space has to be a shared platform, not only a space to come to work.

The co-working space is modern, and consists of quite a large space, designed to inspire and spur creativity; it is functional and, most importantly, provides space for reflection, thinking, and planning, with innovative architectural and technological tools to write, draw, and share. HEC Montreal also offers areas for entrepreneurs to network, meet, and initiate meetups and events.

Regarding the strengths of this program, Cisneros attests to the fact that

> We were constantly receiving very positive feedback from our partners, as well as the entrepreneurs, on our educational processes and achievements. We received financial support from government agencies, reaffirming our role in the entrepreneurial landscape; yet we were eager to crack our programs' strengths. I can list some that we came up with: we are experts in business modeling, thus providing value to our startups that wish to sharpen their models prior to penetrating the market; we are fast; we are international, which means that we have signed agreements in several countries to offer 'soft landing pads' to our entrepreneurs; our programs are multisectorial, multidisciplinary and diversified. Yet, I see our main strength in the co-working space concept. It has shaped our unique blended-value model of: academics–researchers–experts–entrepreneurs–policy-makers, who altogether are an integral part of our ecosystem, deeply engaged in our programs, and facilitating the learning process. We frequently say that academics and researchers contribute with the 'know', experts and policy-makers with the 'know-how', and entrepreneurs with the 'know how to be'.

Today, students, alumni, and any entrepreneur from any sector can apply to entrePrism. The tenants and alumni have contributed original and very frequently scalable projects, such as Cousmos,[17] focusing on the culinary heritage of couscous, assembled through an intensive R&D process and offering unique know-how and healthy meal solutions; Dataperformers,[18] a startup that helps companies train their formerly *lazy data* to perform at an elite level using state-of-the-art AI solutions; Picolo Vélo,[19] the first Canadian producers of high-performance wood-frame bicycles; or Maya Mia[20] soaps that are handmade locally using all natural ingredients, for a mixture of Quebec's inspiration and Mexico's essence. The team is pushing the startups to be active in Montreal's various events, meetups and competitions—from which many projects have raised more money based on their achievements. Cisneros is constantly seeking more collaborations in art-preneurship, AI, and more, to exploit the entrepreneurial concepts that the team preaches to the fullest.

Questions on the Case Study

1. Cisneros states that the shared space at HEC is an educational 'concept'; explain this statement based on 3–4 ideas discussed in this chapter. What is your conclusion, is it a unique educational concept?
2. In your opinion, what are the 3–4 major challenges that entrePrism should focus on to sustain its leading position in the Quebec landscape? Explain your response.
3. Search the internet for two other shared spaces for entrepreneurs in Montreal and write down their names and website addresses. Imagine that founders of a food-tech startup are asking for your advice on enrolling in these two competing venues. What would you suggest? Explain your response.
4. Cisneros and his team are exposed to an opportunity to replicate their concept in the Asian market. List 4–5 questions that they should ask prior to making a decision on the feasibility of the opportunity.
5. Look for entrePrism projects on the web. In your opinion, in which way did entrePrism promote them, based on the case study and on other material on the web? Accordingly, provide Cisneros with ideas for improvement and future directions.

Reflective Questions

1. Look for one co-working space in Europe, one in Africa and one in Latin America. Discuss their similarities and differences. What are your conclusions?
2. A government association asks for your advice in opening a unique place for entrepreneurs in your country, which will emphasize the values and main ideas of the sharing economy. Write a one-page plan for the government association based on the concepts described in this chapter.
3. Write a one-page suggestion for WeWork on how to sustain its leading position as a co-working space in the entrepreneurial landscape.
4. Search the internet for 2–3 startups that have failed, and write down their names and details. Construct a plan based on the sharing-economy concepts to assist them in reopening their businesses. Explain your response.

5. Watch Optimizing Space Itself with WeWork's Adam Neumann | Disrupt NY 2017 at: https://youtu.be/-EKOV71m-PY. List questions for Neumann that invoke the sharing-economy concept as an EE channel for educating entrepreneurs, and suggest five other concepts for him to develop, such as WeLive.[21]

Notes

1 Fear of missing out.
2 See at: www.coursera.org/
3 See at: www.udacity.com/
4 See at: www.udemy.com/
5 See at: www.digitalbusinessacademyuk.com/
6 The survey was conducted by the author in 2018 for research purposes; responses were received from France, Germany, the Netherlands, Serbia, Slovenia, Croatia, Greece, Turkey, Israel, India, China, Taiwan, Mexico, the United States and Canada.
7 See at: www.entrepreneur.com/article/305949
8 See at: www.wework.com/
9 See at: www.edspace.io/
10 See at: www.tahoemountainlab.com/
11 See at: www.mokrinhouse.com/
12 See at: www.kantoorkaravaan.nl/
13 This innovative program was created by HEC Montréal with the support of the Mirella and Lino Saputo Foundation and the Quebec Ministry of Economy, Science and Innovation (January 2016).
14 Personal interview by me.
15 Manaf Bouchentouf is the executive director and Pierre Provost is the coordinator of entrePrism.
16 This is the case for the Certificate of Entrepreneurship and Business Creation.
17 See at: https://cousmos.ca/fr/
18 See at: www.dataperformers.com
19 See at: www.picolovelo.com/
20 See at: maya-mia.com/
21 See at: www.welive.com/

References

Balakrishnan, B. K. P. D., Muthaly, S., & Leenders, M. (2016). Insights from coworking spaces as unique service organizations: The role of physical and social elements. In L. Petruzzellis & R. S. Winer (Eds.), *Rediscovering the Essentiality of Marketing, Developments in Marketing Science: Proceedings of the Academy of Marketing* (pp. 837–848). Cham, Switzerland: Springer. https://doi.org/10.1007/978-3-319-29877-1

Belk, R. (2014). You are what you can access: Sharing and collaborative consumption online. *Journal of Business Research*, 67(8), 1595–1600.

Belleflamme, P., Lambert, T., & Schwienbacher, A. (2013). Individual crowdfunding practices. *Venture Capital*, 15(4), 313–333.

Bouncken, R. B., & Reuschl, A. J. (2016). Coworking-spaces: How a phenomenon of the sharing economy builds a novel trend for the workplace and for entrepreneurship. *Review of Managerial Science*, 1–18.

Brinkmann, S. (2012). *Qualitative Inquiry in Everyday Life: Working with Everyday Life Materials*. London: Sage.

Bruton, G. D., Khavul, S., Siegel, D. S., & Wright, M. (2015). Entrepreneurship theory and practice. *39*(1), 9–26.

Etemad, H., Wilkinson, I., & Dana, L. P. (2010). Internetization as the necessary condition for internationalization in the newly emerging economy. *Journal of International Entrepreneurship*, *8*(4), 319–342.

Fuzi, A. (2015). Co-working spaces for promoting entrepreneurship in sparse regions: The case of South Wales. *Regional Studies, Regional Science*, *2*(1), 462–469. https://doi.org/10.1080/21681376.2015.1072053

Gold, L. (2004). *The Sharing Economy: Solidarity Networks Transforming Globalisation*. Aldershot, UK: Ashgate.

Hargittai, E., & Walejko, G. (2008). The participation divide: Content creation and sharing in the digital age. *Information, Community and Society*, *11*(2), 239–256.

Harrison, R. (2013). Crowdfunding and the revitalisation of the early stage risk capital market: Catalyst or chimera? *Venture Capital*, *15*(4), 283–287. https://doi.org/10.1080/13691066.2013.852331

Huwart, J.-Y., Dichter, G., & Vanrie, P. (2012). Coworking: Collaborative Space for Microentrepreneurs. *EBN Technical Notes*, *1*, 1–24.

Johri, A., & Pal, J. (2012). Capable and convivial design (CCD): A framework for designing information and communication technologies for human development. *Information Technology for Development*, *18*(1), 61–75.

Kahle, L., & Hansen, K. H. (2009). Work in progress – globalization and business innovation: How do we best prepare millennial-generation engineering students for complex challenges? In *Proceedings of the 39th IEEE Conference on Frontiers in Education* (pp. 715–716). IEEE. https://doi.org/10.1109/FIE.2009.5350664

Katz, J. A., Roberts, J., Strom, R., & Freilich, A. (2014). Perspectives on the development of cross campus entrepreneurship education. *Entrepreneurship Research Journal*, *4*(1), 13–44.

Katz, M., Lucani, D. E., Fitzek, F. H., & Seeling, P. (2014). Sharing resources locally and widely: Mobile clouds as the building blocks of the shareconomy. *IEEE Vehicular Technology Magazine*, *9*(3), 63–71.

Kempf, D. (2013). *Shareconomy*. Hanover, Germany: BITKOM.

Kenney, M., & Zysman, J. (2016). The rise of the platform economy. *Issues in Science and Technology*, *32*(3), 61–69.

Mishra, C. S. (2017). *Creating and Sustaining Competitive Advantage: Management Logics, Business Models, and Entrepreneurial Rent*. Cham, Switzerland: Springer.

Möhlmann, M. (2015). Collaborative consumption: determinants of satisfaction and the likelihood of using a sharing economy option again. *Journal of Consumer Behaviour*, *14*(3), 193–207.

Mollick, E. (2014). The dynamics of crowdfunding: An exploratory study. *Journal of Business Venturing*, *29*(1), 1–16. https://doi.org/10.1016/j.jbusvent.2013.06.005

Mullan, E. (2011). What is digital content? *EContent Magazine*, www.econtentmag.com/Articles/Resources/Defining-EContent/What-is-Digital-Content-79501.htm, retrieved March 5, 2014.

Parrino, L. (2015). Coworking: Assessing the role of proximity in knowledge exchange. *Knowledge Management Research & Practice*, *13*(3), 261–271.

Peters, M. A., Besley, T., Araya, D., & Peters, M. A. (2014). *The New Development Paradigm: Education, Knowledge Economy and Digital Futures*. New York: Peter Lang.

Richter, C., Kraus, S., Brem, A., Durst, S., & Giselbrecht, C. (2017). Digital entrepreneurship: Innovative business models for the sharing economy. *Creativity and Innovation Management, 26*(3), 300–310.

Sahm, M., Belleflamme, P., Lambert, T., & Schwienbacher, A. (2014). Corrigendum to "Crowdfunding: Tapping the right crowd." *Journal of Business Venturing, 5*(29), 610–611.

Schmitt, U. (2015). The promise of autonomous personal knowledge management devices to be a key educational technology for growing a 21st century knowledge society. Paper presented to the *Emerging Technologies & Authentic Learning within Higher Vocational Education Conference* (pp. 1–3), Cape Town, South Africa.

Shapiro, C., & Varian, H. R. (1998). *Information Rules: A Strategic Guide to the Network Economy*. Brighton, MA: Harvard Business Press.

Short, J. E., Bohn, R. E., & Baru, C. (2011). *How Much Information? 2010 Report on Enterprise Server Information*. San Diego, CA: Global Information Industry Center at the Graduate School of International Relations and Pacific Studies.

Signer, B. (2010). What is wrong with digital documents? A conceptual model for structural cross-media content composition and reuse. In J. Parker, M. Saiki, P. Shoval, C. Woo, & Y. Wand (Eds.) *Conceptual Modeling – ER 2010, Lecture Notes in Computer Science, Volume 6412*. (pp. 391–404). Berlin: Springer.

Spinuzzi, C. (2012). Working alone together: Coworking as emergent collaborative activity. *Journal of Business and Technical Communication, 26*(4), 399–441.

Sultan, N., & van de Bunt-Kokhuis, S. (2012). Organisational culture and cloud computing: coping with a disruptive innovation. *Technology Analysis & Strategic Management, 24*(2), 167–179.

Sundararajan, A. (2016). *The Sharing Economy: The End of Employment and the Rise of Crowd-based Capitalism*. Cambridge, MA: MIT Press.

Thille, C. (2010). Education technology as a transformational innovation. In *White House Summit on Community Colleges: Conference Papers* (pp. 73–78). Retrieved from www.ed.gov/college-completion/community-college-summit.

*Weijs-Perrée, M., van de Koevering, J., Appel-Meulenbroek, R., & Arentze, T. (2018). Analysing user preferences for co-working space characteristics. *Building Research & Information*, 1–15. https://doi.org/10.1080/09613218.2018.1463750

World Bank (2013, January 1). Crowdfunding's potential for the developing world. www.worldbank.org

7
THE NEW BREED OF PROGRAMS AND ACADEMIA'S ROLE

'Entrepreneurship Can Be Taught!'

Since entrepreneurship has been established as a domain that can be taught, yet entrepreneurs have an instinctive urge to do, act and operate prior to, or simultaneously with, learning, reflecting or planning, creative ways of teaching need to be developed.

Classroom teaching requires flexibility, creativity, and collaboration. There are various creative methods aimed at preparing entrepreneurs for success, along with providing them with the learning experience that will transform learning into an accessible, relevant and valuable process. Aligned with opportunity-exploitation models, three main streams can be used to stimulate entrepreneurial teaching, all based on the principles of opportunity-identification, opportunity-exploration and opportunity-creation models.

- Opportunity identification—hinging on an observed, existing problem, need or gap that warrants a solution that is innovative and different from the systems or methods used to manage such needs.
- Opportunity exploration—providing smart solutions for complex problems. Complex problems exist, renew themselves and are difficult to solve or control (Glouberman & Zimmerman, 2002). Different stakeholders with different interests define them, as well as the threatening extent of such problems, differently. As such, when companies introduce their complex problems, entrepreneurs' solutions should be a 'one-shot operation', and, therefore, a complex problem can stimulate many innovative ideas that could develop into different new businesses.
- Opportunity creation—the drive to develop a new business from scratch, through either already having a solid idea for a business or being fascinated to

learn how to develop a business idea. This refers to introducing 'something' new, essentially, to make a change. Creation means that the entrepreneurs are ready to disrupt the known and established comfort zones, and fuel them with revolutionary solutions.

For example, people frequently lack change in their wallet, and are, therefore, unable to purchase some item at a specific time. An opportunity-identification stream would lead entrepreneurs to observe the situation, define the inconvenience and provide innovative ideas and solutions that can then be duplicated to resolve other such inconveniences or to serve other users. The opportunity-exploration stream would refer to exploring the situation for companies (e.g., banks, commercial firms, restaurants) that have addressed this as a complicated need, and find smart solutions. Opportunity creation might provide a solution for the inconvenience, but on a much more widely encompassing scale than a smart solution, making it a game changer; an example might be developing the blockchain platform, which offers a solution for the inconvenience, but is, in fact, aimed at developing a more open, accessible, and fair financial future.

A variety of educational forms can be developed from these three streams, either individually or in combination, such as identification and creation. Table 7.1 demonstrates how each stream can be used in educating entrepreneurs.

To increase learners' attention and intensify their sense of value accumulation from the various tendered programs, a mixed-method of EE is required. The following ways to tackle education contribute to learners' acquisition of skills, knowledge, experience and networks. Each of the following can be pivoted to the opportunity-driven streams of identification, exploration and creation.

Gamification

The use of gamification in educating entrepreneurs is an innovative teaching technique, part of the 'use of game mechanics in non-gaming contexts' to create gameful experiences (Deterding, Dixon, Khaled, & Nacke, 2011; Hamari, Koivisto, & Sarsa, 2014). It is mainly used as an incentive to encourage students to stay interested in educational pursuits by incorporating game mechanics, incentive systems, and other ideas borrowed from the game world to create a game layer on top of existing educational systems. Gamification is defined in research as the use of game attributes outside the game context with the aim of affecting learning-related behaviors or attitudes that, in turn, strengthen the relationship between instructional design quality and outcomes. The main idea behind gamification in education is to boost learners' motivation, strengthen engagement, change behaviors, and boost innovation. It increases educational effectiveness, while research also stresses its psychological influences in elevating learners' competencies related to becoming entrepreneurs, for example, *curiosity, challenge,* and *control*. Gamification, as part of the big idea of the 'classroom of

TABLE 7.1 Opportunity-driven streams in EE, education forms and expected results for the learners

	Education forms	Expected results for the learners
Opportunity identification	a) Providing knowledge, figures, statistics on trends, successful inventions, investments in startups, etc. b) Inspirational talks with founders and entrepreneurial teams; mentors and experts in the entrepreneurial field c) Hands-on practice – searching for gaps by regularly following leading media property, profiling startups, reviewing new products; interviewing consumers to sketch their needs; operating market simulations to understand people's behavior, etc.	a) Enabling the search for gaps b) Being inspired by those who are already in the field; gaining confidence and being exposed to role models c) Identifying needs by 'being in the field', feeling and sensing the opportunities; better understanding people's behaviors in specific situations, as another route to identifying opportunities, even if these are not yet problems or needs
Opportunity exploration	a) Involving companies from different sectors to introduce their, or their industry's, complex problems b) Developing an ecosystem that predominantly copes with similar complex problems c) Creating smart solutions, being accompanied by the same companies that introduced, or are affected by, the complex problems d) Structuring a diverse group of participants in this learning process: leading figures from academia, industry and government, along with people from different sectors, industries, life experience, expertise, etc.	a) Exploring a phenomenon with different lenses, rather than applying already existing solutions to solve complex problems b) Testing, figuring out and interpreting the problem through the eyes of the bodies that are affected by it c) Ensuring that the explored problem and its subsequent smart solution are supported by companies, which can then provide the platform and infrastructures to implement the solutions in real ventures d) Practicing a new approach of self-learning by compounding different foci, interests, specializations, etc.; acquiring revolutionary new problem-solving skills by blending such different approaches to a solution
Opportunity creation	a) Stimulating creativity in the education process b) Practicing for real (not a simulation) by pitching to investors, looking for talent, recruiting staff members, deciding on mentors and experts to escort the team, among others c) Encouraging learners to join several programs, even simultaneously, which address challenges that differ from those that the business is facing	a) Enhancing and deepening the ideation process b) Getting away from traditional pedagogies to enable learners to manage the roadblocks to creating new ideas; providing a platform for taking risks and making mistakes, enhancing resilience to disappointments c) Embracing knowledge, mindsets, and expertise compounded with different teaching techniques to sort out the idea/business's uniqueness and value proposition

the future', aims to tailor a variety of game-based learning initiatives for best fit to different styles of learning (Caponetto, Earp, & Ott, 2014; Dagnino et al., 2015; Hamari et al., 2016; Landers, Bauer, Callan, & Armstrong, 2015; Simões, Redondo, & Vilas, 2013).

Another view of games as an educational tool for entrepreneurs regards them as learning promoters that provide learners with the opportunity to strategize their moves, test hypotheses, and solve problems, while 'being manipulated' by the game's elements, goals, achievement levels, and reward systems. Games should include narrative plots, animated agents that inform the players of the context and rules of the game—all embedded within the learning context, and further interactive cues and feedback to engage players and motivate them to remain in the game (Ang & Rao, 2008; Csikszentmihalyi, 2000; Dondlinger, 2007).

Gamification serves a variety of functions, such as:

- Increasing knowledge retention.
- Retaining information over time.
- Improving performance in the focal theme.
- Building long-term memory of facts, procedures and processes.
- Testing procurement of knowledge.
- Obtaining experiential, challenging, innovative learning.
- Obtaining shared, co-created new knowledge.
- Working jointly:
  - more fun;
  - synergetically adding more insights on the material;
  - developing new knowledge;
  - providing smarter solutions for complicated situations, and differently interpreting those situations.
- Embracing the outside—catering to the education system, games can include the ecosystem, and offer opportunities to gain more acumen from 'playing' others' parts.

Games are adaptive, mobile education platforms that benefit learners by offering learning methods that are more agile than conventional ones, providing immediate feedback on performance, and giving the learner more control of the learning pace, structure and interests. The learning process is no longer limited to the teacher's teaching method, it extends to the circle of direct and indirect participants involved in the process; the responsibility for a meaningful experience and value is shared by the teacher, learner, course and game developers, and the focal contributors of the addressed situations (e.g., case studies, video interviews, etc.). Nevertheless, games are expensive to develop and run, and it is difficult to monitor the reliability and validity of their success (Bellotti et al., 2013; Domínguez et al., 2013; Hamari et al., 2014; Huotari & Hamari, 2012).

Practice, Internship

Experiential approaches to EE (Dewey, 1938; Kolb, 1984; Lewin, 1942) highlight the pragmatic 'learning by doing'. Learners are involved in real-world practices to gain skills and tools that are relevant to the delivered subject, by enlarging the scope of their experiences to feeling and sensing, rather than just repeating. Furthermore, practicing enables absorption of psychological competencies, for example, resilience, hope and gratitude, among others, that are individual and, therefore, aligned to each learner's hub of motivations, aspirations, concerns, strengths, etc.

Practice has been found to support learners' engagement in the educational process due to changes in the learning dynamics, especially since organizations and the individual are both learning organisms. Student entrepreneurs are more prone to:

- Be interested in a variety of distinct fields that are relevant to their entrepreneurial process, idea or performance, yet not affiliated to one discipline, for example, business models, production processes, data mining, etc.
- Perceive networking and co-creation as valuable, albeit informal learning.
- Praise the learning experience.
- Embrace learning from anything in the surroundings, while formal education is no longer seen as comprising the bulk of learning.
- No longer separating learning in academia, courses or training from learning through the entrepreneurial process.
- Thinking or mindsets that are altered by technology.
- Supplementing the 'know-how' and 'know-what' with the 'know-where', that is, determining where to find knowledge.

Practice requires reshaping the educational process, by involving the ecosystem in the development and activation of the process, and (re)defining the win–win situation for the participants of the educational process, such as companies that provide internships, communities and governmental bodies that encourage practice, etc. The control and manageability of the bodies' leading platforms for entrepreneurs (incubators, accelerators, centers for innovation, academia, etc.) are decreasing, and new challenges are arising, such as dealing with emotional impact, cognition, reflection and experience processing, team-related challenges, and the role of innovation in the practical context, among others.

Practice can be performed on or away from the platform, but should be processed and reflected upon to enable entrepreneurs to transfer the experience into learning outcomes. Practical activities include 'selling a product', 'pitching to investors' or 'organizing a meetup'; these can either be performed 'in class' in front of relevant figures from the field, or outside the classroom, by taking part as a learner in the activity of a specific startup, say a company striving for innovation and creativity, or one with a more general, unstructured business routine (Cooper, Bottomley, & Gordon, 2004; Desplaces, Wergeles, & McGuigan, 2009; Heinonen, 2007; Heinonen & Poikkijoki, 2006; Penaluna, Coates, & Penaluna, 2010; Shepherd, 2004; Taatila, 2010; Tunstall & Lynch, 2010).

Virtual, Digitalized Learning (Figure 7.1)

The pervasive increase in the technological complexity and diversity of virtual learning environments, along with entrepreneurs' tendency to be 'early adapters', have boosted the proliferation of sophisticated virtual education methods. In contrast to the structured learning that takes place in the classroom, knowledge transfer, simulations and games in the virtual space are all part of an open-ended environment in which entrepreneurs can design and create their own objects, coordinate in real time, reflect and share; as well as connect more naturally to the real-life situations that they are apt to encounter (Dickey, 2005; Hew & Cheung, 2010; Sitzmann, 2011).

Virtual reality (VR) technology—These games and simulations are meant to enhance work-related knowledge and skills. The technology introduces vivid gamification teaching methods, while being mainly designed as a game-based environment where students can apply a concept in different contexts, and their performance can be assessed. Research shows that VR fosters engagement in the learning process; 'live' experiences promote ability-based and skill-based learning outcomes; yet, its knowledge-based effectiveness, including retention and transfer of learning from the virtual to real environment, is still in doubt. Some studies have addressed the design of the task and settings of the VR sessions, for example, combining them with face-to-face sessions, working individually rather than collaboratively when learning through games, and designing VR instruction, among others (Bossard, Kermarrec, Buche, & Tisseau, 2008; Vogel et al., 2006).

Digitalized learning—In many countries, higher education reforms have moved digital learning to center stage, to provide a learning space that is not restricted to the classroom, time, place or specific pedagogy. Digital learning is mainly defined as a strategy based in the internet and technology that facilitates students'

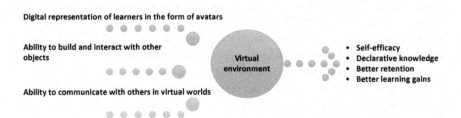

FIGURE 7.1 Virtual learning perspectives—the illusion of being in a different space and time

learning by returning control of their learning process to them in components such as time, place, path and pace. The proliferation of internet-access devices has given students the ability to learn anytime. As technology develops and becomes more sophisticated, agile and user-friendly, digital learning is becoming a natural option for learning. Digital learning requires a combination of technology, digital content and instruction to create different digital learning programs.

Technology facilitates how students receive content. The delivery of content is also simplified; students can receive it from a desktop, laptop, iPad and even smartphone. However, the content—the *what*—requires new teaching approaches, as students' concentration span is greatly reduced when exposed to digitalized learning contexts and environments. Moreover, as most of the digitalized sessions are conducted individually, rather than in a conventional classroom setting, students lose interest faster than in shared sessions. Therefore, the digitalized contents are shorter, to the point, and blended with material such as videos, games, simulations and tests, as well as mixed synchronized and unsynchronized sessions. As already noted, some combine digitalized and face-to-face programs.

From the teaching viewpoint, digital teaching provides more room to create interactive, engaging, flexible learning materials and use a wide range of digital and multimedia formats. Teachers that employ digitalized measures are more focused on how the learning is designed, how learning teams are structured, the nature of the learning environment, and how they can guarantee that students absorb and interpret the content accurately and equally. The focus of teachers of digitalized teaching is not technological or digital; rather, these refer to the ways in which learners can retain knowledge, control their learning process, and then transform learning into valuable knowledge that is aligned with their entrepreneurial tasks.

The transformation in teaching toward digitalized programs is aligned with the market's expectations and needs; as such, it is deemed a meaningful step forward in the relevance of the content and structures employed in conventional learning environments.

Virtual hackathons, incubators and accelerators—Such forms of incubation are expected to become more and more prevalent in the coming years. Early-stage entrepreneurs can search for, and choose, the best fit to promote their businesses and their teams' entrepreneurial skills and competencies by not having to restrict themselves to specific locations, countries or time.

Some virtual incubation or accelerator programs are for use in the classroom to increase engagement, accomplishing this through exclusive virtual content, for example, videos, audio, templates, and articles, among others. Others target entrepreneurial businesses that are distantly located, by providing support services, business assistance, counseling, administrative support, mentoring, introduction to resources, business networking, business-plan review, referrals to professional services, and access to sources of capital.

Another type of virtual program offers access to research-relevant information and person-to-person contact, facilitated by a protected document management system, video-conferencing, file transfer, text chat and shared discussion boards. It also includes e-learning support, professional or executive education and training, and online support for collaborative projects (e.g., project management with secure document management, video-conferencing, discussion boards).

Synchronous learning—These tools imitate the 'here and now' effect of learning, although they draw on the internet. As such, this type of learning expands the scope of people and situations to which entrepreneurs are exposed, as they can e-meet in real time with mentors, educators, other entrepreneurs and a variety of stakeholders the world over. The location-based setting of conventional learning restricts entrepreneurs to specific locations, while the odds of finding the best match for mentors, the most valuable ideas or the best potential team members increase when the search range is expanded.

Psychological studies show that the excitement, interest and motivation to start and retain synchronous sessions are higher than for asynchronous ones. The use of simple tools such as Facebook, video chat or Skype to more complex video tools facilitates synchronous programs, including person-to-person mentoring sessions, teamwork, webinars, and virtual competitions, among others.

Synchronous sessions include:

- *Virtual learning environment*—open-source commercial products drawing on the concept of distance learning, such as Blackboard, MOOC, CyberExtension, Desire2Learn, WebTrain Dokeos, ILIAS, Moodle and Sakai. These courses are open to everyone, digitized and accessible over the internet with no barriers. They are of two main types: those that guide the learners like a teacher and those where the learners themselves construct their own course.
- *Discussion boards*—thread-based discussions where participants respond to an initial prompt and to each other.
- *Webinars*—a web-based seminar that can be a lecture, session, presentation, workshop or talk transmitted through the internet, mainly using video-conference software. It is semi-interactive, as the presenter can 'see' the learners' comments, or hear them through VOIP. The learners can share audio, documents and applications with webinar attendees. This is useful when the webinar host is conducting a lecture or information session. While the presenter is speaking, they can share desktop applications and documents. Today, many webinar services offer live streaming options or the ability to record the webinar and publish to YouTube and other services later on.
- *Wikis*—a space that can be created and edited through a simple online database. It allows users to add, remove, edit and change content. Each article contains a discussion page where editors and readers can talk about

the document. Hence, it facilitates collaboration of writing and ideas. It can be used for content creation and management, as an index for a file library, to create a process manual or FAQs (Frequently Asked Questions), or to share agenda creation, to-do lists, action items.
- *Google documents*—multiple collaborating users can contribute, edit, and format documents simultaneously online in real time.
- *Videos, YouTube and TED talks*—used as learning material—audio and visual content—to explain concepts and course materials.
- *Messages*—such as an email-like environment that can be used for course communication (Pomerol, Epelboin, & Thoury, 2015; Simonson, Smaldino, Albright, & Zvacek, 2012).

Differences between synchronous and asynchronous approaches to educating entrepreneurs are introduced in Figure 7.2.

Summary

Innovative ways of educating entrepreneurs are already inevitable. They provide the learners with a parallel journey—education/learning and entrepreneurial—by adding value to learners in both experiences. The presence of multifaceted, instantly accessible technologies along with the students', especially student entrepreneurs', approach to their learning journey as a functional vehicle toward their future new ventures requires developing more updated and customized tools to grasp student entrepreneurs.

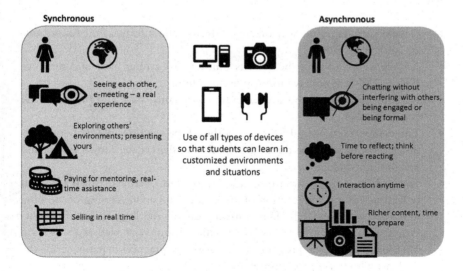

FIGURE 7.2 Synchronous and asynchronous approaches to EL

Attracting these types of students and engaging them in the learning process demands the application of teaching tools that are familiar, interactive, user-friendly and in their 'comfort zone', such as games, instant messenger, discussions, role-play activities, simulations of starting new businesses or use of virtual worlds, delivered through either small, flexible software tools or pervasive portables devices.

Innovative tools for entrepreneurs are emerging, and student entrepreneurs are adapting their mindsets and performance accordingly; their familiarity with, attraction to, and current use of new technologies reflect the effectiveness of educational tools developed for entrepreneurs. Entrepreneurial teaching tools stipulate pre-development considerations, to support the learners' parallel experiences along the journey and to build a deeper understanding of the pedagogies suited to each tool and the expected outcomes.

In this chapter, we introduced and discussed the current tools for teaching student entrepreneurs. As early adopters, these students are thrilled by the more advanced and changing teaching tools. However, achieving results in the multilayered aspects of entrepreneurial learning: knowledge, experience, hands-on, networking, practicing, real-world challenges, etc., demands tailor-made tools that are agile and can be altered as real situations change, or new technologies emerge. A well-established monitoring and assessment mechanism to verify students' retention and ability to make constructive use of the learning process is indispensable along this journey.

Takeaways

For educators and teaching developers:

- Develop programs in a way that leaves formal and informal time for creativity and collaboration.
- A deep knowledge of the various innovative learning tools and methods (Figure 7.3) is imperative to include them in programs.
- Prior to developing and implementing programs, map and prioritize the necessary KSA.
- The content, setting and structure of the EE program should draw on continual research with the direct stakeholders to deliver the most valuable and practical knowledge.
- Practical learning may seem insignificant to some learners, as it is based on reflection, informal absorption of knowledge and a false feeling of 'nothing new has been provided'. This is mainly due to the long tradition of education. It is imperative to include practical learning as well as to develop 'mentor the mentors' programs to translate the practical experience for the students who have gone through it.

For EE participants:

- Embrace innovation in learning. The conventional ways of learning can be deemed your 'comfort zone' while the new ways may seem to be time-consuming (getting used to practical learning, application-based learning, etc.). Yet, research and practice prove that a blend of known and new methods provides the best outcomes and potential for success.
- There are so many options for absorbing EE (Figure 7.3). Look at these as a 'buffet', and choose the methods that you feel most comfortable with.
- Use digitalization. It is free and simple, provides the flexibility that you need to expand your potential and actual ecosystem; you can easily be mentored by, or start a discussion with, potential collaborators from the other side of the world
- Gamification may appear to be 'just' a game. However, from childhood, we learn by playing games; it enables structuring potential scenarios, planning and preparing at a customized pace and while having fun.

Case Study 7—INNOVATING,[1] Accelerator Program in a Technological Academic Institution

TECH U sees gain in pursuing a new idea—even when it doesn't turn up as "the next big thing."

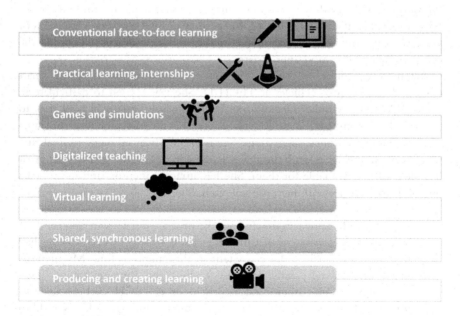

FIGURE 7.3 Types of learning tools

TECH U, a technology-pioneering and applied academic institution, has grown enormously—to hundreds of employees worldwide in various areas and specialties, for example, academic staff, administrative staff, educational program developers, VR specialists, video and media specialists, and technological lab experts, among others. It is part of a wide-ranging global network of academic institutions and technology companies. It provides academic knowledge, internships, training, online learning, virtual facilities, video production and services, and more. TECH U initiated a unique undertaking: INNOVATING, based on the fact that while innovative ideas abound at TECH U, few of those who have conceived them can actually couple them with the required business know-how and cash needed for their development. INNOVATING is a unique program that aims at fostering innovation by providing TECH U employees with the opportunity to pursue their original ideas in-house, in terms of paid time, funding, connections, and development platforms. To realize the program, several barriers that are inherent to industry had to be removed, including IP issues, staffing, funding schemes, and others. For example, what happens when an employee comes up with an idea that falls outside the realm of his or her own department? Regular full-time tasks cannot be effectively combined with the effort of developing something new. How are managers to cultivate employees' talents and outside-the-box thinking, while also fulfilling ongoing responsibilities? The program enables employees who have been selected to participate in INNOVATING to leave their positions for an intensive period of up to six months of R&D, while retaining their salary and benefits; if all goes as hoped, the participant will eventually leave his or her former position and go on to develop the new idea somewhere within the company where it is most appropriate.

Nadina is an editor, working in the multimedia office specializing in smart cities and autonomous vehicles at TECH U. She was chosen to participate in INNOVATING, with her idea of simulating business dilemmas in rural areas to teach students from those areas how to handle such situations, rather than learning from big-city business suggestions. She is in the advanced stages of finalizing her survey on rural areas, with the aim of convincing TECH U management that her idea will be profitable for them. She has attracted mentors and multimedia specialists to assist her with her proposal pitch. She says,

> I have already gained so much from the process, just by working on convincing my management that my project is worthwhile. I have never had the chance to analyze the ecosystem so thoroughly before. My mentors have enriched me greatly, and just to think that they are the accountants, engineers and administrators next door at TECH U. I am keen to go through the process, the departments and the locations of TECH U to work on my project, generate the resources and funds, convince people, and be able to produce it, disseminate it and sustain it.

Accepted ideas are notably a new brand or an expansion of an existing brand. After the initial, written presentation of the idea, the program's staff works with participants to connect the idea to an appropriate environment within TECH U's numerous areas of expertise and countries. Then participants are tasked with the crucial—and highly instructive—endeavor of conducting extensive market research to explore potential market size, competition, the funding needed to bring the idea to fruition, etc. Early on in the process, the program staff identifies the division or department that will be the new idea's home if it is ultimately selected for development. With the professional support of the program's staff, participants next prepare to pitch their idea to a group of venture-capital fund managers, tweaking their plan and honing their skills. If the idea is selected for realization, the next phase is the employee's transition into the new role, during which the transitioning employee trains his or her replacement. Company-wise, at this point, all other resources (budget, programmers, designers, etc.) for the new feature or product are also being prepared, so that development work can begin promptly as the employee assumes the new position.

Throughout the process, participants are supported by the program staff in their original country and synchronously by other TECH U venues worldwide, and receive weekly virtual reviewer feedback on their work and progress. Thus, the entire process is one of growth and personal and professional development. One participant referred to the added value of merely participating in the program, saying that no matter what the outcome, he feels that he has become a different person just for having participated in it.

The program's orientation is to give an appropriate in-house response to employees' 'itch' to innovate, nurture and develop their ideas, and to enable them to return to their position if development is not pursued further. A surprising 20% of the ideas submitted to the program's staff are returning applicants, indicating that their experience in the program has been positive and empowering.

Questions on the Case Study

1. What is unique about INNOVATING? Address 4–5 components discussed in this chapter. Explain how it differs from a 'regular' academic incubator.
2. Now, search the web for an academic incubator, and write down its name and web address. Compare it to INNOVATING's incubation process. What are your main conclusions? Address at least three educational forms discussed in this chapter.
3. INNOVATING asks you to build a virtual digitalized learning plan. List five questions to gain more information on the needs and expectations for such a change. Explain your answer based on the chapter's main ideas.
4. TECH U wants to provide a learning opportunity for its employees in Africa and India. How would you suggest creating a virtual program in Africa and

India, where they lack knowledge on the learning tools that can be applied for their employees? Draw a prototype of such a program.
5. Other tech companies are interested in connecting with academia to build accelerators. What are the main components that these companies should emphasize while developing such a program?

Reflective Questions

1. Search the internet for 3–4 accelerators/incubators from different countries, and write down their names and websites addresses. List the learning tools that they employ. Discuss the 'right choice' for each tool with respect to the accelerator/incubator's goals, location, startup maturity and success stories.
2. Search the web for 2–3 of the most innovative educational programs for entrepreneurs around the world, and write down their names and website addresses. What keywords did you use for your search? Why? Illustrate what is innovative in these programs, with respect to the topics discussed in this chapter. What are the differences between these programs in terms of the innovation they introduce?
3. Search the OpenEducation Challenge www.openeducationchallenge.eu/ in Europe. Discuss its importance, value and ongoing impact for educating entrepreneurs.
4. Look at ISB, Deloitte program for students at: www.youtube.com/watch?v=vWlA6C7EpSg. Search for any further information on the program. What do you think makes the program so valuable for its participants? Why does Deloitte need to be affiliated with academia to operate an incubation program?
5. Explore the two case studies of open innovation accelerators at: www.ey.com/Publication/vwLUAssets/EY-Open-Innovation-Accelerators-Harnessing-the-value-created-through-collaboration/$FILE/EY-Open-Innovation-Accelerators-Harnessing-the-value-created-through-collaboration.pdf. Suggest how other companies can develop such programs for entrepreneurs. Explain your answer.

Note

1 A face-to-face interview with the initiator and driver of INNOVATING. Names of the company, the incubator program and the interviewee have been changed as per the company's request. However, all aspects of the program are displayed as presented in the interview.

References

Ang, C. S., & Rao, G. S. V. R. K. (2008). Computer game theories for designing motivating educational software: A survey study. *International Journal on E-Learning*, 7(2), 181–199.

Bellotti, F., Berta, R., De Gloria, A., Lavagnino, E., Antonaci, A., Dagnino, F. M., & Ott, M. (2013). A gamified short course for promoting entrepreneurship among ICT engineering students. In *IEEE 13th International Conference on Advanced Learning Technologies* (pp. 31–32). Piscataway, NJ: IEEE.

Bossard, C., Kermarrec, G., Buche, C., & Tisseau, J. (2008). Transfer of learning in virtual environments: A new challenge? *Virtual Reality, 12*(3), 151–161.

Caponetto, I., Earp, J., & Ott, M. (2014). Gamification and education: A literature review. In *Proceedings of the 8th European Conference on Games Based Learning Vol. 1* (pp. 50–57). Reading, UK: Academic Conferences International.

Cooper, S., Bottomley, C., & Gordon, J. (2004). Stepping out of the classroom and up the ladder of learning. *Industry and Higher Education, 18*(1), 11–22. https://doi.org/10.5367/000000004773040924

Csikszentmihalyi, M. (2000). *Beyond Boredom and Anxiety: Experiencing Flow in Work and Play.* San Francisco, CA: Jossey-Bass.

Dagnino, F. M., Antonaci, A., Ott, M., Lavagnino, E., Bellotti, F., Berta, R., & De Gloria, A. (2015). The eSG project: A blended learning model for teaching entrepreneurship through serious games. In R. P. Dameri, R. Garelli, & M. Resta (Eds.), *10th European Conference on Innovation and Entrepreneurship* (p. 147). Reading, UK: Academic Conferences International.

Desplaces, D. E., Wergeles, F., & McGuigan, P. (2009). Economic gardening through entrepreneurship education. *Industry and Higher Education, 23*(6), 473–484. https://doi.org/10.5367/000000009790156436

Deterding, S., Dixon, D., Khaled, R., & Nacke, L. (2011). From game design elements to gamefulness. In *Proceedings of the 15th International Academic MindTrek Conference on Envisioning Future Media Environments – MindTrek '11* (p. 9). New York: ACM Press. https://doi.org/10.1145/2181037.2181040

Dewey, J. (1938). *Logic, The Theory of Inquiry.* New York: Holt, Rinehart and Winston.

Dickey, M. D. (2005). Three-dimensional virtual worlds and distance learning: Two case studies of Active Worlds as a medium for distance education. *British Journal of Educational Technology, 36*(3), 439–451.

Domínguez, A., Saenz-De-Navarrete, J., De-Marcos, L., Fernández-Sanz, L., Pagés, C., & Martínez-Herráiz, J.-J. (2013). Gamifying learning experiences: Practical implications and outcomes. *Computers & Education, 63*, 380–392.

Dondlinger, M. J. (2007). Educational video game design: A review of the literature. *Journal of Applied Educational Technology, 4*(1), 21–31.

Glouberman, S., & Zimmerman, B. (2002). Complicated and complex systems: What would successful reform of Medicare look like? *Romanow Papers, 2*, 21–53.

Hamari, J., Koivisto, J., & Sarsa, H. (2014). Does gamification work? A literature review of empirical studies on gamification. In *47th Hawaii International Conference on System Sciences (HICSS)* (pp. 3025–3034). Piscataway, NJ: IEEE.

Hamari, J., Shernoff, D. J., Rowe, E., Coller, B., Asbell-Clarke, J., & Edwards, T. (2016). Challenging games help students learn: An empirical study on engagement, flow and immersion in game-based learning. *Computers in Human Behavior, 54*, 170–179. https://doi.org/10.1016/j.chb.2015.07.045

Heinonen, J. (2007). An entrepreneurial-directed approach to teaching corporate entrepreneurship at university level. *Education+ Training, 49*(4), 310–324.

Heinonen, J., & Poikkijoki, S. (2006). An entrepreneurial-directed approach to entrepreneurship education: Mission impossible? *Journal of Management Development, 25*(1), 80–94. https://doi.org/10.1108/02621710610637981

Hew, K. F., & Cheung, W. S. (2010). Use of three-dimensional (3-D) immersive virtual worlds in K-12 and higher education settings: A review of the research. *British Journal of Educational Technology, 41*(1), 33–55.

Huotari, K., & Hamari, J. (2012). Defining gamification: a service marketing perspective. In *Proceedings of the 16th International Academic MindTrek Conference* (pp. 17–22). New York: ACM Press.

Kolb, D. A. (1984). *Experiential Learning: Experience as the Source of Learning and Development.* Englewood Cliffs, NJ: Prentice-Hall.

Landers, R. N., Bauer, K. N., Callan, R. C., & Armstrong, M. B. (2015). Psychological theory and the gamification of learning. In T. Reiners & L. C. Wood (Eds.), *Gamification in Education and Business* (pp. 165–186). Cham, Switzerland: Springer. https://doi.org/10.1007/978-3-319-10208-5_9

Lewin, K. (1942). Field theory and learning. In N. B. Henry (Ed.), *The Forty-first Yearbook of the National Society for the Study of Education: Part 2, The Psychology of Learning* (pp. 215–242). Chicago, IL: University of Chicago Press.

Penaluna, A., Coates, J., & Penaluna, K. (2010). Creativity-based assessment and neural understandings: A discussion and case study analysis. *Education+ Training, 52*(8/9), 660–678.

Pomerol, J. C., Epelboin, Y., & Thoury, C. (2015). What is a MOOC? In *MOOCs: Design, Use and Business Models* (pp. 1–17). Hoboken, NJ: John Wiley.

Shepherd, D. A. (2004). Educating entrepreneurship students about emotion and learning from failure. *Academy of Management Learning & Education, 3*(3), 274–287.

Simões, J., Redondo, R. D., & Vilas, A. F. (2013). A social gamification framework for a K-6 learning platform. *Computers in Human Behavior, 29*(2), 345–353. https://doi.org/10.1016/j.chb.2012.06.007

Simonson, M. R., Smaldino, S. E., Albright, M., & Zvacek, S. (2012). *Teaching and Learning at a Distance: Foundations of Distance Education* (5th ed.). Boston, MA: Pearson.

Sitzmann, T. (2011). A meta-analytic examination of the instructional effectiveness of computer-based simulation games. *Personnel Psychology, 64*(2), 489–528. https://doi.org/10.1111/j.1744-6570.2011.01190.x

Taatila, V. P. (2010). Learning entrepreneurship in higher education. *Education+ Training, 52*(1), 48–61.

Tunstall, R., & Lynch, M. (2010). The role of simulation case studies in enterprise education. *Education+ Training, 52*(8/9), 624–642.

Vogel, J. J., Vogel, D. S., Cannon-Bowers, J., Bowers, C. A., Muse, K., & Wright, M. (2006). Computer gaming and interactive simulations for learning: A meta-analysis. *Journal of Educational Computing Research, 34*(3), 229–243. https://doi.org/10.2190/FLHV-K4WA-WPVQ-H0YM

8

PORTRAYING THE ENABLING PLATFORMS

Incubators

The Landscape of Incubators

The meaning of incubator comes from the Latin word *incubare*, meaning 'hatch', and refers to hatching a business from the very start and nurturing it from its first steps. Along with the proliferation of business incubators, multiple definitions have emerged, although all are based on the original foundations of incubators [i.e., in the agricultural field: for protecting eggs, plants; in medicine: for protecting premature babies, viz. "a container that has controlled air and temperature conditions in which a weak or premature baby (= one which was born too early) can be kept alive";[1] or "an apparatus with a chamber used to provide controlled environmental conditions especially for the cultivation of microorganisms or the care and protection of premature or sick babies."[2]] The main concepts—container, controlling conditions, premature, cultivation, care and protection—can all be applied to business incubators. The rationale for business incubators' prevalence is that entrepreneurial businesses are considered vulnerable, lacking the required 'conditions' to penetrate the market, and require an incubation program, where the 'right' conditions are met, and business tools are delivered.

Business, or startup, incubators are considered the pioneering concept for nurturing startup businesses and fostering entrepreneurship, providing resources, space, and tangible and intangible services to early-stage companies. Today, as more entrepreneurial companies which are in more advanced stages are still striving to survive in the market, incubators have expanded their prime vision of helping early stages by: (a) helping startups develop until they are able to sustain themselves in the market (not just to 'go-to-market'); (b) applying a long-term approach to incubation programs, by providing space and services for longer periods of time; (c) specialization—many incubators are specializing, mainly in fields requiring intensive R&D processes, for example, sophisticated technology, medical developments, pharmaceutics; and (d) for specialized companies, leading experts are becoming involved in the incubator's activity.

The incubator model relies on providing space and services for a relatively long period of time, for companies at different stages of development; this creates unique relationships among the incubatees and expands the scope of the 'business' done in the incubator. Specifically, by having early-stage and more advanced companies under one roof, customer–supplier relationships emerge, which are represented by a give-and-take in knowledge, technologies, services, advice and products. Studies show that tapping into the strong incubator network, both internal, that is, incubated and graduated companies, and external, that is, incubators' business partners, investors, etc., is of particular value in gaining more opportunities, assistance, advice, and feedback from a professional network. Such reciprocity is exclusive in the context of intensive R&D and innovation-driven companies, which tend to protect and withhold information on their projects, including organizational or marketing information, which is not confidential, and that could provide valuable insights if discussed. In the incubator culture, these types of cooperation prevail. Most business incubators provide support through internal (in-house) and external resources.

Internal Resources

- *Infrastructure*: workspaces 'under one roof', workshops, shared services; rather than cohort-based programs, as typical in accelerators; specifically, a 'factory-builder' concept, that is, offering members use of the incubator's equipment (including machinery, labs, etc.) for prototypes and production.
- *Financial advice/IP teams/legal advice*: business incubators loan their financial advisors, IP teams and legal advisors to the entrepreneurs so that they can make well-informed decisions.
- *Contacts for potential investors*: through organized meetings and mentorship sessions.
- *Coaching and training*: mostly in-house, or hybrid, as detailed below (coaching and mentoring).

External Resources

- *Networking*: connections with partnering institutions, such as academic institutions, government, public or private companies, and with entrepreneurs from the same industry/sector.
- *Coaching and mentoring*: most of the coaching and training are in-house, but for mentorship, experts from affiliated institutions are also involved; for example, an incubator in a research lab involves the lab's experts, and so forth for academic institutions, municipalities or international institutions

such as the United Nations, as well as expert representatives of the incubator's collaborators, for example, policy-makers, researchers, advisors (Grimaldi & Grandi, 2005; Headd, 2000; Knopp, 2007; Rice, 2002)

Incubators: Models and Approaches

The Centre for Digital Innovation (C4DI),[3] a digital incubator based in Kingston upon Hull, UK, is connecting the ecosystem's businesses with fast-track, high-growth members who are keen to run a startup, but without a product or even an idea, through the C4DI team, experts and experienced entrepreneurs; T-Hub,[4] India's largest incubator for startups, which comprises a partnership between the private sector and the government of Telangana along with India's leading academic institutions, delivers multiple cutting-edge programs and inspirational talks, designed to enable incubatees to continuously innovate, scale up and generate deal flows for their business; F10[5] is a Zurich-based incubator in the innovation center of SIX, a financial service provider that operates the infrastructure of Switzerland's financial center. Its primary mission is to support startups' implementation of ideas into successful companies through worldwide collaborations with international finance organizations. For example, a six-month program provides each team with a coach and an external mentor. These examples demonstrate the multiplicity of incubator missions, programs and industry foci, but also emphasize the blurred differentiation between incubators and other EE programs and activities.

An evolutionary overview—Incubators began with the first undertaking in 1959, when the first business incubator in the US opened at Batavia Industrial Center; however, until the late 1970s, the concept of assisting entrepreneurs to survive or grow in the market was too innovative for the ecosystem to appreciate its value. The presumed turning point was in the mid-1980s, with the strong support of the United States Small Business Administration, in the development of incubators through numerous routes, resulting in around 3,200 incubators active today;[6] one-third of these are based in the US, and about one-third in Europe.

While incubators are already a well-established concept, their differentiation from other EE programs, which are proliferating, is still vague. Thus, Smilor and Gill's terming and definition of incubators in 1986, and the expansion of incubators over the years, have resulted in a plethora of definitions and typologies, and it seems that the concept of incubator is conflated with other concepts, such as startup incubators, business incubators, technology business incubators (TBIs), technology parks, technology centers, and innovation centers, where the differences between these concepts fluctuate, seemingly inconsistently. Some researchers and practitioners have stated that incubators are embryonic forms of the existing accelerators—that the accelerator model is, in fact, a new generation of the incubation model; others stress that to prepare entrepreneurs to join an acceleration program, a preparatory incubation program is needed, which is typified as more structured, instructive and conforming to early-stage companies, while still others treat incubators as an independent form of support for entrepreneurs, offering a link between technology, know-how, entrepreneurial talent, and capital. A more recent stream of studies has promoted a more dynamic view of incubation research, led by the notion that the needs of incubated companies and the ecosystem are changing and, accordingly, incubators provide a shared office space facility that offers resources to its incubatees toward a strategic, value-adding intervention process. This more generic and fresh look is the leading perspective in the customized models discussed in this book, and implemented in subsequent stages of EE programs' evolution. With the prevalence of co-working spaces for entrepreneurs, such as WeWork, most of the practical and academic discourse today addresses the role of incubators as property-based initiatives providing a support infrastructure for cutting-edge developments, hence demarcating and differentiating the incubation concept to specialized, high-growth-potential niches. Concurrently, the introduced services are changing to emphasize high-quality networking and frontline professional practices, including research and university specialists, equipment, grants and funds, among others. The evolution and changes in incubators' focus are demonstrated in Figure 8.1.

The main incubator models are:

(1) business innovation centers, with a focus on regional economic development;
(2) university incubators to facilitate technology commercialization;
(3) research incubators embedded in research institutes to valorize research output;
(4) stand-alone incubators, focused on selecting and supporting high-potential ventures;
(5) off-site or virtual incubators, remotely serving startup businesses independent of geographical location.

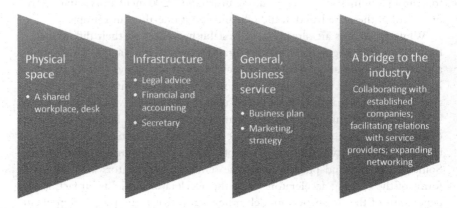

FIGURE 8.1 Incubators' focus and development

As pioneering concepts, the business models of incubators are still simple, although they depend on the affiliated collaborators. In general, incubatees pay for the space and services; when the incubator's funds are involved, equity is determined in advance; in other cases, the incubator is a strategic collaborator, for a determined period of time, in incubated companies for any investment funds generated, regardless of the funding source.

From the investors' point of view, incubators are a home, a place to meet under one roof, where fast-growing, high-potential companies are being incubated with leading experts in a most professional process (Aernoudt, 2004; Amit & Zott, 2001; Barbero, Casillas, Wright, & Garcia, 2014; Bergek & Norrman, 2008; Carayannis & Von Zedtwitz, 2005; Dettwiler, Lindelöf, & Löfsten, 2006; Grimaldi & Grandi, 2005; Hackett & Dilts, 2004; Kilcrease, 2012; Schwartz, 2013; Wise & Valliere, 2014).

The Journey

The incubator process starts with the admission of teams or individuals who may not yet have a rigorous project, but are considered to have high potential in terms of the team's composition, the specific individual or team's expertise, the innovativeness or originality of their project, etc. Through a selection process that includes interviews, simulations, and a determination of team dynamics, among others, entrepreneurship-related characteristics are assessed to consider the applicants' fit to the program. At the inception of the incubation process, sole entrepreneurs are encouraged to team up with others, based on common interests and complementary skills or expertise. The 'journey' is illustrated in Figure 8.2.

The Institutionalizing Perspective

Researchers and practitioners associate incubation programs with 'institutionalizing entrepreneurship', referring to incubators as a sort of add-on for institutions such as government ministries, offices and companies, aimed at developing regions, verticals (professional industries), specific populations, employment, innovation, and export, etc.; municipalities, intending to advance their regional employment and development; embassies and diplomatic offices/missions, targeted to promoting bilateral commercialization of innovations; and institutions connected to professional and specific areas, e.g., biotechnology, aerospace, and pharmaceutics (Cohen, 2013; Deering, Cartagena, & Dowdeswell, 2014; Hochberg, 2016; Kim & Wagman, 2014; Pauwels, Clarysse, Wright, & Van Hove, 2016).

Different types of incubators vary in their missions, such as boosting local entrepreneurship, encouraging student entrepreneurs, or generating returns, and in their formation of strategic connections with universities, research centers,

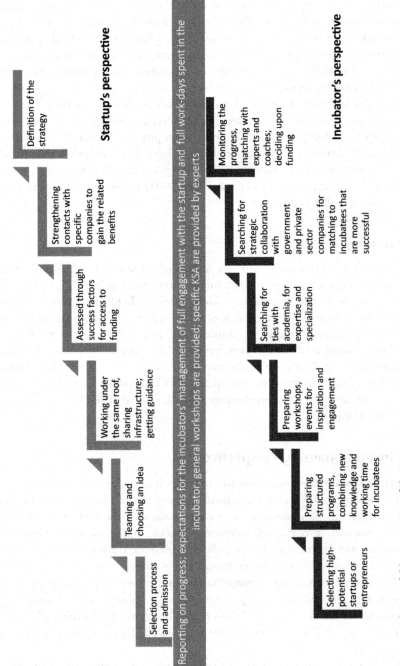

FIGURE 8.2 The twofold perspective of the journey

government and the local economy, depending on their institutional affiliations, as follows:

- The government, the public sector, municipalities foster entrepreneurship for national and regional economic development.
- Academic institutions nurture spin-offs into successful startups through technology-transfer offices, science parks and incubation infrastructures.
- Corporations develop in-house incubation facilities to assist new startups as a means to source new ideas.
- The private sector is rent-seeking, with the involvement of investors as a way to improve the deal flow of their portfolio.

Figure 8.3 exhibits the different strategic connections established by flourishing incubators, and the reciprocal benefits of these connections (Becker & Gassmann, 2006; Clarysse, Wright, & Van Hove, 2015; Grimaldi & Grandi, 2005; Hill & Birkinshaw, 2014; Looy, Debackere, & Andries, 2003; Miller & Bound, 2011).

The evolution of the incubation models clearly demonstrates the changes in entrepreneurs' needs and expectations with time, in the following areas:

- Tangible offerings, mainly space, funds and equipment (for example, machinery to build a prototype; technology, printers, etc.).
- A longer period of incubation (rather than being limited to programs or cohorts).
- In the early years, target incubatees were small businesses; with the opening of collaborations with academia, there has been a shift to more specialized, R&D-intensive companies.
- An institutionalized format, i.e., affiliated to government, academia, municipalities, etc.
- In-house services, with an emphasis on practical, instructive education (coaching, training).
- Simple business models of the incubator.

The shift today is embodied mainly in the wider range of intangible services, aimed at delivering tools to the incubated companies for their competitive advantage in the market; an emphasis on the business process, rather than only on outcomes; a focus on leading professional experts, including equipment, labs, etc., to support the incubated companies; and on mentorship, hence, not only an instructional focus, but a more process-oriented mentoring. The sought-after target incubatees have changed, and clearly represent the incubator's affiliation: municipality incubators attempt to capture more regional entrepreneurs to promote regional development and job creation; labs and academic institutions

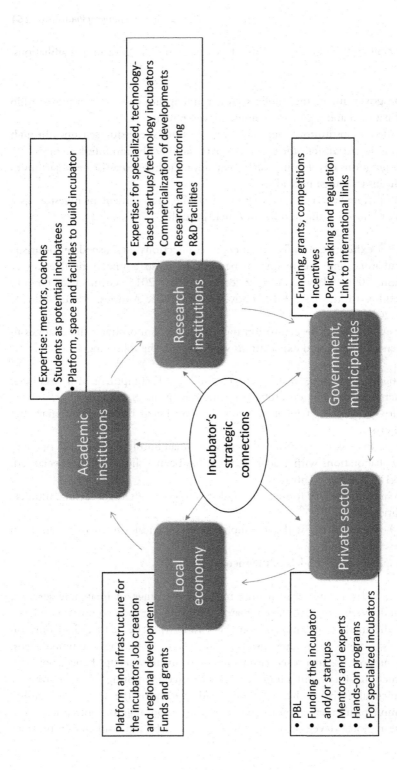

FIGURE 8.3 Incubators' strategic connections

target incubatees requiring more R&D support; international incubators aim at attracting entrepreneurs who can tackle untapped international issues, among others. Experts and collaborators mirror the affiliations as well, and the in-house approach still prevails in incubators.

The extensive shift has appeared more recently through the development of accelerators, spotting the value in access and delivery of the ecosystem, through establishment of communities and blockchain-oriented processes in the 2000s. At this point, with the emergence of accelerators, incubators have moved to the back of the stage, and are considered either a preparatory process for acceleration programs, or platforms capturing more capital-intensive startups, such as technology-oriented spin-offs from universities (Amit & Zott, 2012; Christiansen, 2009; Clarysse & Bruneel, 2007; Cohen & Hochberg, 2014; Isabelle, 2013; Phan, Siegel, & Wright, 2005; Soetanto & Jack, 2013).

AT-A-GLANCE

Governmental incubators—mainly led by the science, innovation, and economy offices/ministries, and intended to create economic prosperity through innovation—maintain a country's position at the forefront of global innovation and elevate the entire economy through technological innovation. Governments confirm that boosting economic growth and fortifying economic performance in job creation, taxation, and private investment, all derive from the high-growth startup sector, and therefore funding programs that support the creation of more companies, and provide them with incentives to encourage startups, choose governmental incubators. There, most of the startup costs are funded and/or subsidized for a long period of time, from 2–7 years, depending on the sector; additional grants are offered for success factors to encourage the incubatees to effectively pursue their business's development; sometimes the startups get tax-free grants, some incubators offer contracts to deliver specific services to the startups on behalf of the government, and there are different types of financially based incentives. Moreover, the incubators provide comprehensive assistance, physical space and infrastructure, administrative services, technological and business guidance, legal advice and access to partners, additional investors and potential customers.

Food for thought:

Is it the government's responsibility to initiate incubators?

AT-A-GLANCE

The World Food Program (WFP), a United Nations incubator, deploys innovative approaches across its global operations to help solve hunger through disruptive innovation. The United Nations considers innovation a critical approach to tackling hunger and is delivering on its mandate to reach Zero Hunger. As such, it opened an incubator that identifies, supports and scales up high-potential solutions for hunger worldwide. It provides WFP entrepreneurs, startups, companies and non-governmental organizations (NGOs) access to mentorship, training, financial support, expert insights and WFP operations. The Innovation Incubator is part of WFP's Innovation and Change Management Division. It encompasses innovation challenges, innovation bootcamps, and sprint programs, among others. It employs cutting-edge tools, and engages external experts, new technology and blockchain. It encourages and supports pilot projects and, through a meticulous methodology, scales them up, and helps in the implementation of new technologies and business models in field contexts. According to the WFP's 2017 Annual Report,* more than 1,000 applicants and around this number of external startups have applied. Projects include Tech for Food, providing job opportunities in the global digital economy for young adults in conflict-affected communities; or a monitoring tool for social protection and nutrition treatment programs that uses handheld devices and contactless payment to capture, integrate and visualize key information and outcomes in real time. The WFP targets health workers working with pregnant women, young mothers and children under the age of two; among others, these have been incubated. The incubator-supported innovations have reached more than 360,000 beneficiaries. As a result in 2017, the incubator was recognized as one of Fast Company's 'Most Innovative Companies' in the food sector, a list that also includes recognized brands such as Starbucks and Chobani.

Food for thought:

What would be the motivation for startups from advanced countries to enroll in the WFP incubator, rather than in corporate or other independent incubators? How can WFP attract more startups?

* See at: https://innovation.wfp.org/year-review-2017/docs/WFP-innovation-accelerator-2017-annual-report.pdf

Summary

Incubators are the pioneering platform of the EE concept, and the leading promoter of this expanding phenomenon. Due to the swift development of new EE programs, which will be discussed in the following chapters, incubators in today's EE landscape are at risk of losing their relevance if they continue with their conventional, general (rather than customized) offerings and overlook the dynamic, varying needs of entrepreneurial businesses and the ecosystem. Yet, incubators that shift to more dynamic systems that intertwine different EE approaches, such as shared spaces, accelerators, PBL and connections to collaborators, will survive. The underlying premise of incubators lies in their tangible deliveries, which are not limited by programs or cohorts; their institutional affiliations greatly affect their activity, target incubated companies and expertise. Incubators are deemed as preparatory programs for accelerators, probably due to their fundamental vision in helping 'premature' companies (adapted originally from premature eggs, plants, and babies); nonetheless, the various models presented in this chapter prove their delivery of unique and stand-alone value. Finally, though incubators' terminology does not naturally include concepts such as ecosystem, communities or blockchain, their affiliation to institutions, such as government ministries, municipalities, and academia, give them access to valuable networks that the incubatees can benefit from, by obtaining advice, customer-supply relationships, potential opportunities, and funds.

Takeaways

For educators and teaching developers:

- Collaborate with strategic partners that can provide multifaceted value to incubatees: expertise, mentorship, opening doors, funding opportunities.
- Strategic partners should represent a wide scope of institutions: governmental, academic, private sector.
- Determine the competitive advantage of the incubators in your ecosystem.
- Innovate and stay relevant, by staying well informed about the competing EE programs in the region.
- Some incubators have positioned themselves as capturing the frontline, high-potential companies or companies in R&D-intensive industries; these incubation programs attract more attention and funding from government and academia.

For EE participants:

- Incubators are known to provide space and tangible facilities; some companies need the free, quiet space to work; others may experience loneliness. Therefore, be aware of the advantages and disadvantages of the incubator's format and prepare accordingly.
- Make the most of your stay in the incubator by leveraging the dwelling with other incubated companies that are at different stages, for advice, inspiration and 'business'.

- Proactively innovate the incubator's process, suggest changes, such as inviting experts, initiating meetups, etc., that are not only useful for your company's progress, but also for the other incubatees and for the incubator itself.
- Prior to deciding on what incubator to apply to, it is important to map its affiliated institutions, for example, academia, public sector, government, as these have a major impact on the mission, activity, target companies and funding opportunities.

Case Study 8 – From a Musical Journey to 2018 Incubator of the Year: The Case of Neotec HUB, Kolkata, India[7]

After a musical journey of self-discovery, on sabbatical from a corporate career in senior management spanning 30 years, Sanjay Sarda finds himself back as the Director of the incubator Neotec Hub.

For this mechanical engineer with postgraduate studies in management and a known figure in India's corporate world, who left everything for his passion—to learn to play the traditional 110-stringed Indian instrument called 'Santoor'—and then started music academies in different parts of India as employee engagement and retention tools for various corporations, the new journey in the startup ecosystem has been a beautiful and rejuvenating experience.

In many ways, according to Sarda, the musical journey and the startup incubator/accelerator journey are similar. He explains that, in music, a connection is required—with one's soul or with God. Once that is established, the positive energy manifests in our being able to pick up any musical instrument and slowly, with inherent passion, start practicing; gradually, we become good enough to perform for an audience. Then we become a conduit of the positive energy flowing through us and our instrument to the audience who, in turn, become 'connected'. Similarly, in the startup ecosystem, our connection is with so many young and talented entrepreneurs with great ideas and dreams. We become connected to this collaborative environment where we realize that there are many areas in which we can contribute and add value, and, thus, we become a conduit for tapping into this positivity. In both cases, it is a 'giving back' to the world at large by recognizing and utilizing the opportunity with which we have been provided.

So, when he was called upon by H. V. Neotia to build, from scratch, a corporate incubator for the mounting number of startups in the soaring city of Kolkata, it was a golden opportunity to be involved in a pioneering project to nurture startups in the region and intensify Kolkata's startup scene.

Neotec HUB was founded under Ambuja Neotia,[8] one of the leading corporations in Kolkata, India, specializing in education, healthcare, real estate and hospitality. The Neotia family has been an integral part of the business scene in Kolkata for nearly 120 years. Through a long and successful entrepreneurial tradition, with various companies evolving under their corporation's umbrella, they have developed into a responsible corporate entity, both socially and environmentally.

In 2016, H. V. Neotia, the Chairman of the group, asked Sarda to start something that could bring Kolkata into the startup ecosystem buzz and Neotec Hub was formed. Sarda's creative nature intertwined with his corporate experience and techno-commercial professionalism enabled him to promptly investigate the need in the Kolkata startup ecosystem and, accordingly, develop the necessary incubator concept.

According to Kalyan Banga, Founder of FusionAnalyticsWorld.com 1 Research & Analytic"

> There are a lot of startups across cities and Kolkata is no exception. In terms of number of startups across major cities, we are lagging far behind since we had a late start, but in five years' time, hopefully, the gap will have narrowed considerably. Kolkata may not be at the fore in leaders' minds, but, surely and steadily, it is marching forward with the strong startup push given by the Government of West Bengal, IIm Calcutta and NASSCOM.[9]

Sarda's probe revealed the reasons for the relatively high percentage of even good startups, with great ideas and good teams, not being able to reach their full potential:

i) Lack of accessibility to the market.
ii) Lack of funds to implement the idea.
iii) Lack of proper, seamless mentoring in various areas, such as ideating, business plans, cash flow, pivoting, scaling up.
iv) Lack of support in corporate governance, taxation, legal and accounts, etc.

The challenge of addressing these reasons for failure prompted Sarda to articulate the vision of Neotec HUB: to convert young entrepreneurs' dreams into reality by designing an incubation program that addresses these four points.

i) Ambuja Neotia has businesses in real estate, education, healthcare and hospitality. Startups who are working in any of these domains are accepted into the incubation program, so that Ambuja Neotia businesses become their first customer, on day 1.
ii) The incubation program offers seed funding to select startups based on performance. Any further required funding is analyzed through the business plan and cash flow. These funds are arranged by either Ambuja Neotia or their consortium of investors.

iii) The incubation program is customized to each startup; mentors who are domain champions and industry doyens are assigned to each startup on an unlimited basis with respect to time or content.

iv) Apart from the state-of-the-art infrastructure, all support systems—digital marketing, accounts, corporate governance, legal, etc.—are provided to ensure hygiene and compliance. In addition, financial modeling support is extended through proof of concept.

The incubation process entails two stages: in the first, consisting of a three-month program, the startups are given a basic program structure and a customized matrix of milestones to achieve. During this three-month period, they are required to finalize the business plan, financial plan, and marketing plan, and be prepared for a panel of experts' evaluation of the batch of startups for the next stage; the second stage, lasting nine months, intensifies the relationships of the selected startups with Ambuja Neotia, with the escort of dedicated mentors from the Ambuja Neotia businesses. The startups get funding against equity while collaboratively working toward the development of a tested product, validated by Ambuja Neotia. The program provides multiple networking sessions with corporations, investors, and other mentors outside of Ambuja Neotia's businesses, and so much more. The principal incubation model, as seen in more and more enabling systems, is to provide young startups access to Ambuja Neotia businesses as first customers.

The Neotec Hub cohort presently consists of 20 startups, ten of which are at the revenue stage. Of these, four are going for a pre-series A round in the December 2018 to March 2019 period.

Neotec Hub has a global presence, with representatives in Israel, the European Union and the US. There are joint ventures with Israeli companies who would like to tap into the Indian market for their product/service/technology. These joint ventures will start operating after 2–3 months in India.

Neotec Hub feels that the success of their incubation will lie in the success stories of its startups. The incubation program is just completing its first year, which may not be time enough for such stories but, undoubtedly, they are just around the corner and will be heard soon.

In August, 2018, CEO Magazine selected Neotec Hub as the best company for 2018 in the Incubator category. CEO is a professional body that gives out yearly awards in different categories, such as Industry, Manufacturing, Marketing, Analytics, IT, Process Industry, Services, etc. According to CEO Magazine, "the sole intention, core values, clear vision and impulsion of the management team, together have anchored the organization firmly."

Recently the global leader of PWC from Australia visited Neotec Hub with a research team to interact with them and learn more about the incubation program. So, here he is at the Neotec Hub incubator, with his team, trying to 'convert startups' dreams'.

Questions on the Case Study

1. List 3–4 components that make Neotec Hub unique.
2. In your opinion, is Neotec Hub a typical incubator? What are the 2–3 characteristics that are typical to incubators and what are the 2–3 characteristics that are not typical of incubators? Explain your answer.
3. Suppose Sarda is invited to replicate the incubator model in your country. What are the five main tips that you would give him? Explain your answer.
4. Search the internet for another incubator in India. Write down the name and website address. Identify three similarities and three differences between that incubator and Neotec HUB. Why do you think these differences appear?
5. Watch: Bill Gross, TED2015, 'The single biggest reason why startups succeed' at: https://www.ted.com/talks/bill_gross_the_single_biggest_reason_why_startups_succeed on incubated companies. Based on the concept of Neotec Hub, give three reasons why Bill Gross's ideas are wrong, and three rebuttals to those reasons.

Reflective Questions

1. Search for different types of incubators on the web (in universities, government-based, regional); write down their names and website addresses. Write a one-page article for a professional magazine for entrepreneurs on the advantages to enrolling in incubation programs, based on the examples.
2. Search the Global Map of Startup Ecosystems—StartupBlink, at: www.startupblink.com/. Suggest 2–3 more categories to be included on the map to help entrepreneurs and startups search for the best accelerator/incubator for their needs. If you have other suggestions to improve the website, list them; explain your answer.
3. Look at XL-Africa, at: www.xl-africa.com/. Explain what makes it compatible for entrepreneurs in Africa. Suppose Microsoft, one of its corporate partners, asks you to develop XL-Asia. What kind of innovative processes would you suggest? Why?
4. Video interview 3–5 tenant entrepreneurs in an incubator, for a three-minute clip. You may find them through friends and co-workers, or by joining/creating a group for entrepreneurs in the social media (Facebook, LinkedIn, WeChat, WhatsApp, etc.). What are the five main insights on the incubator programs for the tenants, managers of these programs, corporations and governments, based on the interviews?
5. The municipality in your home town has put out a call: "Design an incubation program for young entrepreneurs who have taken courses in cybersecurity and wish to develop a business, yet they do not know how to start, what a good idea means, etc." Submit a 1.5-page paper in response to the call.

Notes

1 The *Cambridge Dictionary*, at: https://dictionary.cambridge.org/dictionary/english/incubator
2 The Mirriam Webster Dictionary, at: www.merriam-webster.com/dictionary/incubator
3 See at: www.c4di.co.uk/
4 See at: https://t-hub.co/
5 See at: www.f10.ch/
6 According to: *A Guide to Business Incubation for Elected Officials in NYS, 2008*; NBIA, 2012.
7 Sanjay Sarda was interviewed personally over the phone by me in August 2018.
8 See at: www.ambujaneotia.com/
9 Answer in Quora, December 20, 2016, see at: www.quora.com/Hows-the-start-up-scene-in-Kolkata

References

Aernoudt, R. (2004). Incubators: Tool for entrepreneurship? *Small Business Economics, 23*(2), 127–135.

Amit, R., & Zott, C. (2001). Value creation in e-business. *Strategic Management Journal, 22*(6–7), 493–520.

Amit, R., & Zott, C. (2012). Creating value through business model innovation. *MIT Sloan Management Review, 53*(3), 41–49.

Barbero, J. L., Casillas, J. C., Wright, M., & Garcia, A. R. (2014). Do different types of incubators produce different types of innovations? *Journal of Technology Transfer, 39*(2), 151–168.

Becker, B., & Gassmann, O. (2006). Corporate incubators: industrial R&D and what universities can learn from them. *Journal of Technology Transfer, 31*(4), 469–483.

Bergek, A., & Norrman, C. (2008). Incubator best practice: A framework. *Technovation, 28*(1–2), 20–28.

Carayannis, E. G., & Von Zedtwitz, M. (2005). Architecting gloCal (global–local), real-virtual incubator networks (G-RVINs) as catalysts and accelerators of entrepreneurship in transitioning and developing economies: Lessons learned and best practices from current development and business incubation . *Technovation, 25*(2), 95–110.

Christiansen, J. (2009). Copying Y Combinator, a framework for developing seed accelerator programmes. BA Dissertation at Judge Business School and Jesus College, University of Cambridge, UK.

Clarysse, B., & Bruneel, J. (2007). Nurturing and growing innovative start-ups: The role of policy as integrator. *R&D Management, 37*(2), 139–149.

Clarysse, B., Wright, M., & Van Hove, J. (2015). *A Look Inside Accelerators*. London, UK: Nesta.

Cohen, S. (2013). What do accelerators do? Insights from incubators and angels. *Innovations: Technology, Governance, Globalization, 8*(3–4), 19–25. https://doi.org/10.1162/INOV_a_00184

Cohen, S., & Hochberg, Y. V. (2014). Accelerating startups: The seed accelerator phenomenon. *SSRN Electronic Journal*. https://doi.org/10.2139/ssrn.2418000

Deering, L., Cartagena, M., & Dowdeswell, C. (2014). *Accelerate: Founder Insights into Accelerator Programs*. Boulder, CO: FG Press.

Dettwiler, P., Lindelöf, P., & Löfsten, H. (2006). Utility of location: A comparative survey between small new technology-based firms located on and off Science Parks—implications for facilities management. *Technovation, 26*(4), 506–517.

Grimaldi, R., & Grandi, A. (2005). Business incubators and new venture creation: an assessment of incubating models. *Technovation, 25*(2), 111–121.

Hackett, S. M., & Dilts, D. M. (2004). A real options-driven theory of business incubation. *Journal of Technology Transfer, 29*(1), 41–54. https://doi.org/10.1023/B:JOTT.0000011180.19370.36

Headd, B. (2000). The characteristics of small-business employees. *Monthly Laboratory Review, 123*, 13–18.

Hill, S. A., & Birkinshaw, J. (2014). Ambidexterity and survival in corporate venture units. *Journal of Management, 40*(7), 1899–1931.

Hochberg, Y. V. (2016). Accelerating entrepreneurs and ecosystems: The seed accelerator model. *Innovation Policy and the Economy, 16*, 25–51. https://doi.org/10.1086/684985

Isabelle, D. A. (2013). Key factors affecting a technology entrepreneur's choice of incubator or accelerator. *Technology Innovation Management Review, 3*(2): 16–22.

Kilcrease, K. (2012). The Batavia Industrial Center: The hatching of the world's first business incubator. *New York History, 93*(1), 71–93.

Kim, J.-H., & Wagman, L. (2014). Portfolio size and information disclosure: An analysis of startup accelerators. *Journal of Corporate Finance, 29*, 520–534.

Knopp, L. (2007). *2006 State of the Business Incubation Industry*. Athens, Ohio: National Business Incubation Association.

Looy, B. Van, Debackere, K., & Andries, P. (2003). Policies to stimulate regional innovation capabilities via university–industry collaboration: an analysis and an assessment. *R&D Management, 33*(2), 209–229.

Miller, P., & Bound, K. (2011). *The Startup Factories: The Rise of Accelerator Programmes to Support New Technology Ventures*. London, UK: Nesta.

Pauwels, C., Clarysse, B., Wright, M., & Van Hove, J. (2016). Understanding a new generation incubation model: The accelerator. *Technovation, 50–51*, 13–24.

Phan, P. H., Siegel, D. S., & Wright, M. (2005). Science parks and incubators: Observations, synthesis and future research. *Journal of Business Venturing, 20*(2), 165–182.

Rice, M. P. (2002). Co-production of business assistance in business incubators: An exploratory study. *Journal of Business Venturing, 17*, 163–187.

Schwartz, M. (2013). A control group study of incubators' impact to promote firm survival. *Journal of Technology Transfer, 38*(3), 302–331.

Soetanto, D. P., & Jack, S. L. (2013). Business incubators and the networks of technology-based firms. *Journal of Technology Transfer, 38*(4), 432–453.

Wise, S., & Valliere, D. (2014). The impact on management experience on the performance of start-ups within accelerators. *Journal of Private Equity*, 9–19.

9

THE RISE OF THE ACCELERATION MODEL

Global statistics[1] show that the number of accelerators, incubators and programs for entrepreneurs have risen exponentially. In addition to the introduced variation, statistics show that around 190 programs worldwide are dedicated to facilitating the entrepreneur's journey by providing programs, mentorship, communities, and financial support. According to new findings in the Global Accelerator Report,[2] in 2016, more than $206M was invested into more than 11,300 startups by 580 accelerators. These statistics are constantly rising, on both the startup and investor sides. Concurrently, there has been a continual debate around the misleading trend and potential 'accelerator and incubator bubble', considering them to be a segment of industry, or startups themselves. The main arguments refer to too many companies joining these programs, where mentorship is vague, there is no rigorous monitoring of program quality, the time consumed by an incubated/accelerated business, no prospect for the 'day after', that is, once these programs are completed, as they are mainly limited in duration. In 2012, TechCrunch[3] put out a headline predicting that "90% of incubators and accelerators will fail." This was a significant starting point for doubts and criticism about the proliferation of these enabling systems. Others claim that the success of accelerators indicates that only the top-tier, highly selective programs (such as Y Combinator and TechStars) have been successful in building startups that go on to raise money from outside investors. The opposing arguments stress that there is nothing particularly insidious about these programs; most of them do not take equity, and most of their alumni feel that, at the very least, they have gained a deeper understanding of the entrepreneurial journey and the ecosystem, and they have met with individuals and companies that may propel their advancement in the future. From the investors' perspective, the accelerator trend is new in venture investing and, as yet, there are no meticulous data to compare acceleration programs to the 'regular' later-stage venture capital firms, in financial terms, for example, acquisitions, exits or initial public offerings (IPOs). One reliable indicator of a successful program is how much funding graduates can continue to attract in their first year or two after graduating; yet, it is still difficult to find follow-on venture funding. However, some statistics show that startups which launched with the assistance of an accelerator and failed to quickly find traction were mainly ignored by investors after just a year or two.[4]

Enabling systems for entrepreneurs and startups offer facilitation by providing:

- Mentorship programs for entrepreneurs and founders of startups, with renowned mentors, either professionals in consulting entrepreneurs, or former serial entrepreneurs who wish to 'give back'.
- An introduction to a wide array of leading figures from the entrepreneurial scene who would be difficult to meet otherwise.
- A platform paved by experience in the field—meeting with entrepreneurs, venture capitalists, angel investors, leading corporate executives.
- The opportunity to pitch ideas in a public pitch event, or 'demo day', and to a large group of potential investors.
- Skill-related coaching/training workshops.
- Networking and creation of thematic communities.

The diversity of the programs has created some ambiguity in their definition; many programs call themselves 'accelerators' but do not strictly meet the formal definition (Cohen, 2013; Cohen & Hochberg, 2014; Hochberg, 2016; Hochberg & Kamath, 2012; Hochberg, Cohen, Fehder, & Yee, 2014; Kim & Wagman, 2012; Kortum & Lerner, 2000; Yitshaki & Drori, 2018).

Models and Trends

The Seed Acceleration Rankings Project[5] ranks the top accelerators in the US to deepen knowledge of, and acquaintance with, the different accelerator programs and their relative success, based on longevity, founders' satisfaction from a survey of the entrepreneurs who graduated from the programs, and the alumnus network generated from the companies that have graduated from the program. Bearing in mind that many of the metrics related to finance, fund generation, valuations, strategic collaborations and innovative developments might be either undisclosed or imprecisely stated by the accelerators due to the sensitivity of the information, the ranking analysis still discloses the entrepreneurial landscape in terms of interest in specific fields, industries and models. For example, both AngelPad and Y Combinator, which were ranked in the highest tier in 2015 and 2016, focus on early-stage startups, and are generic, rather than thematic; both emphasize lifelong entrepreneurial preparation; for example, they teach entrepreneurs how to pitch their startups to potential key partners, and how to close a deal once they have generated interest. Their attention to money and investment from the accelerator is marginal; they treat it as financial aid, rather than as a traditional investment in a startup. The second tier, including accelerators such as Alchemist, Amplify LA, MuckerLab, StartX, Techstars, and the University of Chicago's New Venture Challenge, introduces a variety of new programs that, apart from the traditional accelerator programs such as a university or academia-centered accelerator like New Venture Challenge and StartX, offer high-quality mentorship combined with prompt gaining of traction and network expansion (Techstars), or focus on diversity, as in 500 Startups Accelerator.

Within the past decade, since the development and implementation, in Cambridge, Massachusetts, of the first accelerator model, Y Combinator, the abundance of accelerators has been rising, with a global presence of around 400 of them today. Y Combinator, founded in 2005, followed by Techstars, founded in 2006 in Boulder, Colorado, clearly symbolize a transformational stage in the startup scene. Many aspiring and high-achieving startups, in any industry—not necessarily tech-driven— enroll in accelerators. Research regards accelerators as a new generation of the incubation model, aimed at accelerating entrepreneurial businesses by providing intangible services, such as mentoring and networking, and the relevant content knowledge to cohorts of ventures over a limited time. One of their main premises is a reliance on business development to develop startups to scaleups and unicorns; hence, during this time-limited support, they introduce a platform for intense relevant and valuable connections, meetings, content delivery and monitoring to enable rapid progress (Christiansen, 2009; Cohen, 2013; Cohen & Hochberg, 2014; Drori & Wright, 2018; Kerr, Nanda, & Rhodes-Kropf, 2014; Vanaelst, van Hove, & Wright, 2018).

Networks—Accelerators extensively endeavor to create significant networks around their programs, which include top mentors from the entrepreneurial, finance, investment and academia sectors, to ensure the richness and fullness of their deliveries. In addition, they try to obtain long-term engagement of the mentors to give their accelerated startups access to top figures during and after the program. As such, they offer, and gain, continual value: (a) for their accelerated startups, by preserving their contacts with top figures, thus optimizing their likelihood of succeeding through the sharing of information and resources that are critical to entrepreneurs; (b) for the accelerator itself, as a profitable business, it needs to maintain the engagement of these top figures for support and branding, and to attract subsequent cohorts.

The network is, therefore, critical to the startups' establishment of significant connections with mentors, and with former startups and actively accelerated startups. These relationships extend the scope of collaborations for the startup. For the accelerators, creating and continually expanding their surrounding network by retaining their mentors and adding startups to their portfolio is a most effective strategy for attracting the best candidates in the next cohort, the best investors and, consequently, potential financial support. Moreover, successes of businesses accelerated in the accelerator reflect the latter's quality, thus enhancing the attraction for potential candidates. Through robust, well-managed networking activity, the members of the network are informed of the success stories, and can then pass them along to their family and friends. In addition, the accelerator application process screens a large population of startups, thereby helping investors, banks, and companies that are interested in finding entrepreneurs; otherwise, the cost of searching for 'trained' entrepreneurs is high and risky. Finally, networks can serve for business model purposes, such as big data, for academic purposes and for research, such as in constructing case studies, and for government monitoring and implementation, such as the country's startup ecosystem, or support systems required on a national level. Networks can be established digitally, in meetups, at guest lectures or events, among others, creating an effective platform for reaching the accelerator's goals. For example, MassChallenge[6] is a non-profit organization on a mission to make it as easy as possible for entrepreneurs to launch and grow new ventures. Through its massive networking, MassChallenge has accelerated more than 1,500 startups which have raised more than $3bn in funding, generated more than $2bn in revenue, and created more than 80,000 jobs in total. This not-for-profit organization is passionate about creating a global movement to support entrepreneurship, and reprioritizing the impact of its startups and networks in the global economy (Hochberg, Lindsey, & Westerfield, 2015; Hochberg, Ljungqvist, & Lu, 2007; Wenzel & Koch, 2017).

Accelerator activities—Accelerator activities are varied. Most accelerators are generalists, as innovative ideas and businesses in different sectors and industry may fit the program. However, in recent years, a breed of thematic accelerators has emerged; these are more focused on different vertical industries, such as fin-tech, health care, social, etc. In fact, many such accelerators have emerged from companies that strive to innovate with new accelerated ideas that can then be implemented with their support. An example is Startupbootcamp,[7] which helps early-stage tech founders scale up their companies by providing direct access to an international network of mentors, partners, and investors. Each program focuses on a specific theme: fin-tech, insure-tech, digital health, real estate, and education, among others.

In point of fact, there is still no well-established definition for an accelerator; rather, they encompass a range of activities and goals that include mentorship, curriculum, and experience in, for example, events and small seed investments. The activities and platforms of accelerators are listed in Table 9.1 and Figure 9.1 (Clarysse, Wright, & Van Hove, 2015; Cohen, 2013; Feldman & Zoller, 2012; Hochberg, 2016; Winston Smith & Hannigan, 2014).

TABLE 9.1 Accelerator activities and platforms

Goals	Activities
➢ Seed investment	➢ On a competitive basis ➢ By pre-mentoring ➢ Preparation for pitches ➢ Preparation of business models, plans, presentations ➢ Office hours offered by professionals in finance, marketing, strategy
➢ Mentorship	➢ One-on-one: mentor accompanies the startup ➢ Mentors provide office hours ➢ Mentors give guest lectures ➢ Mentors periodically assess the startup's progress ➢ Key players, such as investors or representatives of giant corporations that are striving for internal innovation, often serve as mentors, for the purpose of getting an early look at the startups, business plans, team dynamics, and progress over the term of the program
➢ Information, knowledge, data	➢ Lecture, training and workshops: face-to-face, online, hybrid and gamification-based ➢ Meeting with experts ➢ Practical experience ➢ Visits to leading companies/startups ➢ Access to databases, research, reports—general or of a specific escorting corporation ➢ Digitalized tools and apps
➢ Co-working/ co-location	➢ Sharing a space with other startup companies in private or public co-working spaces ➢ Enabling fruitful connections for the startups by creating shared office hours with professionals, inspirational talks, and shared services, including kitchens, dining rooms, logistic assistance ➢ A 'showroom' for investors and other key players in the ecosystem to meet with passionate startups/entrepreneurs with great ideas
➢ Exposure	➢ Exposure to the local ecosystem, including startups, corporate companies, global companies, government sector ➢ International exposure, for example, meetings with international delegations of entrepreneurs, bodies interested in supporting entrepreneurs, academia ➢ Media – interviews, editorial, etc. ➢ Events – local, global, in-house, for the whole startup community
➢ Network	➢ Offering opportunities to pitch to multiple investors ➢ Demo days, events in and for the ecosystem ➢ Access to the accelerator's networks

> Communities
> - Building a thematic community around the accelerator
> - Creating reciprocal value for the startups participating in the accelerator and for the stakeholders taking part in the accelerator's community
> - Foundation to create new businesses
> - A place to develop a pool of clients, suppliers, referrals, exposure, advice, etc.

Accelerator business models—Accelerator programs have implemented alternative revenue strategies to maintain solvency prior to their portfolio startups' ROI. These consist of alternative revenue-generation models in the short or long term, as well as acquisition of financial support for their daily operation, including mentorship, expertise, office hours, infrastructure, and for special events sponsored by the ecosystem, including demo days, competitions, bootcamps, etc. They include:

- *Startups tenants*—charging fees for mentorship, services, space; in the long term, equity revenues.
- *The corporate model*—corporate sponsorships and partnerships; hosting events, partnering on a global scale with major corporations to create corporate accelerator programs for each company. Also crucial for connecting startups with incumbents to promote proof of concept for another long-term financial source.
- *Investors, angels*—investors strive to select the most promising early-stage companies, which could bring them a prompt ROI; accelerators spread risk across more portfolio companies than investors, and they can 'mold' the startups to the companies' strategies, while participating in their programs; the investors thus hedge their bets and increase their odds of picking a promising company. Accelerators can serve as a deal aggregator, and provide a real option for investors, who can learn about a batch of ventures before taking a larger financial stake in them.
- *Mentors, experts*—support program operations; guest lectures, mentorship and training free of charge.
- *Government and institutional firms*—sponsorship, financial support, dissemination and grants for promoting entrepreneurship, startups or specific segments, such as female entrepreneurship, immigrant entrepreneurship, etc.

(Brunet, Grof, & Izquierdo, 2016; Pauwels, Clarysse, Wright, & Van Hove, 2016; Vanaelst et al., 2018; Winston Smith, Hannigan, & Gasiorowski, 2013; Yitshaki & Drori, 2018).

Financial models—Financial models include:

- The prevalent business model of accelerators originating from the private sector is based on a long-term relationship with the nurtured startups, predominantly grounded in exits, which include mergers, acquisitions, and/or IPOs. Global reports show that accelerators in the United States and Canada comprise the greatest number of startup exits, but global exits are still uncommon events in Europe, Latin America, or Asia.
- Alternative funding sources: some accelerators raise funds from investor–partners for a single cohort, for a few companies in their portfolio, or a specific accelerator event/mission. The investors of the fund can be regarded as angel investors, in that they serve as mentors, and provide office hours and overall care for the startups. In addition, some venture capital and investment companies support accelerator programs, principally or exclusively, for early access to the portfolio companies rather than for the expected direct return on the contribution to the accelerator, as this gives them preemptive rights to establish a relationship with these companies. Another funding source comes from the corporate or financial and global companies that support accelerator programs, or some portfolio companies that are differentiated from a corporate accelerator. In such cases, the partnership of the accelerator with the supporting companies is maintained by providing business-related services, office hours, sometimes seed money for the portfolio companies, and sponsorships and other financial aid for the accelerator, while their main goal is to nurture startup projects that align with their products, services or vision. In the accelerator Alchemist,[8] Cisco is one of the supporting companies; and DHL, Samsung and Pfizer are supporters of Plug and Play.[9] Another source of sustenance is the accelerators themselves, by selling space, mentorship, and guest lectures. They are keen to be the first to engage with innovative ideas stemming from startups, to be more experienced and professional in pivoting their range of activities, approaching new niches and overall, being the first to attract investors for their accelerator's programs.
- Non-profit: there is a significant and growing proportion of accelerators that are not-for-profit. They can be found mainly in academic institutions and public institutions, and a large proportion of them exist in the Middle East and Africa. Moreover, some leading accelerators that are not in this category do not take equity stakes in the portfolio companies, for example, MassChallenge, and Microsoft accelerator. These accelerators' model is characterized by typically not taking equity, a social–environmental orientation, and a focus on industries with a specific public benefit, such as health-tech and ed-tech; moreover, these accelerators introduce new opportunities for disadvantaged groups, such as minorities, the poor, disaster victims, individuals with special needs. They may be either privately or publicly funded, mainly by bodies supporting a cause or mission.[10]

- Academic accelerators: this type of accelerator is mainly interested in the educational perspective, and provides their participants with the platform to obtain the necessary KSA to generate a competitive advantage over their entrepreneurial competitors in the market. Thus, they do not tend to invest in their portfolio companies, and do not ask for equity, or, if they do, for only a very small amount, considered earnest fees. These accelerators gain the academic institution's support and fund their activities by intertwining their sessions and programs with the academic curriculum. The schools and faculties that engage in academic accelerators gain more diversified, innovative programs and educational techniques, and attract more students, while subsidizing the activities.

From the startup viewpoint—Startups pay for participating in accelerators due to the perception that they are 'one-stop shops' that reduce costs over the long run and provide a good fit in the search for partnerships, investors and venture capitalists. The accelerator is seen as the primary enabler of the most common financial support model for a startup by exposing the startups to the ecosystem, initiating meetings with key players that may open doors for the next round of funding, and jointly developing the startup into a robust business that is prepared for external investment. An indirect, yet impactful, role of the accelerator is the 'funneling mechanism', defined as self-directing to a specific 'place' which, through the startups' wish to be part of the accelerator, extends its traction, and it becomes a more attractive 'place' to be aligned with. Being an alumnus of Y Combinator, Techstars or Microsoft accelerators, for example, is a selling point; startups are willing to pay for this. When payment is required only when first money has been generated, usually after bootstrapping, the payment is feasible.

Processes, practices and approaches—We live in an accelerated world, according to *Forbes* magazine[11] in the 2016 article 'The state of the startup accelerator industry'. Accelerators are crucial for entrepreneurial business development and growth, from the viewpoints of both the early-stage business and the ecosystem. The latter will more readily 'accept' a new entrepreneurial business when it has gone through an accelerator. The early-stage business gains more confidence, in addition to skills and networking, by participating in an acceleration program. Accelerators have created rigorous networks and communities around them, so that early-stage startups can be furthered by, as well as foster, the established companies included in the network. The crucial role of accelerators in the development of entrepreneurial businesses calls for meticulous decision making with respect to choosing the most suitable accelerator.

Drawing on the Kauffman Foundation,[12] the three main categories of accelerator processes and practices that need to be addressed are: vertical, specializing in specific industries; horizontal, grounded on different platforms; and institutional, that is, corporate- or government-led accelerators initiated by either a corporate or governmental office, with mission- or trade-related tasks.

Horizontal accelerators are designed for those startups targeting a specific product or technology, with customers that can come from various markets; thus, the developed product or service meets similar customers' needs across different market niches. Vertical accelerators are designed for startups targeting a specific industry, trade or customer type (e.g., health, education, technology, energy, media, fashion); and institutional accelerators promote their institution's interests, for example, a leading technology of a corporate company that could be used for different purposes (corporate), or a governmental cause or mission such as promoting bilateral relationships, or advancing employability in deprived areas.

The process—In most cases, the process is linear, as presented in Figure 9.1. According to one of the managers of Microsoft's accelerator:[13]

> we see so many talents, and they are in love with their ideas; in fact, with the entrepreneurial process they envision, too. But since they are in an early stage, most of them are first-timers, and we are already aware of the gap between the dreams and plans, and reality. So they go through a process. Things are structured, designed and monitored. We provide the startups with some freedom, seen in our customized and agile culture. But they have to meet the milestones. Our Demo Day is a celebration of their journey. We bring Microsoft's CEO in Israel for Demo Day to convey the importance of this event for their future development.

New approaches for acceleration programs—these include:

- *Scaleup programs*—targeting more established startups to help them in sales, distribution, penetration into big, global markets.
- *Seed funds*—mainly for portfolio startups to develop their proof of concept, drawing from portfolio companies' continual requests for more funding. Accelerators allocate more time and money to seed funds than to training programs. In addition, accelerators are starting to establish side funds for follow-on funding.
- *Extended or unlimited period*—due to the longer time spent on R&D and production for the more sophisticated products, using innovative technologies, accelerators have extended the acceleration period (not the 'incubation' period), to enable startups to prepare for roadshows, demo days and investor events.
- *Expanding scope of services*—accelerators provide complementary services, such as space for companies to stay after the program, business support, and code academies.
- *Intensified partnership with the corporate companies*—a new breed of accelerator models embed the corporate world and the ecosystem in the accelerator's strategy and activities in various ways, ranging from the more common ones, such as mentorship by corporate representatives, and increased exposure of the startups and the corporation within the accelerator program to

Selection process

Interviews, evaluation methods, practical-based selection (proof of concept, beta sites)

Kickoff

Exposure to networking, mutual expectations, contracts

3-month "incubation"

Meeting the mentors, setting milestones, reflecting on the process, advancing through feedback

Exposure to experts, specialists, guest lecturers, to deepen knowledge and expertise and to pave the way for relationships that may produce potential partnerships

Startup's commitment of full dedication to, and engagement in the entrepreneurial journey

Events

Thematic events in the entrepreneurial process, such as in marketing, finance, innovation, digitalization, penetrating global markets, etc.

Professional events, meetups and sharing concepts and tips in the vertical specification, e.g., in-tech, fashion-tech, ad-tech, etc.

Mid-selection process

Evaluators' process, drawing on the startups' members, the mentors, the accelerator's managers, the relevant ecosystem members, for deciding on the maturity, engagement and feasibility of the business, to determine its fit to the acceleration phase

3- to 9-month "acceleration"

Acceleration starts with an incubation process, which allows the incubated companies to achieve the level needed for an acceleration process

An accelerated journey for the startups, in meeting with the ecosystem, convincing them to engage the company's products/services, and gaining faith, traction and funds

FIGURE 9.1 The accelerator process

more advanced modes, including responding to corporate needs through the startups' products/services, use of the corporation's products/services, technologies, processes for the startup's production or marketing processes, or matching startups to a corporation as a venture builder, that is, the corporation develops itself, or a new spin-off, through a combination of the startup's developments, shared resources and passion, which are stimulated in both the accelerator and the corporation.

- *Startup for Enterprise' approach*—accelerators focus on 'reshaping' their portfolio startups from day one for and with ecosystem partners, to provide the startups with the first, significant stakeholder, for example, customers, suppliers, investors, media, advocators, etc. The partner has the option to share ownership of the startup or purchase the startup outright down the line.

Taken together, the acceleration model is typified by:

- Being mainly focused on early-stage tech startups.
- Setting their main goal as developing startups into investment-ready businesses.
- Offering a time-limited program (3–6 months on average), and not necessarily at a specific venue/location.
- Typically offering pre-seed investment, usually in exchange for equity.
- Close connection to business angels, and, recently, more connections to corporations, as their business model.
- Offering a variety of services along the program, all-around intensive professional mentoring and networking opportunities.
- Emphasizing the informal processes facilitated by the accelerator, such as a supportive peer-to-peer environment; entrepreneurial culture; development of unplanned contacts that can be leveraged into projects beyond the focal one.
- Introducing the 'fast and long-term' blend, which refers to intense interaction and constant monitoring toward rapid progress along with a life-long 'promise' to embrace the graduate startups, through continued networking support beyond the program, establishment of communities, and a 'giving back' approach (for example, alumni become mentors, the accelerator's ambassadors, etc.).

Scaleup Accelerators

Startups that have reached a more mature level are designated as scaleups; they will become 'unicorns' if their value exceeds €1bn, and a 'decacorn' if their value exceeds €10bn. Accelerators strive to escort startups to these levels. A scaleup accelerator transcends its deliveries to its stakeholders with the purpose of proving the startup's opportunities to outreach its value in the market. It reinforces national and, especially, international collaborations with the industry, the entrepreneurial ecosystem and academia and provides opportunities for more harmonious interactions with entrepreneurship initiatives, for example, venture capital companies, investors, etc., with experts and mentors, and academia, to gain more accurate insights from cutting-edge research. It fortifies networking competencies and experiences; opens doors to the global and international markets; delves into the needs and procedures related to IP protection; and continually emphasizes new trends to be embedded in the startup's activities. One of the main hurdles encountered by scaleup accelerators is related to the startups' time commitment; the programs are intensive and demanding while, concurrently, the startups must promptly step forward in penetrating new markets, which may include frequent trips and meetings. The need to expand the ecosystem to a global arena is another hurdle that scaleup startups face. Many scaleup accelerators operate a hybrid model, in which the startups are required to attend a week-long initiation at the hub of their choice but are free to travel for their marketing activities; distance content, video conferences, virtual meetings and digitalized courses are also major enablers for a successful program at this stage of development. Active, formal alumnus participation is an important factor for life-long learning and community creation. The Microsoft ScaleUp program,[14] operated in eight global locations, attracts enterprise-ready startup companies to expediate their business activity by providing connections to fortify sales with access to top Microsoft partners and customers; learning and inspiration, by building relations with proven Microsoft sales leaders, hence a path for the accelerated startups to scale up their growth globally; and an alumnus network that fosters peer support and networking around Microsoft activity (Clarysse, Wright, & Hove, 2016; Iborra, Sanchez, Pastor, Alonso, & Suarez, 2017; Vanaelst et al., 2018).

Corporate Accelerators

Corporations running acceleration programs in tandem or on behalf of corporations have become a dominant new source of funding innovation and strategic partnerships. Corporations have seen the substantial value in developing 'outside' innovation by the new, enthusiastic startups to gain, internally, new vitality that can then stimulate their staff, modernize their processes or change their approaches to technology, channels, marketing, etc., and, externally, by 'importing' new processes that are, on the one hand, developed outside the corporation, thus bringing innovation and cutting-edge knowledge and capacity, while on the other hand, developed inside the corporation and, thus, customized to the corporation's needs.

There are many examples of corporate accelators, operated in three different ways: internally (Wayra and Microsoft Ventures), outsourced (Barclays, Kaplan, and Disney), or partnered (Citrix and Red Hat). Consolidation of accelerators and corporate missions can be seen across industries and continents. Statistics and research in this field are sporadic, yet the leading implication reveals a corporate trend in which more than half of the accelerators worldwide are at least partially funded by corporations, and over two-thirds of them are aimed at generating revenue from services sold to corporations; around half of the revenues aimed for accelerators come from corporate partnerships.

The corporate accelerator trend is encouraged by three main players: (a) the corporate interest in startup innovation, and through the discovery of efficient and effective ways to engage with startups. Corporations realize that they must innovate to stay relevant and competitive for their stakeholders; yet, their sheer size, internal processes, and speed of operation, which lacks agility while being weighted down by bureaucracy, make it complicated for them to innovate while startups that are agile and flexible, and consider their development to be a 'life or death' proposition, can provide the corporation with the required innovation in new and surprising ways, as it stems from an external source, and can potentially provide a higher degree of competitive advantage; (b) accelerator managements' interest in partnering with the corporation arises from their understanding that corporations can help them fund operations in the short-to-medium term, and, subsequently, improve the prospects of their portfolio companies that can potentially raise funds from the supporting corporations; (c) the existing and potential early-stage startups that grasp the value provided from both a corporation and an accelerator, thereby multiplying their opportunities to be funded, merged, acquired or developed in other ways, including gaining higher levels of exposure, opening doors and subsequent partnerships.

Institutional Accelerators

Like corporate accelerators, other institutions, driven by similar motivations, open accelerators. These include government offices, task forces and missions, embassies, consulates, municipalities, regional offices, while, internationally, the European Commission, the Organisation for Economic Co-operation and Development, the United Nations and other bodies can partner, support or even initiate their own accelerators. Accelerators supported by these institutionalized bodies nurture startups that can provide higher and new developments for a cause, including social, environmental, regional, health-related, education-based, and many other causes with which governments are involved. In general, the government and other stakeholders support the accelerators' activities; they tend to initiate competitions for grants, scholarships and other endowments. Institutional accelerators can open doors to government-related bodies, locally and globally.

Summary

The number of accelerators worldwide has vastly increased, proving the value attributed by entrepreneurs and the ecosystem (e.g., government offices, private sector, corporations, academic institutions, etc.) to these programs; on the other hand, a concurrent wave is emerging that wonders whether this is a 'bubble'. The differences between accelerators and incubators are contingent on empirical definitions and a delineation of their goals, activities and successes; the vision of being a main facilitator to startups is shared, but the operational aspects diverge.

Accelerators consider a series of attributes as more effective in facilitating start-ups' maturity to penetrate their competitive market, by fortifying, in the most customized way, the relevant KSA and providing the 'right' environment that can cultivate creativity and innovation. Among those attributes, accelerators provide seed investments; mentorship from the entrepreneurial, financial and corporate industries; the information, knowledge, and data necessary to craft marketing, production and financial strategies; co-working spaces, though this is not mandatory; exposure to the ecosystem, opportunities to pitch, to be interviewed in the media and to leverage the accelerator's exposure to the startup's purposes; valuable networks; and being part of a community. Corporate accelerators use similar attributes to nurture new ideas within the company, to promote innovation, embed innovative ideas in the corporation, test their new developments through the startups' use (of a new technology, a new market strategy, etc.), and motivate and activate employees while providing entrepreneurs with a platform for their betas and being their first clients.

Accelerators are treated as part of a large ecosystem; they aim to directly promote entrepreneurship while their circuitous impact on the private and public sector, the government, the economy and regional development, is immense; thus, all of the involved bodies should be incorporated into the programs' planning and implementation.

Takeaways

For educators and teaching developers:

- Innovate! Innovate every segment of the program—the content, duration, delivery, business model—to attract more and new interest from potential startups and the ecosystem.
- Hook up with the industry to delve into their needs, trends, innovation, developments, to be able to launch programs that align with the most current trends.
- Create corporate partnerships to expand your deliveries, opportunities and sources of support.
- Link to academic and research institutions to share complementary knowledge; use research and teaching to gain more insight into the program's best practices and success factors, as well as to promote the entrepreneurial arena by demonstrating data, stemming from the accelerator's cohorts, for more research.

For EE participants:

- Joining programs in accelerators is a prevailing trend today. Scout for the best, most suitable and most affordable program for your startup, by asking alumni, mentors, and potential clients to decide if a program should be chosen, and which one.
- Map real needs, not the popular ones that may not be relevant to your business, then prioritize them. Search for the accelerators that specialize in the areas in which your business needs lie.
- Interview the people responsible for the programs in the accelerators; prepare your questions in advance, and make sure you have a thorough idea of each point that you raise.
- One of the main benefits of accelerators is in preparing, opening doors, and facilitating. These are not magical devices that will automatically turn ideas into successful ventures. It is imperative to regulate expectations accordingly.

For stakeholders:

- Be connected to an accelerator via sponsorship, mentorship, financial support.
- Stay abreast of the different types of involvement, to be able to diffuse the connection with different accelerators; for example, supporting a program, supporting a portfolio startup, nurturing teams of tenant entrepreneurs, etc.
- Connect corporate/business needs and expectations to the portfolio startups' development to gain from the innovation introduced for their businesses.

Case Study 9—Techstars

Techstars embodies the ideal model of entrepreneurial culture creation and community formation. Techstars was established in 2006 in Boulder, Colorado, quite modestly, but with a determined vision: *using the power of networking*. David Cohen invited his friends David Brown and Jared Polis, and convinced a well-known investor, Brad Feld, to start a business that empowers and supports entrepreneurs. They were all already engaged in the idea of boosting area startups through a powerful network. Techstars has grown forcefully, and, according to *Forbes* magazine, as of August 2018, its accelerator program has produced over 1,000 companies valued at over $8bn; more than 3,300 founders running 1,300 businesses have participated in its almost 50 accelerators. According to one of its participants in New York City:

> this is the best thing I have ever experienced in my life, though it was demanding and a very intensive 90-day bootcamp, but I would definitely do it again! Techstars works like a huge family, there are endless connections,

and you are encouraged to use most of them. Along with its rich networks, you are treated like family, everything is personalized; everyone is attentive to your needs, prompting positive vibes; so, you are confident that anything can be reached, you just need to dare to try it. I was surrounded by mentors and corporate experts, who worked with us very rigorously on our product strategy; at the same time, we met with experts with whom we worked in depth on our marketing strategy, along with other amazing mentors who were more concentrated on our business models, but all of them were really focused on our team. They pushed us to work hard on team formation and operation. It was a hectic and overwhelming time. I came back to the co-working space where I had worked before attending the Techstars program with so many insights and so much work to do, and it is amazing to get the feedback from the managing team here on the maturation of my business, and the changes in my self-confidence, including in managing the co-founders' team; this is thanks to my participation in Techstars.

Techstars is known for using the power of the network, mentorship and giving back to form a unique culture and stimulate the entire community; it documented how its model works and gave it to the world for free. Advocating the role of mentors in the entrepreneurial journey, Techstars believes that entrepreneurs should work with several different ones, who may give them different, sometimes contradictory, advice; this 'trains' the founders to make decisions by prioritizing and evaluating advice. Techstars also offers their successful model to corporations, such as 'Powered by Techstars'; sports tech: Nike Accelerator; entertainment tech: Disney Accelerator; education tech: Kaplan Accelerator; mobile health tech: Sprint Accelerator; and fin-tech: Barclays Accelerator.

In an interview with David Brown,[15] co-founder of Techstars, the development of the conceptual idea of creating a culture, ecosystem and valuable networks is revealed while deeply intertwined with Techstars' documented primary values.

DK: Can you describe the story of Techstars from your perspective as one of the founders, who is also a serial entrepreneur? What were your motivations to start Techstars? Where did the idea come from? How did people around you react to your idea? Who supported you, and what were the main opportunities and challenges?

Brown: In February 2006, David Cohen sent me an email about an idea he had to help entrepreneurs succeed. That email led to conversations with Brad Feld and Jared Polis. Later in 2006, the four of us officially incorporated Techstars. From the beginning, our focus was on the entrepreneur, or as we say at Techstars, the founder. We were determined to create a program that would focus on the founder. Today, we say that Techstars is Founders First.

DK: Techstars is known to bring innovation to the startup landscape. What specific types of innovation does it introduce, and to whom? Would you define it as disruptive innovation?

Brown: At Techstars, we focus on the entrepreneurial team before we focus on the specific innovation or idea. When we screen applicants for the Techstars Mentorship-Driven accelerator program, we have six criteria. They are team, team, team, market, progress and idea. The idea is important, but the team is the most critical, which is why it takes up the first three spots. To be disruptive, early-stage startups must have a strong team that can weather a storm together, that have demonstrated the ability to execute and have clear roles (who does what) in the company.

DK: How exactly do you define Techstars? On the website it is defined as a network, but it also offers acceleration and scaleup programs. This question is especially interesting to me due to the proliferation of programs for entrepreneurs (accelerators, incubators, labs, innovation centers, open innovation platforms . . .).

Brown: Techstars is a worldwide network that helps entrepreneurs succeed. It has a number of programs to support all founders—from Techstars Startup Weekend to Techstars Mentorship-Driven accelerator programs to Techstars Innovation Bootcamps. We want to support entrepreneurs throughout their journey. We like to say that Techstars is here for founders from idea to IPO. In fact, Techstars produced the first company from a tech accelerator to go public—SendGrid.

DK: What is your view regarding the growing numbers of programs that are offered to entrepreneurs? How is it affecting the entrepreneurial landscape, the startups, investors, other stakeholders?

Brown: I am excited to see growing support for entrepreneurs around the world. These additional programs that focus on the entrepreneurs to help them grow their businesses and create jobs in their community are laudable. We don't view them as competition for Techstars.

DK: And . . . how is the massive competition affecting Techstars? Its tenants? Its mentors? Its investors? How do you explain Techstars' success over time?

Brown: The power of the Techstars networks has driven our success. At Techstars, we actively focus on the 'give first' philosophy, which means to give help, advice, introductions, etc. with no expectation of anything in return. Building a successful company takes more than funding. Through the Techstars network, our companies can reach out and make connections to help grow their company.

DK: How similar/different is Techstars 2018 relative to your vision/its first year?

Brown: Techstars started with ten companies in one accelerator in 2006. We had the opportunity to define the model for an accelerator program.

	We have helped more than 1,600 startups since our inception. We are now approaching 50 accelerator programs around the world. We have added Techstars Startup Weekend, Techstars Startup Digest and Techstars Startup Week. We remain fully committed to helping entrepreneurs succeed and growing our Techstars network to support startups everywhere.
DK:	What are your next steps and future for Techstars? For your own career?
Brown:	Techstars is the last job I'll ever have. It's the best job in the world—I get to work with some of the best and brightest minds building a great future for all of us.

Questions on the Case Study

1. Techstars is continually ranked as a leading accelerator program; find 2–3 articles on the internet indicating accelerators' rankings. In your opinion, how has Techstars been able to maintain its high ranking for so long?
2. From the interview, how, in your opinion, does Brown see Techstars as 'disruptive' and how is this implemented in Techstars? Provide three arguments suggesting different 'disruptive innovation' features of Techstars' program.
3. Search for 2–3 leading accelerators in the world; write down their names and website addresses. In your opinion, what are the 3–4 major competitive challenges for Techstars with these accelerators? Explain your answer.
4. Use your social media, including interest groups, blogs, and chats, and search for entrepreneurs who are participating or have participated (or can introduce you to others who have participated) in Techstars' program. Record a one-minute video interview with them on their experience. What are your conclusions on Techstars' impact on the entrepreneurial landscape based on these interviews? Alternatively,[16] write a one-pager for three participants of Techstars AFWERX and Techstars Autonomous Technology Accelerator with the U.S. Air Force at: https://youtu.be/fxW7JNTZGXo. What are your conclusions on Techstars' impact on the entrepreneurial landscape based on these testimonials?
5. Watch *Techstars' David Brown Keynote – Making Luck Happen* – Startupfest 2017, at: https://youtu.be/gKqB-HiiIlc. Prepare ten questions for a follow-up interview with Brown on Techstars, on points that he has not (thoroughly) addressed in the lecture in Montreal. Explain your choices.

Reflective Questions

1. Look for one accelerator in Europe and one in Asia; write down their names and website addresses. Compare the activities that they offer and their business models, based on the points discussed in this chapter. Discuss their

similarities and differences; explain them through an ecosystem look. What are your main conclusions?
2. A governmental association asks for your consultancy in opening a scaleup accelerator for immigrants in your country. What are the five main questions that you need information on to plan the scaleup accelerator? Explain your response.
3. You are asked by a large, international corporation to prepare an advertisement for their corporate accelerator. What are the five most important topics that you would include in the ad? Explain your response.
4. Look at: 'Startupbootcamp 8 most asked questions about applying for an accelerator' at: www.startupbootcamp.org/blog/2015/07/8-most-asked-questions-about-applying-for-an-accelerator/. Choose three frequently asked questions and indicate which ones you have chosen; read the responses, and answer them differently, based on the topics discussed in this chapter. What are your main conclusions?
5. Diego Molino is the co-founder of Ubiqua,[17] an SaaS startup in Panama. In the TEDx talk at: https://youtu.be/Al1MA9CeZiM, listen to Molino's views on how startups can create an environment of constant learning and continuous improvements, and write a 1.5-pager of the best acceleration model in terms of fostering creativity and innovation.

Notes

1 See at: www.seed-db.com/accelerators
2 See at: http://gust.com/accelerator_reports/2016/global/
3 See at: https://techcrunch.com/2012/10/14/90-of-incubators-and-accelerators-will-fail-and-why-thats-just-fine-for-america-and-the-world/
4 TechCrunch 2013, 'The startup accelerating trend is finally slowing down', by Mark Lennon. See at: https://techcrunch.com/2013/11/19/the-startup-accelerator-trend-is-finally-slowing-down/
5 See at: www.seedrankings.com/
6 See at: https://masschallenge.org/
7 See at: www.startupbootcamp.org/
8 See at: https://alchemistaccelerator.com/funds/
9 See at: www.plugandplaytechcenter.com/corporations/
10 See at: http://gust.com/global-accelerator-report-2015/
11 See at: www.forbes.com/sites/groupthink/2016/06/29/the-state-of-the-startup-accelerator-industry/#5afb34de7b44
12 See at: www.kauffman.org/currents/2015/04/3-emerging-trends-in-the-accelerator-model
13 Face-to-face interview with me.
14 See at: https://startups.microsoft.com/en-us/scale-up/
15 David Brown was interviewed by tme.
16 Only if you cannot locate tenants or alumni of Techstars through your social media platforms.
17 See at: https://ubiqua.me/en/

References

Brunet, S., Grof, M., & Izquierdo, D. (2016). *Global Accelerator Report 2015*. Gust.com

Christiansen, J. (2009). Copying Y Combinator, a framework for developing seed accelerator programmes. BA Dissertation at Judge Business School and Jesus College, University of Cambridge, UK.

Clarysse, B., Wright, M., & Van Hove, J. (2015). *A Look Inside Accelerators*. London, UK: Nesta.

Clarysse, B., Wright, M., & Van Hove, J. (2016). A look inside accelerators in the United Kingdom: Building technology businesses. In P. H. Phan, S. A. Mian, & W. Lamine (Eds.), *Technology Entrepreneurship and Business Incubation: Theory, Practice, Lessons Learned* (pp. 57–86). London, UK: Imperial College Press. https://doi.org/10.1142/9781783269778_0003

Cohen, S. (2013). What do accelerators do? Insights from incubators and angels. *Innovations: Technology, Governance, Globalization, 8*(3–4), 19–25. https://doi.org/10.1162/INOV_a_00184

Cohen, S., & Hochberg, Y. V. (2014). Accelerating startups: The seed accelerator phenomenon. *SSRN Electronic Journal*. https://doi.org/10.2139/ssrn.2418000

Drori, I., & Wright, M. (2018). Accelerators: Characteristics, trends and the new entrepreneurial ecosystem. In M. Wright & I. Drori (Eds.), *Accelerators: Successful Venture Creation and Growth* (pp. 1–20). Cheltenham, UK: Edward Elgar.

Feldman, M., & Zoller, T. D. (2012). Dealmakers in place: Social capital connections in regional entrepreneurial economies. *Regional Studies, 46*(1), 23–37.

Hochberg, Y. V. (2016). Accelerating entrepreneurs and ecosystems: The seed accelerator model. *Innovation Policy and the Economy, 16*, 25–51. https://doi.org/10.1086/684985

Hochberg, Y. V., & Kamath, K. (2012). 2012 Seed accelerator rankings. *Seed Accelerator Rankings Project*. http://yael-hochberg.com/Accelerator%20Companion%20FINAL.pdf

Hochberg, Y. V., Cohen, S., Fehder, D. C., & Yee, E. (2014). 2013 Seed accelerator rankings. *Seed Accelerator Rankings Project*. www.seed-rankings.com

Hochberg, Y. V., Lindsey, L. A., & Westerfield, M. (2015). Resource accumulation through economic ties: Evidence from venture capital. *Journal of Financial Economics, 118*(2), 245–267.

Hochberg, Y. V., Ljungqvist, A., & Lu, Y. (2007). Whom you know matters: Venture capital networks and investment performance. *Journal of Finance, 62*(1), 251–301.

Iborra, A., Sanchez, P., Pastor, J. A., Alonso, D., & Suarez, T. (2017). Beyond traditional entrepreneurship education in engineering promoting IoT start-ups from universities. In *2017 IEEE 26th International Symposium on Industrial Electronics (ISIE)* (pp. 1575–1580). IEEE. https://doi.org/10.1109/ISIE.2017.8001481

Kerr, W. R., Nanda, R., & Rhodes-Kropf, M. (2014). Entrepreneurship as experimentation. *Journal of Economic Perspectives, 28*(3), 25–48.

Kim, J.-H., & Wagman, L. (2012). Early-stage financing and information gathering: An analysis of startup accelerators (Working Paper no. 2142262, Social Science Research Network). *SSRN Electronic Journal*. https://doi.org/10.2139/ssrn.2142262

Kortum, S., & Lerner, J. (2000). Assessing the contribution of venture capital to innovation. *RAND Journal of Economics, 31*(4), 674. https://doi.org/10.2307/2696354

Pauwels, C., Clarysse, B., Wright, M., & Van Hove, J. (2016). Understanding a new generation incubation model: The accelerator. *Technovation, 50–51*, 13–24.

Vanaelst, I., van Hove, J., & Wright, M. (2018). Revolutionizing entrepreneurial ecosystems through US and European accelerator policy. In M. Wright & I. Drori (Eds.), *Accelerators: Successful Venture Creation and Growth*. Cheltenham, UK: Edward Elgar.

Wenzel, M., & Koch, J. (2017). Acceleration as process: A strategy process perspective on startup acceleration. In I. Drori & M. Wright (Eds.), *Accelerators*. Cheltenham, UK: Edward Elgar.

Winston Smith, S., & Hannigan, T. J. (2014). Home run, strike out, or base hit: How do accelerators impact exit and VC financing in new firms? *Academy of Management Proceedings, 2014*(1), 13811. https://doi.org/10.5465/ambpp.2014.13811abstract

Winston Smith, S., Hannigan, T. J., & Gasiorowski, L. L. (2013). Accelerators and crowd-funding: Complementarity, competition, or convergence in the earliest stages of financing new ventures? *SSRN Electronic Journal*. https://doi.org/10.2139/ssrn.2298875

Yitshaki, R., & Drori, I. (2018). The 'give and take' of mentorship processes within accelerators. *Academy of Management Proceedings, 2018*(1), 15669.. https://doi.org/10.5465/AMBPP.2018.15669.

10
THE EVOLUTION OF INNOVATIVE ENABLING PLATFORMS

The entrepreneurial landscape is crowded, growing exponentially, and fueled by ongoing innovations and developments. As a result, entrepreneurial businesses are tackling challenging conditions, including vast competition, saturated markets, irrelevance of their products or services to specific markets, and inconsistency in attracting stakeholders. Such conditions are forcing entrepreneurs to learn how to survive, sustain their businesses and grow 'by doing', making them the best 'employees of the future', equipped with the future-proof skills of proactivity, quick learning, and rapid reactions to unexpected situations, among others. In an attempt to assist entrepreneurs in managing these challenging conditions, innovative programs are burgeoning; they strive to exceed the structures of conservative education, as entrepreneurs have already gained their own 'learning-by-doing' experiences; concomitantly, they have to innovate and demonstrate unique value, as there are many programs dedicated to assisting entrepreneurs, with some of them developed in the academic and corporate worlds. Since many of these innovative programs are initiated and matured by entrepreneurs, based on their own experiences, they seem to overlap in some cases, fuse too many 'verticals' and exhibit innovation in already established areas. Based on the models of accelerators and incubators, this chapter discusses some of the leading programs, by demonstrating their disruptive innovation, the clients they serve, and the stakeholders that surround them.

Overall, the innovative enabling programs share similar core values and goals; their diversity can be categorized as follows (Figure 10.1).

Open Innovation Platforms (OIPs)

OIPs, such as open innovation accelerators, incubators or networks, represent a revolutionary paradigm shift in approaching innovation; these platforms employ

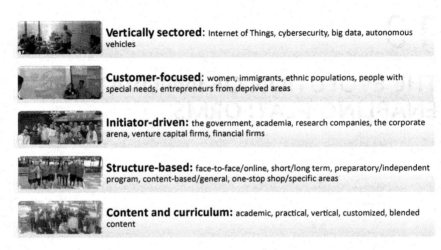

FIGURE 10.1 The main factors categorizing enabling systems for entrepreneurs

innovation emerging from startups, but emphasize its capture and incorporation in corporate processes. OIPs match the corporation's needs—startups—and the corporation's processes, by channeling the best attributes of the startup's products, services or ideas and the entrepreneur's passionate, creative mindset and vibes into the corporation to gain an advantage in their market, as shown in Figure 10.2. The introduced value is reciprocal: (a) for the corporations, which go through a structured process of mapping their problems, difficulties and needs; they obtain various approaches from startups as they tackle these problems and solve them; they benefit from various startups' innovative ideas, coming from different verticals; they also benefit from the exclusive startup and entrepreneurial mindsets, vibes and passion; finally, they join, rather than compete with their potential competitors, that is, startups, and can then acquire them, thereby diminishing the risk that such startups bring to the ecosystem. It is historically well established that many companies, as well as industries, become irrelevant in the face of startups' introduction of new technologies and processes. Moreover, by collaborating with startups, the corporation gains insight into those startups to deepen their understanding of 'what's going on' and for potential investment or acquisition. Their internal development is enhanced by exposing their employees to fresh technologies and ideas; (b) for the startups and entrepreneurs, who are working for their first client or corporate strategic partner; this is most important for their survival in light of the growing number of failures among nascent startups; by being attached to, and embraced by, a corporation, startups gain a great deal of exposure to the complicated business processes that they will need to implement, to the media, and to leading figures. The startups learn how to collaborate in beneficial ways, although they still have to be attentive, as most OIPs 'match' one corporation to several startups, and each of those startups has to work as hard as possible to be the one selected to sustain its activities with the corporation; finally, startups learn how to enhance their agility and creativity by looking for avenues to respond to the corporations' needs, through their own services, ideas, technologies or products. The corporations do not 'play' the expected game with their corporate and startup competitors, but, rather, gain fresh perspectives and new approaches that are not hampered by their own corporate culture and processes. In addition, they can take advantage of the survival-driven ways in which entrepreneurial businesses endure, by applying them to their own corporate processes; (c) for the EE developers and managers who benefit from a deeper engagement with the industry, mainly the corporate industry, which has been left at least partly 'out of the loop' in the entrepreneurial landscape, but only for funding or mentoring. The OIP developers embrace the corporate world, in fact, they provide their services to corporations, to at least the same extent as to startups; corporations will pay for getting the best innovative solution, on time, from people who are enthused to work on the solution and excited about getting it done. For EE developers and managers, who have based their financial models on startups' rent payment, or equity in the startups' future investment, such a revolutionary approach is more secure and more profitable.

There are various types of programs delivered by OIPs: web portals that encourage the corporations to set out the needs and problems to be solved; competitions and challenges to be solved by startups, based on the corporations' problems and needs—termed PBL methodology; collaborations with accelerators or incubators to mentor startups that are dedicated to responding to the corporations' needs.

The target participants of the OIP can be:

- Corporations in general or in specific professional verticals.
- Startups from the ecosystem that are:
  - In their developing stages, and have a firm idea about the product/services they are developing. These may contribute to the corporation with 'anything' that is innovative and brings a fresh approach, and that can provide a solution to the participating corporations (even by pivoting the business), for example, technology, product, marketing, pricing, financing, etc.
  - In their ideating stage—they are still looking for the best idea. In this case, they can start developing a solution for the corporation, which can then be developed into different products/services for different customers.
  - Innovative ideas from inside the corporation, to work part-time with the external startups on innovative solutions.
  - External mentors to escort the startups along their solution-development process.
  - Internal mentors to be hands-on and ensure that the external startups are providing solutions that are aligned with the corporation's needs.

The need   Match & collaborate   Innovation

- Corporation's existing problems to be solved
- Corporation's need for external innovation to be embedded

Startups (SUs) are driven by multiple ideas, cutting-edge technologies and the passion to actually start; but face difficulties in locating clients, strategic collaborators and funding

Open innovation platforms "match" a startup with a corporation and introduce:

Bringing "new" innovation	Time-consuming	Agility
• Unexpected solutions for the corporation's needs • Innovation based on SUs' existing (sometimes after proof of concept) processes	• SUs' existing products/ideas, or current processes • SUs' attentiveness • SUs' vulnerability to time to market	• For introducing innovation - simpler for SUs to alter, change, pivot at any stage of the development • To gain clients - SUs are agile in locating clients

Corporations get external innovation   SUs work for their 1st client

FIGURE 10.2 The revolutionary evolution of enabling systems

One of the main outcomes of the new OIP concept is the formation of a surrounding community; this enables a continual reaping of values: startups employ their speed, agility and risk-taking approach to explore ideas that answer the corporations' needs, in a faster, more focused and less expensive way; while the corporations bring their commercial scale and depth of experience to help validate, launch and grow the startups' ideas. As such, they become the start-ups' beta sites on the one hand, and their builders on the other, by allowing startups to use the corporation's tools, machinery, expertise, etc., to develop their ideas; (d) for other stakeholders, such as academia, which benefit from such collaborations, especially when innovation development in the university's labs is involved; investors can act in a more secure environment, as a leading corporation is working closely with the startup, and is prepared to incubate and incorporate its products/services/processes; and the entrepreneurial ecosystem can benefit greatly from the creation of a new form of community.

Individuals' Personalized Platforms

In this era of acceleration programs, mentorship and pitches to investors can be accomplished digitally. Entrepreneurs may justify their time spent in enrolling in acceleration programs, for example, by looking for options that are customized and personalized. Face-to-face and virtual platforms are developing, though they are in their infancy; these provide a one-stop shop, an aggregation of EE services for the entrepreneur and the startup. From this 'buffet'-driven platform, participants can choose the programs, mentorship, networking, and events that suit their needs, perceived needs, perceived outcomes, and value gained. The participants in these platforms are mainly nascent entrepreneurs who are somehow involved with the ecosystem, hence they are more focused on a specific service (e.g., mentoring, acceleration program in a specific vertical or to specific stages of the business, among others); their time dedication to the business is crucial, either due to a specific deadline or to the prediction of potential competition, etc.

Educational virtual tools and courses are another way to personalize enabling programs, by building the demanded skills and competencies through virtual courses, interactive textbooks, inspirational talks and virtual webinars and conferences. Such tools can be useful for entrepreneurs who are more disciplined in organizing their time and assignments, mainly student entrepreneurs who can more easily capture the value of such digitalized, educational contents.

Innovation Factory

Hewlett Packard Enterprise[1] offers a combination of advanced technology, consulting, and process reengineering to help IT make the transition to an innovation factory for a digital economy; IBM opened an innovation factory to pilot innovation around cloud computing, to enable "innovation by putting a structure around the innovation process and providing tools for innovators and early adopters to publish, experiment, provide feedback, and enhance innovations";[2] IDEO[3] is leading change creation through design in an innovation factory model; IdeaLab is looking for "big problems in the world that have technology solutions and test many ideas in parallel. When one shows great promise, we recruit a great team, spin it off into a company, and help them grow a successful business",[4] and AccorHotels has developed an internal platform for collaborative innovation that enables promoting exploration, testing and implementation of the best ideas in the field of hospitality. This blend of different businesses, large and global, chains and consulting companies only partially represents a new model for companies to stay relevant in today's dynamic world by introducing innovation; yet, because embedding innovation demands testing as well as taking potential risks, for example, spending money, time, human resources and technology, while the fit of the innovation to the company's needs is uncertain, the innovation factory model enables remixing and combining capabilities and technologies to create new value. Based on Hargadon and Sutton's (2000) knowledge-brokering cycle approach, innovation factories make use of the following intertwined practices: (a) capturing good ideas: from company employees, outside entrepreneurs, students or active startups which, in sharing their ideas, create collaborative innovation, and anyone can comment on ideas that have already been shared and exchanged freely with peers the world over; (b) keeping ideas alive, by spotting old ideas that can be used in new places, new ways, and new combinations, rather than inventing from scratch; (c) imagining new uses for old ideas, through sharing, brainstorming, involving everyone—including retired employees and past and present stakeholders of the company, to inspire with their stories about the company, to engage in older practices; (d) test the best ideas. As innovation factories are company-based, they are strongly connected to the company's core values, processes and capabilities, and testing innovation is less risky. The company is the best place to accelerate innovation, by using its infrastructure and resources and its being hands-on regarding the development of the innovation process, including the possibility to cease, change or pivot it (Hargadon & Sutton, 2000; Kaplan, 2012; Rinne, 2004).

The innovation factory model is essentially useful for the company in bringing innovation in unique ways and remotivating and re-energizing employees who are facing innovation and entrepreneurial processes. It is most useful for entrepreneurs and startups, mainly those that are vertical-focused, that is, their products/services are specified to an exclusive field, such as cloud computing, hospitality; however, more generically vertical fields, such as expertise in IT and design, can also be a valuable fit for the startup. These startups are either lacking a niche or marketing channels, or are aspiring to make a change in the industry. In either case, they are contracting with a company that strategizes innovation as its core mission to serve its processes via its in-house resource—the innovative development of the startups.

Venture Builders

A venture builder is a company that creates companies by using shared resources, for example, capital, teams, partnerships, etc., to launch solutions that then operate as fully operational companies. *In its most basic form, the venture-building company is a holding company that owns equity in the various corporate entities it has helped create.* The venture builders identify problems tackled by entrepreneurs, then partner with a potential company or a leading figure to co-create an idea; with the venture builders' assistance in the business field, and the leading figure responsible for raising the funds, venture builders create metrics for achieving the best market fit or traction, and then assemble the support for that company to achieve its goal. Such models can be seen as a 'place' for matching co-founders to enhance the levels of a startup's performance and success. Though there are various models of venture builders for startups, documentation in this area is still scarce (Diallo, 2015; Kessler & Frank, 2009; Morris, Webb, Fu, & Singhal, 2013). Venture builders focus on identifying business ideas, then providing the startup with the resources to develop and implement those ideas; resources include matching ideas to talents, building the 'right' teams for them, locating partnerships and funds, assisting in managing the business. The venture builder model is, thus, valuable for venture capital companies and corporations, either as consulting or in-house services. Some of the most notable venture builders include Obvious Corp., which spun off Twitter and Medium; Hard Valuable Fun, which produced Affirm.com and Glow.com; Betaworks, whose portfolio includes Instapaper and Blend; Germany's Rocket Internet, putting out PayMill, Jumia, FoodPanda, etc.; the Netherlands gave us StarterSquad, the self-proclaimed "European version of Betaworks". Startups can enjoy a full solution to advance their development, as most of the core activities required by the startup can be provided by the venture builder. As such, it may be a valuable model for startups that wish to advance or scale up some of their products, or even ideas, by partnering with an existing company.

Startup Factory

The startup factory is a unique form that brings resources to high-growth startups and locates the competencies that can be achieved, hence providing the entrepreneurial platform upon which startups can develop. A startup factory is an organization that creates, houses, and nurtures startup companies. The startup factory strives to offer startups infrastructure, mentoring, networking and any sought-after support to intensify their performance (Gawer & Cusumano, 2002; Ketchen, Sandler, & Sandler, 2015; Kohler & Baumann, 2016; Lapowsky, 2014). Some researchers claim that a startup factory is a form of venture builder; others describe it as a model that can be implemented in incubators and accelerators. The difference from a more conservative acceleration process lies in the startup factory management's mission to 'match' the best experts, talents, technologies, management tools, etc., to the startup's idea. An analogy for this concept might be a cubes game—taking an idea and building the best business to pursue it and scale it up. This model can be better used in co-working and shared spaces, where resources are more accessible. It can fit most innovative, feasible ideas of individual entrepreneurs, including scientists who develop their ideas in labs, or immigrant entrepreneurs who have no network, but have developed bright and innovative ideas but have not yet established any means to develop and commercialize them.

Impact Hubs

Impact hubs build entrepreneurial communities that reciprocally bring and deliver impact to startups and entrepreneurs. The concept behind these hubs corresponds to the entrepreneur's independent behavior and mindset; rather than 'matching' the best resources and talent with entrepreneurs and their ideas, entrepreneurs choose the resources and talent that they locate through the communities. These hubs are, thus, impactful and play a substantial role in entrepreneurial development at its various levels: the personal level, that is, the founder's career development as an entrepreneur, the business level, the community level, and the national and global levels. The largest and most impactful Impact Hub[5] network, acknowledged by the United Nations Office in Geneva as a driver of community engagement, focuses on innovative solutions for emerging socially and environmentally pressing issues. Others, such as Startup Grind, envision connecting by making friends, not only contacts, giving, not taking, and helping others, even before helping oneself. These impact hubs coexist in virtual and hybrid communities dedicated to entrepreneurs in chapters around the world, through competitions and challenges, and they sustain their relevance by creating communities and are invigorated by community creators and specialists through instant-messaging platforms and social media.

Startup Studios

Startup studios, also called venture studios, generate ideas for startups either internally or by partnering with entrepreneurs. They act as second co-founders, hence hold a mandate to build the team, while offering the studio's infrastructure and resources to the startups. Studios are based on the success of an idea's maturation into a business, and, therefore, they endeavor to develop the best ideas and assist with the best-matching means for the startup to grow. Startup studios attract business ideas in-house or from their network, and assign internal or external teams from the ecosystem to develop them, for example, technology experts, business developers, marketing managers, etc., fostered by experts and internal resources, to create strong businesses. Their main premise is in concurrently developing different projects that will go on to be developed into separate businesses.[6] Such models can fit either vertical-focused entrepreneurs and startups, or entrepreneurs with the zeal to pursue an idea and need a studio with various 'tools' to create it. Recently, there has been a shift to studios assigned to more mature startups that are striving to scale up. Similarly, the underlying concept of these studios is to foster businesses with their tools, networks and resources.

Venture Labs, Co-labs

The venture lab and co-lab models have developed through the congregation of academia–commercial companies–startups, driven by the transformation of lab-based innovations into early-stage companies though an emphasis on business-related processes and entrepreneurial competencies. This strategy leads to the creation of an ecosystem of aspiring entrepreneurs in a business lab environment that cultivates innovation and inventions, as well as production and commercialization competencies. Thus, entrepreneurial researchers, scientists and students with an aptitude for new venture creation can be galvanized through exposure to business creation of their inventions. Such labs lower the entry barriers to entrepreneurship for inventors and people with great ideas by encouraging and enabling them to test their inventions.

Venture labs also prevail in the corporate world with substantial R&D activity; for example, a venture lab to foster innovation was developed at Lucent Technologies; the IBM innovation space employs a venture lab model (Apgar, 2006; Chesbrough & Socolof, 2000; Curley & Formica, 2010; Kientz et al., 2008). Georgia Tech's Venture Lab,[7] launched at Georgia Tech in 2001 and then adopted by other research universities in the United States, provides comprehensive assistance to Georgia Tech faculty members, research staff and students who want to form startup companies to commercialize the technological innovations that they have developed. Some venture labs are dedicated to regional development as part of their strategy, of both the entrepreneurial landscape and employment opportunities.

Boot Camps

Startup boot camps are characterized as intensive, rapid skill-training programs, mainly as part of a competitive selection process for acceleration or incubation programs. These camps rely on project-based, experiential learning principles, aimed at rapidly improving the participants' entrepreneurial skills, though some programs are adapted to either the accelerator/incubators' demands or the bottom-up needs revealed by information from entrepreneurs, students, mentors, etc. The underlying principle is a 'ready-to-work' model that introduces the benefits of enrolling in a boot camp rapidly and globally. This kind of program varies in duration, depth, curriculum, and focus, and subsequently, in access to entrepreneurial opportunities.

Boot camps introduce cutting-edge content, which is usually based on international best practice and a digitalized platform, as both provide entrepreneurial skills and competencies through short-term programs akin to rapid vocational skills training; they also hone their value as an imperative component in the entrepreneurial education landscape.

According to the World Bank Report 2017,[8] there are five main types of boot camp: pre-boot camp providing basic entrepreneurial/business/tech skills to prepare students for the 'ready-to-work' model; ready-to-work boot camp—an intensive, short-term, full-time, rapid skill-training program that prepares participants for entrepreneurial capabilities, for example, pitching to investors, preparing a business plan; a boot camp model that extends the training approach to practical or 'on-the-job' training to equip participants with a higher level of required skills and capabilities to develop a product/service, mainly focused on technological skills; mini boot camp—very short-term training programs aimed at stimulating the zeal in entrepreneurship; and early education boot camp, mainly to trigger interest in tech-related skills and capabilities at an early age. Other categorizations refer to *verticals*—tech-related, fin-tech, digital health, and customer-focused, such as Akirachix in Kenya[9] "helping young women develop a capacity to be competitive [and] allowing them access to opportunities in the information technology industry"; *strategic initiators* or *partners* such as accelerators and incubators, governmental offices, academic institutions, the corporate boot camps; for example, the General Assembly in New York City[10] is a pioneer in education in the most highly demanded skills and a leading 'factory' for boot camps, aimed at providing dynamic training to close the global skills gap; their graduates are then attractive to startups, or become entrepreneurs; and *geographical locations*, for example, VamosA[11] in Latin America, or Global Entrepreneurship Bootcamp.[12]

AT-A-GLANCE: STARTUPBOOTCAMP

Startupbootcamp* operates in Amsterdam, Berlin, Copenhagen, Eindhoven, Israel, Istanbul and London, and, shortly, in San Francisco. Stimulated by an internship, Alex Farcet, co-founder and CEO of the European accelerator Startupbootcamp, went through DHL in Hungary in the early 1990s, and he started making himself useful to other entrepreneurs, helping them find funding for their startups. He even made an angel investment of his own in a grocery delivery business.

Startupbootcamp operates an intensive three-month program, tapping into their international network of alumnus founders, corporate partners and investors. The managing team believes in meeting entrepreneurs around the world in person, through events and business conferences, to get to know the potential applicants and to get a better grasp of entrepreneurial needs. The selection process includes registrants' meetings with an investment team, mentors, and corporate partners, concluding with 8–12 teams being invited to join the three-month program. Thus, both selected and rejected teams gain from the selection process. For three months, the selected startups collaborate with mentors, partners, and investors to scale up their businesses, in addition to getting a per-team budget to cover living expenses during the program, free office space, and exposure to exclusive partner deals from leading technology providers such as Amazon, HubSpot, SendGrid, and others. On Demo Day, leading figures are invited who wish to assist in scaling up the businesses. At the Berlin venue, one of the managers[†] stated that:

> in the digital health field, you need to identify the most engaged, professional and innovative teams. We have created a selection process modeled on *X-Factor*, which is fun, current and, most importantly, prepares the selected teams for the subsequent program. We have many success stories that we can definitely consider to be an outcome of our bootcamp program.

Food for thought:

What are the advantages of operating a rigid selection process for a program that is preparing entrepreneurs for accelerators (which are also selective)?

[*] www.startupbootcamp.org/
[†] Interviewed by me.

Summary

The various innovative programs for entrepreneurs and the entrepreneurial landscape are portrayed, and examples of these programs' operation are presented. The programs derive from a common vision of promoting entrepreneurship and educating entrepreneurs in the most required skills to generate a competitive advantage, which will allow them to survive and grow in the dynamic entrepreneurial market. These different programs stem from various approaches, needs and interests, based on the initiators' and strategic partners' goals, the tenants' needs, and the corporation challenges that require entrepreneurs' solutions, among others. The chapter presents the more innovative programs and platforms prevailing today, although there are other programs that are either scarcely documented or more marginal that are not included here. Moreover, since research in this area is still in its initial stages, there seems to be some discrepancy and overlap in the construction of the programs' titles, goals, and activities; as such, programs that are defined as providing specific content or structures eventually provide other deliveries. Such differences can also be found across sectors—for example, startup labs initiated by academia or government—and across countries.

Takeaways

For educators and teaching developers:

- For new programs, be proficient in developing educational materials, to be able to introduce value.
- Become methodically acquainted with existing programs running in your country and internationally, including their impact on the entrepreneur, as a basic foundation to develop the new program that you would like to operate.
- Each program has different effects on, and relevance to, different types of entrepreneurs, depending on the levels of development, sector, entrepreneurial experience, and national or regional culture.
- Craft programs with a close link to shareholders' needs, expectations and requirements; then, seek the shareholders' feedback on the operated programs.
- Be attentive to customers' feedback on the program's value; preferably, formally solicit feedback and comments to be able to make adjustments in the next operation of the program.
- The more strategic connections with industry, academia and government are crafted, the more value is delivered to the tenants of the programs. They get to know their ecosystem more thoroughly, and can develop relations to be employed beyond the program's duration.

For EE participants:

- There are many programs proposed for entrepreneurs. They fluctuate across many components, for example, structure, duration, success. Understanding that there are multiple programs is important as a preliminary mindset, even before considering a program.
- Programs can contribute to various needs, for example, the founder's needs, the team's needs, the business' needs, the product's needs, among others. It is your mission to verify that the initially stated deliveries of the EE program are executed to full satisfaction.
- Enquire about the programs that exist; some of them provide a 'testing period' to ensure that the program responds to your needs.
- It is not compulsory to attend the program in its entirety, if it does not fit your expectations. Time is a precious asset for entrepreneurs, and wasting it is not an option.

- Tangible and intangible factors can affect your decision on an EE program; you should not ignore your intuition; even the most popular program, if it 'feels' unsuitable, should not be chosen.

Case Study 10—SOSA NYC: A Disruptive Concept of an OIP[13]

Recently named one of the 100 most influential people in Israel by TheMarker, as well as one of the ten Israelis making a mark on New York's tech scene, Guy Franklin started his career path as an accountant at Ernst and Young in Tel Aviv, then relocated as a senior accountant to Ernst and Young in New York City. Powered by his technological savvy and experience gained in the army, Franklin first founded Israeli Mapped in NY,[14] an interactive platform that maps the Israeli startups operating in New York, to demonstrate Israeli innovation to the world. He identified the large numbers of Israeli startups in New York City and understood that he could promote them in the New York community and in the relevant startup ecosystem in New York; in Franklin's words

> embracing the newcomer startups by introducing them to a community, thus facilitating their adaptation to New York City, hastening their acquaintance with their Israeli peers, who can advise them, as well as with the New York investors, corporate people, potential clients and many other relevant players.

The interactive, crowdsourcing-driven mapping was rapidly boosted to hundreds of Israeli startups that were 'motivated' to join due to FOMO[15] syndrome; startup participation expanded exponentially. Franklin figured out that the mapping had created a community in which the startups, and financial and corporate players, were eager to partake. Driven by substantial media coverage, the spotlight on the Israeli startups in New York heightened and the resultant community expanded. At a strategic crossroads, SOSA Tel-Aviv,[16] founded in 2014 by 25 leading Israeli figures from the investing and high-tech entrepreneurship fields, invited Franklin to bring more value to its existing global network by opening SOSA NYC. Franklin was captivated by SOSA's mission to bring stakeholders from all industries under one roof, to foster business partnerships by providing disruptive innovation to the corporations and startups. He says,

> New York is known as the world's financial hub, with Wall Street's clout extending worldwide, and the leading center of expertise in sectors such as fin-tech, insure-tech, retail, energy, and media, among so many others; it is the best place to sustain and scale SOSA's mission.

He deeply supported, and, therefore, actually implemented, SOSA's view that disruption is the only way to stay relevant, and he strove to develop SOSA NYC into a growing, agile platform that would bring value to any key player involved in its activities. SOSA is an OIP, grounded in delivering disruptive innovation to corporations that wish to integrate more innovation and gain a competitive advantage; such innovation from outside the corporation can promote either finding or developing new ways of engaging with customers, innovating business processes with new digital platforms, and embedding new technology in existing processes, products or services, among others. These 'giants' see the strategic partnership with SOSA as a 'must' for creating valuable innovation. Franklin's endeavors are focused on mobilizing the most suitable innovative solutions, stemming from passionate startups' inventions, to respond to the corporations' needs and expectations. SOSA's team consists of analysts and innovation experts who scout for the solutions with the best fit, which exist, are in the development stages, or can be developed by startups in the ecosystem. The corporations support startups dedicated to developing their solutions; from their standpoint, a startup's success signifies a successful proof of concept that can then be embedded in the corporation. From the startups' standpoint, SOSA connects them to New York's key players by employing their inventions and innovations for the corporations' needs, thereby giving them their first corporate client. Startups can more easily penetrate the market through a big client, and become more attractive to stakeholders, including investors. Franklin, who is a socially conscious and engaged manager, considers the exclusive working space that SOSA offers in New York City as a 'showroom'. It provides startups with a space to work, share and network; concurrently, corporate representatives visiting the exclusive working space can meet with the startups, feel the vibes and sense the overall potential of working with Israeli startups.

From this perspective, SOSA brings new concepts to the enabling system landscape by pinpointing corporations as primary customers while offering strategic connections to startups through a community, training sessions, meet-ups, and an exclusive working space, aimed at enabling and facilitating the best conditions for startups to develop their businesses as innovative responses to corporate needs.

In October 2018, SOSA was chosen by the city of New York to build the city's official Global Cyber Center and to transform NYC into the cyber capital of the world.[17]

Questions on the Case Study

1. List the three most substantial components provided by SOSA to its startups and entrepreneurs, which they cannot easily get elsewhere. Explain your answer.

2. How can SOSA ensure that it still provides entrepreneurs with their needs, while its declared focus is on providing services to established companies?
3. List three advantages and three challenges that an OIP, such as SOSA, introduces into the entrepreneurship landscape. Explain your answer.
4. Search the web for SOSA's activities in other locations. In your opinion, what is the advantage of developing different locations for an OIP?
5. SOSA uses its co-working space and corporate fees as its business model. Suggest 3–4 other innovative business models for OIPs in general, and SOSA NYC in particular. Explain your answer.

Reflective Questions

1. Look for boot camps in three different countries, and write down their names and website addresses. List their main activities; discuss their similarities and differences. In your opinion, are the differences based on their different locations?
2. A private company in Africa is considering opening an internal entrepreneurship program that will promote the entrepreneurial ecosystem in Africa, and will stimulate its workers so that they will be more innovative and creative. As the company's consultant, and in order to plan the program, what are the five main questions that you would like to ask the management? What information would you want to accumulate?
3. There are many criticisms of the EE program 'bubble'. Search for these on the web, then discuss 3–4 main components of this criticism. What is your opinion of this criticism, and why?
4. Watch 'What is a start-up studio? An interview with Suman Lal at Italian Tech Tour 2017' at: https://youtu.be/aI_Ng04Azws. Make three arguments for why the studio could *not* work for entrepreneurs, then respond to your own arguments, trying to explain how it could eventually work. What is your conclusion?
5. Watch '7 Promising startups that went bust' at: https://youtu.be/XLMKku4HbrY. Choose two of these startups and advise on the best program to revive them. Explain your choice. What are your conclusions and what are the implications of your suggestions?

Notes

1 See at: https://h20195.www2.hpe.com/v2/getpdf.aspx/4aa6-4282enw.pdf?
2 See at: www.ibm.com/developerworks/websphere/zones/hipods/
3 See at: www.ideo.com/about
4 See at: www.idealab.com/
5 See at: https://impacthub.net/
6 See at:https://medium.com/the-weekend-reader/startup-studios-the-new-way-to-build-great-companies-6e55b7fe6412; https://techcrunch.com/2018/05/17/fctry-wants-to-be-a-new-type-of-startup-studio/

7 See at: https://venturelab.gatech.edu/
8 CODING BOOTCAMPS building future-proof skills through rapid skills training, at: https://moringaschool.com/wp-content/uploads/2018/05/118627-WP-PUBLIC-P163475-78p-CodingBootcampsFutureProofSkills.pdf
9 See at: http://akirachix.com/
10 See at: https://generalassemb.ly/about
11 See at: www.vamosa.co/
12 See at: https://gebootcamp.com/
13 Face-to-face interview with Guy Franklin, General Manager of SOSA NYC and the founder of Israeli Mapped in NY.
14 See at: www.israelimappedinny.com/
15 Fear of missing out; for example, see at: https://psychcentral.com/blog/fomo-addiction-the-fear-of-missing-out/
16 See at: https://sosa.co/
17 See at: https://sosa.co/industry-expertise/cyber/

References

Apgar, D. (2006). *Risk Intelligence: Learning to Manage what We Don't Know*. Boston, MA: Harvard Business School Press.

Chesbrough, H. W., & Socolof, S. J. (2000). Creating new ventures from Bell Labs technologies. *Research-Technology Management, 43*(2), 13–17. https://doi.org/10.1080/08956308.2000.11671337

Curley, M. G., & Formica, P. (2010). Accelerating venture creation and building on mutual strengths in experimental business labs. *Industry and Higher Education, 24*(1), 7–10. https://doi.org/10.5367/000000010790877326

Diallo, A. (2015). How "venture builders" are changing the startup model. *VentureBeat, 18*, 201.

Gawer, A., & Cusumano, M. A. (2002). *Platform Leadership: How Intel, Microsoft, and Cisco Drive Industry Innovation—Do You Have Platform Leadership?* Boston, MA: Harvard Business School Press.

Hargadon, A., & Sutton, R. I. (2000). Building an innovation factory. *Harvard Business Review, 78*(3), 157–166.

Kaplan, S. (2012). *Business Model Innovation Factory: How To Stay Relevant when the World Is Changing*. New York: John Wiley.

Kessler, A., & Frank, H. (2009). Nascent entrepreneurship in a longitudinal perspective: The impact of person, environment, resources and the founding process on the decision to start business activities. *International Small Business Journal, 27*(6), 720–742. https://doi.org/10.1177/0266242609344363

Ketchen, D. J., Sandler, K., & Sandler, K. (2015). Substitutes for Silicon Valley: The case of the Round House Startup Factory. *Journal of Organization Design, 4*(3), 31. https://doi.org/10.7146/jod.22391

Kientz, J. A., Patel, S. N., Jones, B., Price, E., Mynatt, E. D., & Abowd, G. D. (2008). The Georgia Tech aware home. In *Proceedings of the Twenty-sixth Annual CHI Conference Extended Abstracts on Human Factors in Computing Systems—CHI '08* (pp. 3675–3680). New York: ACM Press. https://doi.org/10.1145/1358628.1358911

Kohler, R., & Baumann, O. (2016). Organizing a venture factory: Company builder incubators and the case of Rocket Internet. *SSRN Electronic Journal*. https://doi.org/10.2139/ssrn.2700098

Lapowsky, I. (2014). The next big thing you missed: Tech superstars build "startup factories". Retrieved September 27, 2018, from www.wired.com/2014/11/startup-factories/

Morris, M. H., Webb, J. W., Fu, J., & Singhal, S. (2013). A competency-based perspective on entrepreneurship education: Conceptual and empirical insights. *Journal of Small Business Management, 51*(3), 352–369. https://doi.org/10.1111/jsbm.12023

Rinne, M. (2004). Technology roadmaps: Infrastructure for innovation. *Technological Forecasting and Social Change, 71*(1–2), 67–80. https://doi.org/10.1016/J.TECHFORE.2003.10.002.

11
THE ROLE OF THE ENVIRONMENT IN FOSTERING ENTREPRENEURSHIP

The Reciprocal Impact of the Ecosystem on Entrepreneurship

Research has established the role of ecosystems in fostering entrepreneurship. Ecosystems affect its emergence, its direction of development, specific evolving trends, and its expected accrued value, through network externalities, and urban and regional policies aimed at attracting and supporting entrepreneurs.

In 2010, Professor Daniel Isenberg published an article in the *Harvard Business Review* entitled 'How to start an entrepreneurial revolution', stressing that

> the private and nonprofit sectors too must shoulder some responsibility. In numerous instances corporate executives, family business owners, universities, professional organizations, foundations, labor organizations, financiers, and, of course, entrepreneurs themselves have initiated and even financed entrepreneurship education, conferences, research, and policy advocacy. As we shall show later in this article, sometimes private initiative makes it easier for governments to act more quickly and effectively, and all stakeholders—government and otherwise—should take every chance to show real leadership. (Isenberg, 2010, p. 3)

Isenberg proved the imperative role of each member of the ecosystem in enabling entrepreneurship to thrive and grow. Yet, entrepreneurship that is boosted through the ecosystem's networks can arise only when the ecosystem is assembled, well connected and shares similar goals and interests. Strong ecosystems develop when the relations of the ecosystem and entrepreneurship are reciprocal, perceived to add value, and sustainable. As such, both the interlinkages between the ecosystem's components, and those of each component with entrepreneurship are important factors in these dynamics. A strong ecosystem in the UK originated with a governmental office that assembled lawyers, accountants and startups. Peter Jones,[1] the initiator of this ecosystem's network, used an instant messaging application to provide a platform for information, e-meetings, and short discussions among members. According to Jones,

> Since it is demonstrated in the application who has left, by an indication 'Mr. X has left the group', it was easy to detect why some members left; the ones who could not see an instant value of participating in this network, left the group. Interestingly, I indicated that the group was for service providers for startups; so it attracted mainly lawyers, accountants, and some other advisors. Then, when it started to bring value, other people, not in the service provider category, asked my permission to join the group. So we had an interesting situation in which people that I was sure fit the group did not necessarily survive it; others, that I thought would find the group irrelevant, were most active.

Shahar Matorin, the Israeli manager of the community's ecosystem, confirmed:

You have to work on the community relevance constantly, be actively attentive and attract various members to the community, yet, stay focused. This means that when you characterize your ecosystem in a way, in our case, as managers of other ecosystems and communities, you have to stick to it. Yet, you will generate more value and impact if you think creatively by inviting such managers from different regions, industries, sectors, different 'characters', etc.

How Is Value Created in an Ecosystem?

Entrepreneurs are looking for individuals, bodies, and systems that can advance their entrepreneurial activity in various ways: information, know-how, opening doors, connecting to other players, expanding relevant networks through the ecosystem's connections, referral, sharing, getting inspired, among others. Nascent and more established entrepreneurial businesses will see value when a fit between their exact need and the solution, or potential solution, is materialized. For example, a young German startup developing gamification for drivers in autonomous cars joined an ecosystem after attending an international conference in their field and receiving disappointing feedback on their concept and potential feasibility. One of the ecosystem's members, a government officer of the trade and industry office, suggested introducing them to some colleagues to refine their concept. The startup's founders have found their participation in this ecosystem most useful, although the introduction and connections are still not finalized, and the results are still unknown.

From the ecosystem bodies' perspective, the connection with entrepreneurs and startups provides potential customers, suppliers and service providers, a deeper acquaintance with innovation and development, and a way to engender the success that startups can conceivably reach. In addition, being linked to startups and entrepreneurs is largely considered to be 'cool'; entrepreneurs are deemed creative, vibrant, go-getters, and these characteristics can be transferrable.

While, theoretically, the relationships between entrepreneurs and their ecosystem seem well-adjusted and promising, research has proved that they are constantly changing, being reshaped, and dependent on the dynamic interests of the ecosystem's components and structures.

Rivanda Azevedo is part of the managing team of a Brazilian pharmaceutical startup developing a neurobased device designed to prevent migraine attacks. She established relationships with the government for public subsidies on the development of the device, with a research center for the expertise, and with a public hospital to gain some insights from the staff on the device's efficiency. At maturation, when the device was in the advanced production phase, Azevedo sought more hospitals to test the device's functionality and received invitations from private hospitals; these were seriously addressed by the existing players, who held different interests. The public hospital cut ties with Azevedo and the team. This example can repeat itself in ecosystems, by constantly activating the ecosystem's structures and dynamics. Ecosystems are expected to be dynamic and mobile, and to progress through changes in the relationships and informal contracts among its constituents.

The startup ecosystem is mainly meant to encompass seven major factors, as shown in Figure 11.1, whose roles in affecting the emergence and direction of entrepreneurship in a specific ecosystem fluctuate across regions, industries and specialties.

To nourish the robust core that the ecosystem builds and proactively triggers, the following ingredients are needed:

- Know-how, R&D, networks.
- Talent, experts, encouragement to study STEM.[2]
- Global mindset and communication skills.
- Entrepreneurial culture.
- Infrastructure for entrepreneurship emergence, startup development.
- Regulations and public policy oriented to and supporting entrepreneurship.

The ecosystem's reciprocal impact on entrepreneurship affects the startup's regional development, and molds its shape, style and dynamics; for example, strong financial companies in an ecosystem prompt higher speed, financially driven growth of startups in the ecosystem; a powerful low-tech industry presence in an ecosystem will inspire more entrepreneurial businesses related to

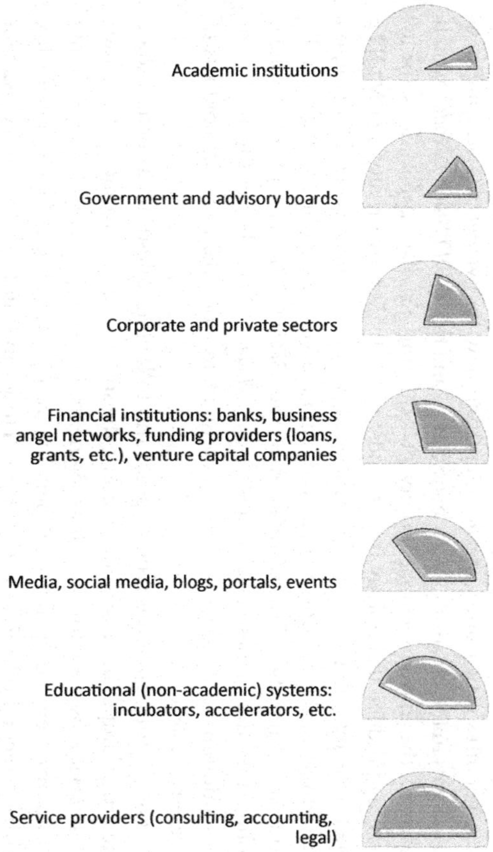

Academic institutions

Government and advisory boards

Corporate and private sectors

Financial institutions: banks, business angel networks, funding providers (loans, grants, etc.), venture capital companies

Media, social media, blogs, portals, events

Educational (non-academic) systems: incubators, accelerators, etc.

Service providers (consulting, accounting, legal)

FIGURE 11.1 A full-range ecosystem

its specialties, as complements or suppliers of products and services. These dynamics raise potential conflicts of interest, which may either advance the ecosystem through vigorous restructuring, or impair the trusted connections and destroy it.

To facilitate the theoretical framing of the relationships between entrepreneurial businesses and the stakeholders in the ecosystem, the following four ecosystem models, demonstrated in Zahra and Nambisan (2011), are presented: the *Orchestra Model*, in which the keystone, dominant companies 'conduct' the ecosystem; hence, startups create new products and services that integrate with the products of these dominant companies, or complement them by adding value; the *Creative Bazaar Model*, in which a dominant company scouts for new innovation across wide, diverse sources, as in a bazaar, and then offers its infrastructure to produce this innovation, commercialize it and introduce it to the market; the *Jam Central Model*, when there are no dominant companies, and new ventures play a primary role in creating new knowledge and steering new paradigms in the creation of new ecosystems; and the *MOD Station Model*, which refers to the entrepreneurial activity of exploring alternate applications for an existing product/technology in new and diverse markets by modifying ('MOD') the dominant company's product knowledge to create new value. Drawing on these models, the discourse of Azevedo and the Brazilian public hospital can be understood through a transformation of the *Orchestra Model*, with the hospital conducting the orchestra, to a *Jam Central Model*, where the startup no longer sees a dominant 'conductor'; subsequently, many potential or actual conflicts of interest can arise.

The Startup Genome report[3] poses the following questions to demonstrate the crucial importance of understanding the structure and dynamics of the entrepreneurial ecosystem for each of its segments. For entrepreneurs, "Where should I start my new company?" "When I'm ready, where should I open up my startup's second office?"; for investors, "How can I find new startup investment opportunities around the world instead of simply settling for solely investing in my local startup ecosystem due to familiarity?" "Given the lack of information out there about emerging startup ecosystems, how do I evaluate which ones I should focus on for finding new opportunities?"; for policy-makers, "What initiatives should I prioritize in my startup ecosystem to maximize growth?" "How should I measure the progress of these initiatives?"; and for all stakeholders, "What is the best way to strengthen the overall vibrancy and entrepreneurial spirit in my ecosystem?"

The structure and performance of the ecosystem are presented in Figure 11.2 through its institutions and bodies, and the involved processes and dynamics (Brant, Myers, & Runge, 2017; Brunt, Lerner, & Nicholas, 2012; Howell, 2015; D. Isenberg, 2011; D. J. Isenberg, 2010; Li, Godley, Belitski, Li, & Manwani, 2015; Zahra & Nambisan, 2012).

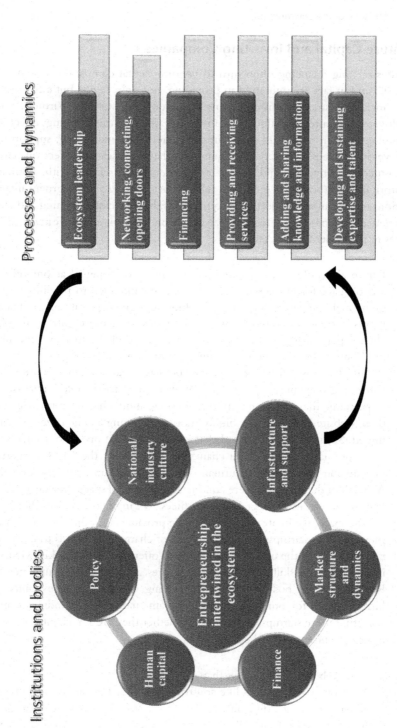

FIGURE 11.2 Structure and processes—the ecosystem's performance

Venture Capital and Investing Companies

Startups seeking financing often turn to venture capital companies, which can provide, and in fact are interested in providing, not only capital but a full solution, including strategic introductions to potential customers, partners, and employees. Venture capitalists and investors are primarily seeking effective technology-driven models to invest in and believe that mentoring, supporting or developing their acceleration programs can have a cascading effect on startups' outcomes. Investors and angels can provide entrepreneurs with: business mentoring, monitoring and guidance, relevant networking and congruent introductions to customers, funders and acquirers, funding, pricing, planning and exit experience and strategies. Oded,[4] a partner in one of Ernest and Young's (EY) offices in the United States, said:

> I have always been fascinated by innovation. We opened at our offices a cool space for entrepreneurs; at first, it was intended to provide entrepreneurial companies financial consulting in a quiet, private place. Then, it was decorated differently, and at the same time, more entrepreneurial clients spent more time in this cool space, beyond the financial consulting hours. One day, the two young, enthused founders of a fashion-tech startup that was still immature were about to make a crucial decision on expanding their business to Asia. My team and I tried to convince them to postpone their decision until their business model had been finalized on their website. But the two highly motivated young women were determined. So, in order to 'save' the situation, we asked one of our clients, a CEO of a large fashion retail chain, to talk to them; the CEO suggested introducing them to the chairman of one of the main textile factories in Asia. All of the meetings were conducted in our cool space. We decided to open an acceleration program at our offices. We invite our startup clients to use the space; we invite our client service providers for office hours, where they meet the startups; everything is free of charge. My plan is to collaborate with one of the universities nearby, to offer a full range of knowledge, information and skills, as well as deepen research on the startups' needs. Recently, at our board of directors' meeting, we raised the possibility of hiring a team for our acceleration program, naming it, branding it and attracting more startups, regardless of whether they are EY clients, to promote the entrepreneurial ecosystem in our region.

Furthermore, Rebecca Wessell[5] says that
Captaining a new enterprise is like constructing a parachute after you've been thrown out of a plane: it's difficult, it's dangerous, you're pressed for time and a wrong decision can be fatal. When faced with the pressures of starting a new company, your ability to act quickly, decisively and correctly will depend on

experience, skill and knowledge. If you are short on any of these attributes (not uncommon for the first-time entrepreneur), mentoring can make the difference between survival and doom.

Investors and venture capital companies see the development of the entrepreneurial business through the financial aspects, and thus contribute greatly to entrepreneurs' understanding and decision-making process. Finance guides you to the right trends, to set a reasonable price for your product, and to explore broadly and carefully your potential strategic partners," says Oded. He concluded:

> One startup that had produced an IoT device to monitor the flame on the stove while away from home was about to sign an agreement with a global company, which was unwarranted and greedy, financially, marketing-wise and branding-wise. The founders could not see beyond the large sum of money. At the EY acceleration space, our experts could guide the founders in their strategic decisions.

More and more, investors and angel groups are not driven exclusively by directly financing or investing in startups; instead, they are becoming the source for critical information and data that align the needs of investors, angels, entrepreneurs, and the startup to create, support and strengthen the entrepreneurial community. This could be through building an educated, professional and well-informed ecosystem that either nurtures startups, or educates investors and angels, through webinars, teaching sessions, reports, research, data, and more. Angel Capital Association[6] is the largest professional angel development organization in the world. It focuses on educating professional angels to make more high-quality investments, thus indirectly strengthening the entrepreneurial mesosystem; New Enterprise Associates[7] (NEA) is a large venture capital firm with mentorship programs for product design entrepreneurs in the fields of technology and health care. NEA draws on the premise of creating a venture capital company that will help entrepreneurs build transformational, disruptive businesses. Pipeline Angels[8] arranges boot camps and funding pitches for female entrepreneurs who need early-stage investments. The boot camps feature mentoring, education and practice sessions; 500 Startups[9] specializes in early funding and mentorship for minority-based ventures. They feature a Seed Program with four months of mentoring, $150,000 in seed money and other support; and Accelerator Ventures[10] is a venture capital company that provides a full range of strategic assistance to the startups that it is tracking for investment. Investors and venture capitalists who are prone to nurture startups offer:

- Robust, cutting-edge financial consulting, in a familial atmosphere.
- Space for consulting, networking, and benefiting from contact with the company's clients, suppliers, partners, etc.
- Experienced, professional office hours by service providers, who are either in-house experts, or clients willing to support the startup community.

- Full-term commitment to escorting the startup; this is exclusive to investors and venture capitalists due to the type of relationship, which is not necessarily guaranteed by other enabling EE systems.
- Events, competitions, meetups, company newsletters.

While investors and angels have been known for decades to be financially driven mentors and enablers for entrepreneurs, they have stepped ahead in recent years to provide a full range of financial as well as non-financial and non-funding-driven strategic support and mentorships. Some companies are supporting incubation and acceleration programs, either in-house, or in collaboration with other companies, mainly for the whole community, and not specifically for their customers.

Banks Embedded in the Entrepreneurial Offerings

The World Bank[11] is a leader in recognizing the crucial significance of entrepreneurship to the economy, and assigned the Innovation and Entrepreneurship team of the World Bank's Financial Access, Finance, Competitiveness & Innovation Global Practice, aimed at enabling the exchange of global experience, knowledge, research and investments, to advance entrepreneurial ecosystems and to be involved in fostering policies, strategies, regulations and investments. The World Bank supports a range of programs, from advisory services, loans and a global trust-funded program to business incubators and innovation hubs. Mainly, it constructs a global network for entrepreneurs and practitioners to exchange knowledge and practices. The Silicon Valley Bank has provided services that are specifically designed for startups for more than 30 years, including cash management and investment solutions, online and mobile banking, valuations, M&A, reporting and advice, and resources for startups such as blogs, webinars, and networking events; Square Capital focuses on helping businesses grow by providing funds to hire team members and purchase new equipment; Chase, as a part of J. P. Morgan Chase & Co., is one of the largest consumer and commercial banking institutions in the world, having one of the best online user interfaces, free business debit cards, mobile banking, and remote check depositing, along with business solutions such as standard business bank accounts, payment processing options, and credit cards.

The goal of serving entrepreneurs and their investors is widespread across banks; introducing plans specifically created for startups and offering packages that are affordable and attractive to startups, with free debit cards, transactions, and free online bill paying, along with additional features that meet the startups' needs.

Several banks are launching and co-supporting development programs for specific verticals in the startup scene, such as fin-tech, digital health, and cybersecurity. The programs can be in-house, and include knowledge and education on the vertical, banking-based trends and best practices for startups to employ, or programs supported by banks that are conducted in external accelerators, incubators or hubs. Banks also take an active part in developing applications and enabling systems for entrepreneurs; some banks sponsor pitch nights, develop online courses for entrepreneurs or an internet application for business plans, for example. Through such active involvement and support, banks stay relevant and up to date; they are more hands-on in the entrepreneurial trends and dynamics and can promote the ecosystem with their resources. In some cases, banks unite for specific projects, such as supporting a technological trend in the region, a specific vertical or group (immigrants, women, people in need). As such, the banks deliver a powerful message to the ecosystem of their support of entrepreneurship. The bank gains vibrant and innovative businesses as potential clients and can leverage its competitive advantage by demonstrating higher involvement with the startup scene and cutting-edge developments, along with value creation for its clients and the ecosystem as a whole.

Banks fortify their impact by internally fostering entrepreneurship to cultivate new, innovative ideas from their staff for the bank's use, such as innovation hubs, creativity sessions, and programs allowing a cohort of employees to spend time ideating and then producing systems and processes to be implemented in the bank. The banks' support of entrepreneurship takes various forms, as demonstrated in Figure 11.3.

Public Sector Participation

Professor Isenberg's recommendations, directed to the government, on how to support the entrepreneurial ecosystem, were summarized in 'How to start an entrepreneurial revolution' as follows:

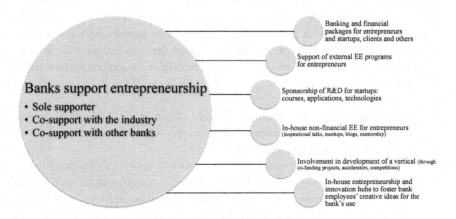

FIGURE 11.3 Banks' directions in supporting entrepreneurship

> Engaging the private sector, modifying cultural norms, removing regulatory barriers, encouraging and celebrating successes, passing conducive legislation, being judicious in emphasizing clusters and incubators, subjecting financing programs to market rigors, and, above all, approaching the entrepreneurship ecosystem as a whole will allow governments to create economic growth by stimulating self-sustaining venture creation.
> (Isenberg, 2010, p. 11)

Governments play an important role in entrepreneurship emergence and growth through governance, regulations, policies, a general 'vibe' of acceptance, and embracing new entrepreneurial ventures; these are a necessary prerequisite to supporting and stimulating entrepreneurship emergence and activity. The governments' main mission is the creation of an environment characterized by increasing knowledge creation, responses to emerging untapped and unsolved problems in areas such as employment, health, sanitation, food, education, and more, reduced regulation, and enhanced regional policy development, which can be accomplished by tangible and intangible support of entrepreneurship, that is, introducing products and services that may solve the unaddressed issues that governments are responsible for, and extending employment and regional development around them.

Research findings prove that governments' support systems are a major stimulus to entrepreneurship activity and growth and, subsequently, catalysts for job creation and economic and regional growth. Therefore, governments use entrepreneurship as one of the most important instruments for promoting their economy, reducing unemployment, creating innovation, commercializing inventions and developments, enhancing academic and research levels through grants and support, connecting bilaterally on innovations, and more. In many countries, public policy initiatives are becoming more entrepreneurship-oriented, although entrepreneurship typically 'happens' without policy intervention; policies *enabling* entrepreneurship may foster its emergence and the reciprocal benefits for entrepreneurship and the government. This could be furthered by introducing knowledge spillovers, finance and human capital through government institutions, regulations and support systems. Governments promote entrepreneurship through the following sources:

- Knowledge spillovers—through finances allocated to R&D investments, research universities and institutions, innovation competitions, conferences and events, social media and blogs.
- Boosting innovation—through formal public networks, by supporting, praising and rewarding successful innovations, as well as unsuccessful businesses that have failed commercially but developed innovation processes that can ultimately serve as the seedbed for the emergence of other innovations; actively assisting in mobilizing innovation to other initiatives.

- Acknowledging entrepreneurs, treating them as national role models, regardless of their outcomes; transmitting this message at school, by proving that entrepreneurship is rewarding and viable, and that the capabilities required to become entrepreneurs can be taught.
- Investments in real estate and infrastructure that encourage entrepreneurship—allocating regional spaces for entrepreneurs, incubators, accelerators, and other programs; enabling free internet, digitalized technologies and other facilities; offering a friendly way to get to investors, grants and support systems, among others.
- Developing the image of a positive emotional sentiment to a place, such as New York, Silicon Valley, Tel Aviv or Frankfurt, developed into locations that are attractive to entrepreneurs

(Acs, Audretsch, & Lehmann, 2013; Baumol, Litan, & Schramm, 2007; Kremer & Williams, 2010; Kwon, Heflin, & Ruef, 2013; Laursen, Masciarelli, & Prencipe, 2012; Lerner & Tirole, 2004; Stenholm, Acs, & Wuebker, 2013).

As government-sponsored initiatives draw on the responses to emerging problems, most ministries, for example, health, economy, education, finance, employment, industry, etc., are embarking on making entrepreneurship the national champion within their unique fields; as an instance, the ministry of health is endeavoring to increase the presence of startups in health-related specializations to increase their national impact by commercializing health-related innovations inside and outside the country, creating more health-related jobs through proliferation of related startups, developing more faculties, schools and educational programs in health, etc.; therefore, ministries promote, financially support and encourage the following:

- Initiating, fostering, implementing and monitoring regulations and public policy that encourages, rewards and acknowledges entrepreneurship.
- Garnering public funding to start entrepreneurial, innovative businesses; supporting businesses' growth in specific areas and specialties; financing later stage businesses, through the involvement of private investments.
- Encouraging, funding and being involved in programs of public incubation and acceleration.
- Funding entrepreneurship programs and helping to encourage and legitimize entrepreneurial learning and practice in universities.
- Harboring innovations, inventions and developments, and protecting them through IP, patentable technologies, copyrighted creative outputs, or trademarked service concepts.
- Advocating regulations, policies and rules that will encourage and foster entrepreneurship.
- Stimulating networks and startup ecosystems; certifying research, innovation and tech centers, hubs, mentors, experts; providing assistance for entrepreneurs through mentors, digitalized systems, courses, training.

- Orchestrating the ecosystem's blend of actions for entrepreneurship by offering win–win 'packages' to each of the ecosystem's agents; coordinating entrepreneurial activity and interests across the ministries to create sharing and alignment rather than competition and rivalry.
- Facilitating global activity; bilateral relationships for startups; research connections and commercialization that are international and global.
- Crafting incentive plans for scientists and researchers; encouraging tech-transfer activities.
- Initiating and encouraging the implementation of policies that affect social values and attitudes toward entrepreneurship to reduce the stigma of failure and enhance the appreciation of entrepreneurial activity in society.
- Being a role model for entrepreneurship and innovation by implementing it in public sectors, for example, developing accelerators within public companies, employing public companies' infrastructures to assist startups in producing their innovation, testing inventions in public companies, etc.
- Governing, not managing, the startup scene by simplifying procedures, mitigating barriers, supplying solutions

(Blackburn, 2016; Michael & Pearce, 2009; Ribeiro-Soriano & Galindo-Martín, 2012).

Private Sector Outreach

Startup with Google[12] is a platform that provides tools, best practices and the Google community for founders to advance their businesses; Amazon AWS Marketplace[13] makes it easy for startups to grow and scale up by providing visibility and traction in the market, and allowing time to focus on the core business; eBay StartUp Cup[14] introduces several challenges to support new regions; for example, in Berlin, eBay StartUp Cup Challenge is an intensive six-month business model competition in which selected participants receive mentoring to hone their business models and the top three teams win cash prizes; Virgin Startup[15] is a not-for-profit organization that helps entrepreneurs in the UK with funding, resources and advice; and the *New York Times*,[16] as a global media organization, provides early-stage investments to digital media startups to support their own innovation efforts. These are only a few examples that demonstrate the rising involvement of the corporate world in the startup and entrepreneurial arena. The mission perceived by corporations fluctuates from one company to the next, depending on their interests, the value gained for their own activity and progress, and the perceived impact of their honing on the ecosystem and the economy as a whole.

The relationship between the private sector and entrepreneurs is multifaceted; from the entrepreneurs' perspective, the government and public sector are responsible for their businesses' advancement as part of the ecosystem's constant improvement and competitiveness; as such, they may be more 'suspicious' of the private sector's involvement, and especially that of the 'giants', in their entrepreneurial businesses. Entrepreneurs can lose control of their IP, management, production and financial processes when the private sector is involved, as they are uncertain how the processes, particularly technology, that they are implementing will be treated within the private sector's company, for example, pivoted, used for the company's interests, shared with clients, etc. The issue of trust is crucial. On the other hand, the public sector is unable to fulfill all of the entrepreneurial business's requirements, and the private sector can fill the void by introducing various alternative finance mechanisms, which are better customized to the entrepreneur's needs; it brings other resources and incentives that may complement the public sector's provisions, including funding generated from many private sources; it invites entrepreneurs to use the private sector's infrastructure for free, as well as its technology, space, mentors, marketing channels, etc. In addition, the strategic relationship with a private sector company, mainly, though by no means exclusively, with the giants, can be leveraged by the startup to gain new funds; for example, startups that are selected to the Microsoft accelerator are more attractive to other investors down the line, because Microsoft believed in their robustness. As the private sector, in contrast to the government, is for-profit-oriented and focused on both spreading and minimizing risk–return tradeoffs, managing a relationship with the private sector can be challenging for startups, as they are expected to be more business-driven, where money and budget count, and the concept of ROI is crucial. The private sector is fascinated by its involvement in the startup and entrepreneurial arena, by the contribution of innovation and developments that the companies can then use, by gaining more clients, that is, startups that succeed, by a business-to-business model, and by being hands-on in potential funding, M&A, and other forms of strategic alliances, both directly with the startup, and indirectly—through the startup—with its stakeholders. Finally, because the private sector has built the ecosystem through entrepreneurship, it is engaged in contributing to that ecosystem's growth (Bruton, Khavul, Siegel, & Wright, 2015; Leyden & Link, 2015; Mazzucato, 2015; Rudenko, Zaitseva, Mekush, Dmitrieva, & Vasilieva, 2016).

The International Perspective on Entrepreneurship Support

Entrepreneurship is sought after around the world, and, at both the country level and a more centralized international level, it is recognized that advancing entrepreneurship can be better achieved by bilateral and multilayered connections between entrepreneurs and their ecosystems on a global scale. The European Commission, United Nations, and Organisation for Economic Co-operation and Development (OECD), among many other organizations, from public and private initiatives, embrace entrepreneurship and provide the required connections and information to foster global, sustainable ties across entrepreneurial businesses. For example, the United Nation's SEED Initiative[17] endeavors to stimulate and build the capacity of outstanding start-up enterprises executing action on the ground; create a conduit for investment in partnerships; disseminate good practice and lessons-learned from successful partnerships to inspire further new partnerships; and generate evidence-based research to assist policy makers

while the European Commission's Entrepreneurship 2020 Action Plan[18] focuses on entrepreneurial education and training to support growth and business creation, removing existing administrative barriers to entrepreneurship, and creating an entrepreneurial culture in Europe to nurture the new generation of entrepreneurs.

Other global organizations that embrace entrepreneurship are bound around similar missions—fostering entrepreneurship in specific fields, geographical areas or among specific types of entrepreneurial businesses. Although each organization has its own interests, they all concede that for sustainable, entrepreneurial success, uni-organizational support is insufficient and collaborative activity is imperative. Such programs include, for example, the Entrepreneurs' Organization, which provides a forum for sharing ideas, and access to mentorship as well as large-scale networking events; the Young Entrepreneur Council, designed for entrepreneurs under the age of 40, which delivers a platform for sharing, getting advice, brand-building and media opportunities; the Young President's Organization, which offers global educational and networking opportunities for entrepreneurs under the age of 45 with access to a variety of events and the opportunity to seek advice from its large network; the Entrepreneur's Club, an international network of high-tech entrepreneurs, executives and business professionals, which offers events in Silicon Valley, with Steve Blank and Guy Kawasaki as keynote speakers, for example. Ashoka is the largest network of social entrepreneurs on a global scale; and Startup Grind is one of the largest networks of independent startups, offering monthly events and an active community.

An international perspective on entrepreneurship allows accumulation of information, knowledge and know-how across countries, verticals and societies, and furnishes EE to the ecosystem's various players: startups, investors, mentors, service providers, accelerator managers, researchers, EE developers, and more; hence, development of a common terminology of entrepreneurship can advance the ecosystem's trustworthy connections, and intensify the entrepreneurship discipline. Specifically, the global institutes can create an awareness of, and support for, entrepreneurship in rural areas, female entrepreneurship, young entrepreneurs, ethnic entrepreneurs, among others (Bryden, 2010; Copeland & James, 2014; Cornell, 2001; Fairlie et al., 2015; Howitt, 2009; Kiriyama, 2012; Mason & Brown, 2014; Steinebach & Knill, 2017).

Entrepreneurial Cities and Communities

Entrepreneurial cities develop a rich and enabling culture, and induce a higher level and pace of opportunity exploitation, thus attracting compatible residents and businesses to advance the city. The entrepreneurial city represents a nested place in which entrepreneurship can thrive through state spatial policy, new reforms and relevant networks, marking a shift away from 'urban managerialism' to flexible accrual and local economies.

Entrepreneurial cities have been developing for several decades, with the best-known startup and entrepreneurial communities, such as Silicon Valley and Research Triangle Park (RTP)—the largest high technology research and science park in North America—created to spur economic development. Federal support enabled the development of rural areas, mounting communities from within to develop a city through job creation, innovation and mitigation of poverty. The cities' nested initiatives smoothed the connections within the ecosystems; entrepreneurs could meet, discuss, negotiate, share ideas, and be mentored while recognizing that their business yield influences their city's development and prosperity. Entrepreneurship can prosper in regions supplying the required resources, for example, talent, know-how, specialization, and the required dynamics, such as networking, recruiting people, negotiating with investors, receiving mentorship and collaborating with the industry, among others. Approaching startup communities as an ecosystem strengthens the relationship between the startup community and the location-based assets that contribute to a place's entrepreneurial culture; the capacity of the community to embrace ecosystem development becomes conditioned on developing entrepreneurial talent, expertise and proof of concept, hence, planning the city's infrastructure, policies and initiatives with the aim of encouraging and attracting entrepreneurship.

In many cities and regions, local leadership acts more entrepreneurially to fill any voids left by the national government, and customizes entrepreneurial strategies to provide entrepreneurial businesses with their needs. Entrepreneurial cities nurture their entrepreneurs while attracting inward investment, growing economic development and income; they harness multiple forms of enabling state interventions within the region and develop policy agendas for advanced models, such as smart and world-class cities. Entrepreneurial cities and regions mainly address:

- The pursuit of innovation strategies intended to enhance entrepreneurship and economic competitiveness.
- Facilitation of innovation through the establishment of accelerators, science parks, regional innovation hubs; sizing up risk capital; and treating entrepreneurs as role models to cultivate the city's culture.
- Support of entrepreneurial initiatives, inviting residents and non-residents to the city to exploit entrepreneurial activities; proposing headquarters in the city for innovation that does not necessarily originate in the city; holding conferences, inviting local and regional officials to the city; making it a hub of entrepreneurship.
- Collaboration with as many outside cities, regions and industries as possible to gain insights and provide value.

- The leveraging of local strengths, including industry, schools, academic institutions, sports leagues, dance groups, etc. to build a strong entrepreneurial ecosystem; identifying their competitive advantages and leveraging them.
- Strengthening diversified talent in the city to broaden the ecosystem's expertise, mindsets and deliveries: ethnic entrepreneurs, immigrants, people from deprived neighborhoods, people with special needs, prisoners, etc.

(Audretsch & Belitski, 2017; Beal & Pinson, 2014; Cohan, 2018; Cox, 2009; Feld, 2012; Gibbs, Krueger, & MacLeod, 2013; Goldman, 2011; Jouve, 2007; Lauermann, 2018; Macke, Markley, & Fulwider, 2014; March & Ribera-Fumaz, 2014; McCann, 2013; Motoyama & Watkins, 2014; Parnell & Pieterse, 2010; Raco & Street, 2012; Shin & Kim, 2016).

Summary

The ecosystem is a critical enabler of entrepreneurship; from the various stakeholders and the ecosystem's activities, entrepreneurs capture the services, knowledge and networking that can trigger their businesses' performance; from entrepreneurship, the various stakeholders absorb the 'entrepreneurial vibe' that encompasses innovative, robust and creative solutions for untapped topics. Ecosystems coexist with, synchronize and mutually fuel, entrepreneurship with stakeholders. The institutional perspective aggregates extant research and practical knowledge on institutions that embrace entrepreneurship, and can be organized through the four ecosystem models introduced by Zahra and Nambisan (2012). These models conceptualize the relationships of entrepreneurs with investors, venture capitalists, banks, the government, international institutions and associations, the city and the region, and enable tapping into the potentially conflicting interests that can be crystallized into a positive, supporting ecosystem. This four-model conceptualization can be used to induce the ecosystem's constituents, for example, investors, government offices, municipalities, etc., to construct, jointly with entrepreneurial businesses, a viable, supportive ecosystem through identification of the harmonizing mission as well as the interests of the players and entrepreneurial businesses, and agreement on the activity model to be followed by all sides.

This chapter introduces the main mission and activity, as well as the value gained for each constituent of a full-range ecosystem, with regard to embracing and developing an entrepreneurial ecosystem. Venture capitalists and investors want to be involved in a full-solution process with the startups; governments and international institutions are more focused on providing solutions for poorly resolved topics; and cities aim to construct internal entrepreneurial hubs. Entrepreneurs should be able to detect these missions to advance their businesses, as well as to contribute to their stakeholders.

Takeaways

For the ecosystem's players:

- Each of you makes an important contribution to the entrepreneurial landscape. Take part in the support systems, even if this is time-consuming and costly.
- Map your value from contributing to the entrepreneurial scene, and plan subsequent support activity accordingly.
- Be attentive to the opportunities accumulating from your contribution to startups; for example, startups developing an interesting technology, partnering with international bodies, or funded by leading companies, among others, can be useful to exploit.
- Supporting startups is a long-term relationship, and you should be fully engaged in managing and funding that relationship.
- Supporting startups can also bring potential conflicts of interest with other players in the ecosystem in terms of resource allocation, provisions, investments, ROIs, among others. Be prepared for these potential scenarios.

For EE participants:

- Thoroughly understand the ecosystem's support aptitude for their specific needs and expectations by searching the internet, asking stakeholders and interviewing the ecosystem's players.
- The ecosystem is interested in the startups and the whole entrepreneurial landscape. Remember this while asking for support, that is, you are equals, bringing value to each other.
- No one stakeholder is better than another, as the potential for assistance is similar. Yet, the stakeholders' support activity can suit the entrepreneurial business in specific stages of development, fill specific needs, or provide guaranteed unique services. Hence, it is worth opening the search for supporters to all sectors of the ecosystem.
- Support goes beyond funding. It is a relationship that requires processes to help it endure and to exploit it to the fullest. Prepare for this as an integral management component in your business process.
- To gain more impact, congregate with other entrepreneurs and make an offer to the ecosystem players; for example, different startups in the food industry might ask government officials to facilitate the IP protection process, or several IoT startups might pledge jointly for funds from an international program. While startups are skeptical about collaborating at the early stages of business development, adjust your mindset to gain more value from the ecosystem.

Case Study 11—A One-stop Shop for Innovation: J. P. Morgan's In-Residence Startup Program[19]

One of the world's largest banks takes startups from "pitch-ready" to "enterprise-ready."

J. P. Morgan's In-Residence Program is a highly structured, outcome-oriented program that engages in a co-creation process with selected startups, pairing fin-tech innovation with the unique resources—expertise, data, network, etc.—of one of the world's largest financial institutions. The results help drive innovation that, beyond improving the global bank's business, benefits the industry as a whole; that is, it produces an ecosystem-level effect.

Fin-techs entering the area of capital markets and wholesale banking (business-to-business financial services) must navigate issues such as compliance with legal requirements and regulatory issues, access to data for the purpose of large-scale testing, or to venture capitalists or industry partners, gaining expertise, as well as resources, in a host of fields, such as trading, banking, sales, design, data, technology, etc. None of these is typically readily available to a smaller, younger company, placing considerable barriers to startups in this industry.

A large, established, innovation-seeking corporation can supply startups with what they lack in expertise, connections and resources. Intent on transitioning from a finance powerhouse to a leader in innovation and technology, J. P. Morgan has nearly 50,000 employees in tech-related positions and is expanding efforts in AI, big data, and machine learning, among other emerging technology areas. In seeking to address some of the industry's most pressing challenges, or identify new ways of delivering value to its customers, the corporation is strongly motivated to create a partnership with startup technological innovation.

There are several established ways in which corporations interact with startups: deploying capital as strategic investment; engaging with external accelerators and technology hubs; and incubating companies internally. "Through the In-Residence Program," says Harris, co-founder and former head of the program, "J. P. Morgan opted for a fourth way—a collaborative approach to partnering with early-stage companies in a structured, outcome-generating co-creation process, customized to the needs of the company."

This program's engagement life cycle begins with a rigorous vetting process, which examines the product in terms of relevance to J. P. Morgan; the technology—its level of development and how it relates to customers' needs; the potential value, in terms of generated revenue; and the investment needed to enable scaling up the startup. A few of the examined companies are accepted (to date, only a handful of companies are in residence, out of hundreds considered) and begin a highly specialized program, tailored to each company's stage of development and strategic objectives.

The program's administrators leverage vast resources to form a designated team of business and technology sponsors. They work directly with the startup, typically over a period of at least six months, to define desired outcomes, refine measures of success, and identify the best experts and resources to connect with it throughout the program—all aimed at enhancing its ability to create technology-led solutions that can help the entire industry operate faster, more safely, and at lower cost.

The program provides another, crucial, component for fin-tech: access to resources that will enable the iterative and rapid testing of their product. This is exemplified by the residence of Mosaic Smart Data, a UK startup and the first graduate of the In-Residence Program. The company is creating a more efficient, user-friendly way of analyzing the vast amount of electronic and voice trade generated by J. P. Morgan across multiple asset classes. Its goal is to allow the bank to deliver insights to their clients and to provide a more customized and personalized service in the quest to place their clients at the center of everything that they do. With the support of J. P. Morgan, Mosaic Smart Data is now delivering this technology to a wider market, and is currently engaged with more than 20 financial institutions across the sell side, buy side and execution venues.

The program is typically designated for companies with at least an initial product developed, with a view of taking it from 'pitch ready' to 'enterprise ready'.

Questions on the Case Study

1. What is unique about J. P. Morgan's In-Residence Program, and how does it contribute to the entrepreneurial landscape?
2. In your opinion, what are the 3–4 major challenges faced by J. P. Morgan's In-Residence Program today, when there are so many other enabling systems, for example, accelerators, innovation centers, etc., and how would you suggest that the management of the program cope with these challenges?
3. In general, what are the three main pros and three cons to developing in-house, entrepreneurial programs? From your list, which apply to J. P. Morgan's In-Residence Program?
4. Search the internet and gain more insight into J. P. Morgan's In-Residence Program; look for 2–3 other in-house programs of financial firms. Write down their names and website addresses. What are your main conclusions on the In-Residence Program compared to the others that you have located? What is the In-Residence Program's competitive advantage over the others?
5. Watch 'Fortify.vc launches DC's tech accelerator TheFort.vc' at: https://youtu.be/B0PxYAOIeFo

    Fortify.vc is a seed and follow-on investment fund; after making several investments in 2011, it created Distilled Intelligence 1.0, a pitch competition designed to energize startups and investors in the mid-Atlantic region. Fortify.vc reinforced their commitment to supporting the startup ecosystem by launching TheFort.vc in early 2012. TheFort.vc is Washington

DC's Tech Accelerator and home to over a dozen companies working side by side with mentors and venture capitalists in a collaborative and creative workspace.

Write a 1–2 pager on the phenomenon of financial companies assisting entrepreneurship by opening programs, based on the J. P. Morgan and Fortify.vc programs. You are encouraged to find one more such program on the web.

Reflective Questions

1. A group of six immigrants from Southern Asia in your country are asking for your advice; being technologically savvy, they are looking for institutional support to ideate and develop concepts for a startup. What are the five main questions that you would ask them to gain preliminary insight into who might help them? In general, what type(s) of support would you suggest? Explain why.
2. HablemoS is a one-year-old startup located in Mexico that is in the production phase. It develops an interactive platform for synchronous video and live virtual chats. It has already generated funds from the government and has been awarded the most innovative startup in Mexico City. HablemoS' management team is looking for support for its scaling phase. Search for three existing competitors in the synchronous video and live virtual chat niche and write down their names and website addresses. Discuss the potential relationships of HablemoS with each of the competitors, by using the four ecosystem models presented by Zahra and Nambisan (2012). Explain which model fits each relationship that HablemoS might construct with the companies that you have found, and explain your answers.
3. Search for EE and support systems operated by venture capital and investing companies in 3–4 different countries and write down their names and website addresses. Examine the mission, activities and programs provided by each of them; accordingly, discuss each company's exclusive interest in embracing entrepreneurship. What are your main conclusions?
4. Choose the five most entrepreneurial and startup cities in the world and write them down. List 2–3 elements in each of them that make them an entrepreneurial city; then, refer to the main stakeholders who are most strongly promoting the construction of these entrepreneurial cities. Now, define 'entrepreneurial city' in your own words; in what sense does your definition differ from those discussed in this chapter?
5. Discuss the bankers of the future with respect to the relationships between startups, innovation and banks, by critiquing Henri Arslanian's TEDx talk entitled: 'How FinTech is shaping the future of banking, at: https://youtu.be/pPkNtN8G7q8. What are your main conclusions? In your opinion, what is the main implication for future bankers? Explain.

Notes

1 Interviewed by me; the name and some details have been changed.
2 Science, Technology, Engineering, and Mathematics (STEM) Education. See at: https://fas.org/sgp/crs/misc/R42642.pdf
3 See at: https://startupgenome.com/about-us/; https://blog.startupgenome.com/the-2015-global-startup-ecosystem-ranking-is-live/
4 Interviewed by me. The name and other details have been changed per request.
5 Rebecca Wessell, 2018. 'Through mentoring, angel investors offer more than just Money', Startup Nation, see at: https://startupnation.com/grow-your-business/mentoring-angel-investors-money/
6 See at: www.angelcapitalassociation.org/entrepreneurs/
7 See at: www.nea.com/about
8 See at: http://pipelineangels.com/angel-investing-bootcamp/#
9 See at: https://500.co/
10 See at: http://acceleratorventures.com/
11 See at: www.worldbank.org/en/topic/innovation-entrepreneurship
12 See : https://startup.google.com/
13 See at: https://aws.amazon.com/campaigns/awsmp-startups/
14 See at: http://dc.startupcup.com/
15 See at: www.virgin.com/company/virgin-startup
16 See at: www.nytco.com/early-stage-investments/
17 Partnering with governments: government of Germany—Federal Ministry for the Environment, Nature Conservation & Nuclear Safety; government of India—Ministry of Environment and Forests; government of the Netherlands—Ministry for Agriculture, Nature and Food Quality; government of Norway – Ministry of Foreign Affairs; government of South Africa—Department of Science & Technology; government of Spain—Ministry of External Affairs & Cooperation; government of the United Kingdom of Great Britain and Northern Ireland—Department of Environment, Food and Rural Affairs; government of the United States of America—State Department. Partnering with major groups: Swiss Re (Switzerland); UN System; United Nations Environment Program (UNEP) (Kenya); United Nations Development Program (UNDP) (United States of America). Partnering with other intergovernmental organizations: International Institute for Sustainable Development (IISD) (Canada); Collective Leadership Institute (CLI) (Germany); International Union for Conservation of Nature (IUCN) (Switzerland).

See at: https://sustainabledevelopment.un.org/partnership/?p=1649
18 See at: https://ec.europa.eu/growth/smes/promoting-entrepreneurship/action-plan_en
19 A face-to-face interview with Oliver Harris, who ran J. P. Morgan's In-Residence startup program and Ally R. McCloskey, Corporate & Investment Bank FinTech.

References

Acs, Z. J., Audretsch, D. B., & Lehmann, E. E. (2013). The knowledge spillover theory of entrepreneurship. *Small Business Economics*, 41(4), 757–774.

Audretsch, D. B., & Belitski, M. (2017). Entrepreneurial ecosystems in cities: Establishing the framework conditions. *Journal of Technology Transfer*, 42(5), 1030–1051. https://doi.org/10.1007/s10961-016-9473-8

Baumol, W. J., Litan, R. E., & Schramm, C. J. (2007). *Good Capitalism, Bad Capitalism, and the Economics of Growth and Prosperity*. New Haven, CT: Yale University Press.

Beal, V., & Pinson, G. (2014). When mayors go global: International strategies, urban governance and leadership. *International Journal of Urban and Regional Research*, 38(1), 302–317.

Blackburn, R. A., & Schaper, M. T. (Eds.) (2016). *Government, SMEs and Entrepreneurship Development: Policy, Practice and Challenges*. Abingdon, UK: Routledge.

Brant, H. K., Myers, N., & Runge, K. L. (2017). Promotion, protection, and entrepreneurship: Stakeholder participation and policy change in the 21st century cures initiative. *Politics & Policy, 45*(3), 372–404. https://doi.org/10.1111/polp.12201

Brunt, L., Lerner, J., & Nicholas, T. (2012). Inducement prizes and innovation. *Journal of Industrial Economics, 60*(4), 657–696. https://doi.org/10.1111/joie.12002

Bruton, G. D., Khavul, S., Siegel, D. S., & Wright, M. (2015). New financial alternatives in seeding entrepreneurship: Microfinance, crowdfunding, and peer-to-peer innovations. *Entrepreneurship Theory and Practice, 39*(1), 9–26.

Bryden, A. (2010). Standards are boring? Think twice... *Paris Tech Review*. Available at: parisinnovationreview.com

Cohan, P. S. (2018). Boosting your startup common. In *Startup Cities: Why Only a Few Cities Dominate the Global Startup Scene and What the Rest Should Do About It* (pp. 219–235). New York: Springer Media. https://doi.org/10.1007/978-1-4842-3393-1

Copeland, P., & James, S. (2014). Policy windows, ambiguity and Commission entrepreneurship: explaining the relaunch of the European Union's economic reform agenda. *Journal of European Public Policy, 21*(1), 1–19. https://doi.org/10.1080/13501763.2013.800789

Cornell, R. (2001). Putting the young in business: Policy challenges for youth entrepreneurship. In *Territorial Development. LEED Notebook No. 29*. OECD Local Economic and Employment Development (LEED) Programme.

Cox, K. R. (2009). 'Rescaling the state' in question. *Cambridge Journal of Regions, Economy and Society, 2*(1), 107–121.

Fairlie, R. W., Morelix, A., Reedy, E. J., Russell, J. (2015). *The Kauffman Index 2015: Startup Activity | National trends*. Kansas, MS: Kauffman Foundation.

Feld, B. (2012). *Startup Communities: Building an Entrepreneurial Ecosystem in Your City*. Hoboken NJ: John Wiley.

Gibbs, D., Krueger, R., & MacLeod, G. (2013). Grappling with smart city politics in an era of market triumphalism. *Urban Studies, 50*(11): 2151–2157. .

Goldman, M. (2011). Speculative urbanism and the making of the next world city. *International Journal of Urban and Regional Research, 35*(3), 555–581.

Howell, S. T. (2015). Financing constraints as barriers to innovation: Evidence from R&D grants to energy startups. *SSRN Electronic Journal*. https://doi.org/10.2139/ssrn.2687457

Howitt, P. (2009). Competition, innovation and growth: theory, evidence and policy challenges. In V. Chandra, D. Eröcal, P. C. Padoan, & C. A. Primo Braga (Eds.), *Innovation and Growth: Chasing a Moving Frontier* (pp. 15–24). World Bank and OECD Publishing. https://doi.org/10.1787/9789264073975-4-en

Isenberg, D. (2011). Introducing the entrepreneurship ecosystem: four defining characteristics. Retrieved September 26, 2018, from www.forbes.com/sites/danisenberg/2011/05/25/introducing-the-entrepreneurship-ecosystem-four-defining-characteristics/#456ff8e25fe8

Isenberg, D. J. (2010). How to start an entrepreneurial revolution. *Harvard Business Review, 88*(6), 40–50.

Jouve, B. (2007). Brenner Neil, *New States Spaces. Urban Governance and the Rescaling of Statehood. Métropoles 1*, 16 May. http://journals.openedition.org/metropoles/116

Kiriyama, N. (2012). Trade and innovation: Synthesis report. *OECD Trade Policy Papers, 135*. https://doi.org/10.1787/5k9gwprtbtxn-en

Kremer, M., & Williams, H. (2010). Incentivizing innovation: Adding to the tool kit. *Source: Innovation Policy and the Economy*, *10*(1), 1–17. https://doi.org/10.1086/605851

Kwon, S.-W., Heflin, C., & Ruef, M. (2013). Community social capital and entrepreneurship. *American Sociological Review*, *78*(6), 980–1008. https://doi.org/10.1177/0003122413506440

Lauermann, J. (2018). Municipal statecraft: Revisiting the geographies of the entrepreneurial city. *Progress in Human Geography*, *42*(2), 205–224. https://doi.org/10.1177/0309132516673240

Laursen, K., Masciarelli, F., & Prencipe, A. (2012). Regions matter: How localized social capital affects innovation and external knowledge acquisition. *Organization Science*, *23*(1), 177–193. https://doi.org/10.1287/orsc.1110.0650

Lerner, J., & Tirole, J. (2004). The economics of technology sharing: Open source and beyond. Working paper 10956. Cambridge, MA: National Bureau of Economic Research. https://doi.org/10.3386/w10956

Leyden, D. P., & Link, A. N. (2015). *Public Sector Entrepreneurship: U.S. Technology and Innovation Policy*. New York: Oxford University Press.

Li, K., Godley, A., Belitski, M., Li, W., & Manwani, S. (2015). The importance of e-leadership in meeting digital challenges. Retrieved from www.computerweekly.com/opinion/

Macke, D. W., Markley, D. M., & Fulwider, J. M. (2014). *Energizing Entrepreneurial Communities: A Pathway to Prosperity*. Lincoln, NE: Center for Rural Entrepreneurship.

March, H., & Ribera-Fumaz, R. (2014). Smart contradictions: The politics of making Barcelona a self-sufficient city. *European Urban and Regional Studies*, *23*(4) 816–830.

Mason, C., & Brown, R. (2014). Entrepreneurial ecosystems and growth oriented entrepreneurship. *Paris*, *30*(1), 77–102.

Mazzucato, M. (2015). *The Entrepreneurial State: Debunking Public vs. Private Sector Myths*. London, UK: Anthem Press.

McCann, E. (2013). Policy boosterism, policy mobilities, and the extrospective city. *Urban Geography*, *34*(1), 5–29.

Michael, S. C., & Pearce, J. A. (2009). The need for innovation as a rationale for government involvement in entrepreneurship. *Entrepreneurship & Regional Development*, *21*(3), 285–302. https://doi.org/10.1080/08985620802279999

Motoyama, Y., & Watkins, K. (2014). *Examining the Connections within the Start-up Ecosystem: A Case Study of St. Louis*. Kansas, MO: Kauffman Foundation.

Parnell, S., & Pieterse, E. (2010). The 'right to the city': Institutional imperatives of a developmental state. *International Journal of Urban and Regional Research*, *34*(1), 146–162.

Raco, M., & Street, E. (2012). Resilience planning, economic change and the politics of post-recession development in London and Hong Kong. *Urban Studies*, *49*(5), 1065–1087.

Ribeiro-Soriano, D., & Galindo-Martín, M.-Á. (2012). Government policies to support entrepreneurship. *Entrepreneurship & Regional Development*, *24*(9–10), 861–864. https://doi.org/10.1080/08985626.2012.742322

Rudenko, L. G., Zaitseva, N. A., Mekush, G. E., Dmitrieva, N. V., & Vasilieva, L. S. (2016). Improving private sector and government partnership system to support small businesses in the service sector. *International Electronic Journal of Mathematics Education*, *11*(5), 1261–1270.

Shin, H. B., & Kim, S.-H. (2016). The developmental state, speculative urbanisation and the politics of displacement in gentrifying Seoul. *Urban Studies*, *53*(3), 540–559.

Steinebach, Y., & Knill, C. (2017). Still an entrepreneur? The changing role of the European Commission in EU environmental policy-making. *Journal of European Public Policy*, *24*(3), 429–446. https://doi.org/10.1080/13501763.2016.1149207

Stenholm, P., Acs, Z. J., & Wuebker, R. (2013). Exploring country-level institutional arrangements on the rate and type of entrepreneurial activity. *Journal of Business Venturing*, *28*(1), 176–193.

Zahra, S. A., & Nambisan, S. (2011). Entrepreneurship in global innovation ecosystems. *Academy of Marketing Science Review*, *1*(1), 4–17.

Zahra, S. A., & Nambisan, S. (2012). Entrepreneurship and strategic thinking in business ecosystems. *Business Horizons*, *55*(3), 219–229. https://doi.org/10.1016/j.bushor.2011.12.004.

12
EVALUATION, IMPLICATIONS AND FUTURE AVENUES

This chapter assembles the concepts and models discussed in this book using a twofold, summative organization: (a) evaluation of EE programs; (b) suggestions for conceptual organization of EE programs, for research and practice. It draws on the ideas and practicalities emerging from the academic and applied research presented throughout the book, and on insights from the interviews with leading figures in the entrepreneurial landscape, presented as case studies.

Evaluation of EE and Enabling Systems

Professor Daniel Kahneman, the Nobel Memorial Prize winner in Economics for his work on developing prospect theory in cognitive psychology, proved that people base their decisions on perceptions of potential loss and gain values, rather than on the final outcome. This chapter aims to provide a platform for entrepreneurs' decision-making on the best EE programs to pursue, based on the values given to the perceived gains and losses from enrolling in the program.

To determine entrepreneurs' valuation of EE gains and losses, a three-pronged organization is applied, as presented in Figure 12.1. This deepens the probing into EE's capacity and enriches it through a multisided perspective: (a) looking at both process and outcomes; (b) richer data generation, using hard data (number, figures) and soft data (attitudes, emotional aspects, etc.); and (c) broadening our understanding of evaluations in the 'eyes of the beholder' to capture a larger scope of evaluations by ecosystem players in EE. These three prongs are applied to the following principals in EE programs:

- *Multidisciplinarity* in planning and delivering EE.
- *Involving the ecosystem* in EE planning, implementation and outcomes.

226 Evaluation, Implications and Future Avenues

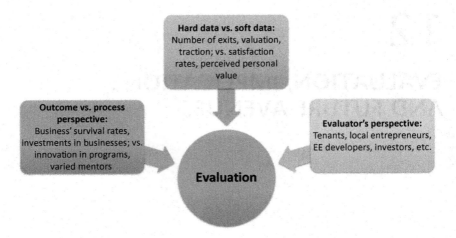

FIGURE 12.1 Conceptual organization for evaluating enabling systems

- Providing *customized value* to the players involved in EE.
- Planning EE for *sustainable impact*.
- *Disseminating* EE programs to various areas, players and missions.
- Learners' and other players' *perceived impact* and *perceived value* are crucial for sustainability and success.
- '*Conventional concepts*' are needed, such as: effectivity, productivity, efficiency and cost.

The Value of the Outcome

Entrepreneurial outcomes and EE outcomes differ, though many student entrepreneurs intertwine the two. The latter include parameters such as number of companies accelerated, number of exits and for how much money, amount of funding for the companies and for the enabling system itself, and number of jobs created in a region, to name a few. Other parameters, contributed by Hochberg and Kamath (2012) include qualified financing activity, qualified exits, reputation with leading venture capitalists, alumnus network, equity taken and stipends.[1] To gain better insight into the outcomes of EE, these parameters can be evaluated through the following lenses.

Refining the focus—There are various indicators of EE outcomes, and a framework should therefore be established. Indicators include a financial look, a view of innovation, a landscape's 'making-the-change' perspective, the success of the tenant/alumni's companies (regardless of the financial aspects associated with the EE program), for example, survival after the program, gaining higher traction, being attractive to stakeholders.

Reference and benchmark—These refer to the frame or point of reference for comparative assessments; for example, financial activity, number of tenants, number of surviving businesses, compared to benchmark numbers, to assess the level of EE success. The outcomes can be compared within:

- EE programs of the same category; for example, an incubator's outcomes versus other incubators, rather than versus a corporate accelerator or a co-working space for entrepreneurs.
- EE programs in the region/country, for example, an incubator's outcomes versus those of any program offered to entrepreneurs, regardless of type—incubators, accelerators, academic programs, institutional-based entrepreneurial centers, etc.
- EE programs in a vertical specialty—for example, an incubator in pharmaceutics is compared to other EE programs in pharmaceutics.
- EE programs for particular groups—for example, programs for immigrant entrepreneurs, for women entrepreneurs, or employing unique models such as virtual incubators, are compared only to similar programs.
- Entrepreneurial factors—a pre–post-based view, giving an estimate of evolution by 'calculating' changes in the entrepreneurial activity of a region; for example, growth of 50% in the region's number of entrepreneurial businesses, job creation, or investments in entrepreneurial businesses in the region, can be used as indicators for EE programs in that region.

These comparisons provide a deeper understanding of EE outputs based on numbers, that is, hard data. However, drawing on Kahneman's theory, these do not necessarily reflect the perceived value of gains and losses incurred with the EE program. Moreover, numbers, figures and data can be interpreted differently, depending on the interpreter's view. The next two constituents address value perceptions by generating insights from soft data, and expanding the search to various players.

Value creation—Perception of value culled from EE is a challenging parameter to assess. People assign various, and constantly changing, meanings to the value that they have gained from participating in EE programs; moreover, these perceptions can change considerably as the program progresses, due to uncontrollable external influences, such as economic changes, political situations, regulation-related developments, etc. Just as venture capitalists get to know the startup beyond the due diligence process, players involved in EE should gain more insight on EE programs' outcomes by delving into the players' approaches and attitudes to these outcomes. Various questionnaires and surveys appear on the web, designed to capture learners' attitudes and satisfaction rates from the process and outcomes. Although perceptions are seized, for example, 'What services or benefits do you most value in an incubator or accelerator program?';[2] 'Are you interested in additional support services combined with training?';[3] among many others, such quantitative surveys can introduce a fractional overview of learners' perceived value created by completing the EE program; qualitative methods can complete the quest. Both quantitative and qualitative data on the value gained by student entrepreneurs are important to produce and share, and can be engendered through:

- The EE program, incubators or accelerators, or other enabling systems in the region/city.
- Government, regional associations, municipalities, bodies engaged in regional development.
- Academia, research centers, labs.
- Corporate—either a specific company or several companies dedicated to entrepreneurial businesses in the region or in a specific vertical.
- Investors, venture capitalists and financial companies.
- Media.

Ways to produce insights on the value gained from EE outcomes through 'soft' data can include:

- Formal pre- and post-interviews with the portfolio companies, for every cohort.
- Periodical formal and informal meetings with alumni, mentors, experts, and players involved in the EE program—to gain a temporal overview (for example, from alumni) and an ecosystem view.
- Informal, unstructured encounters—'documenting' any feedback, comments, insights of players involved in EE, whenever meetings occur, at conferences, meetups, blogs, etc., with the 'documentation' to be stored in a shared cloud file; once in a while, the managers of the accelerator then analyze it.
- Media and social media—raising feedback and comments from blogs, social media chats, etc. There are many web and mobile applications that can track such chats by keywords (e.g., the incubator's name); there is a growing demand for community builders/developers who can also detect feedback and comments.
- Leveraging events—initiating events, programs, competitions for the portfolio companies, and 'embedding' feedback questions in the activities. For example, in a regional competition, the task is to pitch to investors, and address three factors that the company has gained from the EE program.
- Deals—the accelerator asks its alumni to send videos about their companies for public relations and media exposure that the accelerator will operate, in return for a feedback discussion on the program's outcomes from the perspective of several years later.

- Shared undertaking—creating an open source for anyone who is interested in sharing their comments, feedback, and suggestions for the EE programs in the region.

The beholder's view—Various players are involved in EE programs; they hold different views and different interests in the EE outcomes, and it is important to map the evaluators' perspectives. Table 12.1 illustrates outcome evaluation through: the *individual look*, referring to the portfolio company, alumnus entrepreneurs, founders searching for the program that best fits their existing or future invested companies; the *business look*, concerning the views of the managing teams of the EE programs, for example, the accelerator, the corporate hub, the municipality incubators; the *investment/financial look*, referring to investors and strategic collaborators, including angel investors, banks, venture capital companies, corporations that have invested in the business of EE programs and/or in a specific tenant company; and the *institutional look*, reflecting the impact at a regional or national level, based on institutional interests: employment, education, environment, regional development ministries, etc.

Evaluation of the Educational Process

The importance of evaluating the factors associated with the EE process lies in the detection of the boosters of, and hindrances to, the expected entrepreneurial pursuit. Largely, the core mission delivered by the various EE programs consists of similar concepts, such as supporting startups and entrepreneurial dynamics, creating a community of mentors and experts to support the startups, developing skills, capabilities, and advancing trusted connections with the tenant entrepreneurial companies by allowing access to the EE programs' networks.

While outcomes are visible, the process encompasses stimuli for the learners that may evolve over time, or even never bear on performance, yet can be most influential for the learner's entrepreneurial career. Therefore, evaluating the process is challenging; it touches on a multifaceted range of learner capabilities and competencies, which are expected to self-transform into entrepreneurial outcomes. These acquired capabilities are fused with the learner's previous experiences, knowledge and motivations, and, therefore, take on different forms and fluctuate across learners, making them difficult to identify. Moreover, entrepreneurial dynamics are in constant flux and demand congruent changes in EE to provide the learners with a real experience of the entrepreneurial journey. These changes require an ongoing modification of the EE process, which further complicates its evaluation.

In addition, EE is criticized in research for being subject to 'mismatches' between the entrepreneurs' real needs and the acquired KSA, with a key weakness of EE in neglecting to focus on competence, rather than knowledge. In an era of open platforms, knowledge is accessible, and the value of the EE process

TABLE 12.1 Evaluation factors and the level of measurement

Individual look	Business look	Investment/financial look	Institutional look
Business progress: production stage, becoming a licensed company, etc.	Increased traction and interest in the business, by: potential entrepreneurs, potential collaborators, potential investors, government, academia, etc.	ROI in the company in 3–5 years	Increased job creation
Networks: attracting more investments, investors	Networking—attracting an impactful community around the EE program	ROI in the program in 3–5 years	Increase in innovations, inventions, development, hence in IP, trademarks, etc. Rise in bilateral collaborations, including export, import, memorandum of understanding,[4] etc.
Higher valuation of the company by investment (the company develops more value, attracts investments at more mature stages)	Growth in the number of companies that survive one year or more after graduation	Improvement of business-model decisions, e.g., money-for-equity, loans, resources-for-equity, donations, sponsorship	Developments promoting health, environment, education, etc. (new medication, ways to purify water, methods to educate the poor online, etc.)
Attracting more strategic collaborators, sponsorship, support	Growth in tenant firms' ROI in 3–5 years	Increased involvement in company and/or program: number of people from investing companies, equity involved, time spent on mentorship	
Expanding the number of relevant, valuable contacts	Rise in the number of tenant and alumnus firms that have raised money from external investors	Expansion in the 2nd tier network for the investor, based on connections with the EE program's networks (i.e., motivation to continue, EE program is praised by investors, promoting its value, etc.)	Increased attraction to STEM-related education and employment
Improving the team's complementary capabilities	Rise in total value of portfolio companies	Increase in investor company's exposure/attractiveness to the ecosystem	Higher global ranking of a country/region based on innovation rankings
Gaining more media exposure	Rise in exits in 3–5 years	Rise in total value of invested companies	

lies in translating and mediating experimental situations to co-create and build the required abilities, such as exploiting opportunities, making discoveries, and ideating. Tapping into 'sensing' and 'feeling' rather than just 'knowing' can produce more value for the learners (Carey & Matlay, 2010; Edwards & Muir, 2005; Fehder, 2016; Hannon, 2005; Honig, 2004; Hytti & O'Gorman, 2004; Pittaway & Cope, 2007; Pittaway & Edwards, 2012; Vij, 2014; Vij & Ball, 2009; Yu Cheng, Sei Chan, & Mahmood, 2009). Figure 12.2 demonstrates the assorted factors associated with the EE process to be considered when evaluating EE programs.

Table 12.2 links the evaluations of the various process-related factors to the views of the main players in a more systematic fashion.

Summary

An evaluation of EE programs is crucial, challenging, constantly changing, and still not well established in terms of rigorous development of evaluation models, or in differentiating the evaluation process of EE programs from that of any other program; the context, value and impact of these programs are drastically different. In this chapter, the complexity of the evaluation activity is discussed, by showing how the dynamic changing entrepreneurial landscape affects EE programs. The other challenge raised in this chapter is addressed by suggesting different conceptual organizations of factors related to EE, to be addressed by entrepreneurs considering an EE program. Sorting the evaluation by outcomes and processes through different ways of generating the information and by encouraging a broader look through the eyes of different stakeholders is introduced.

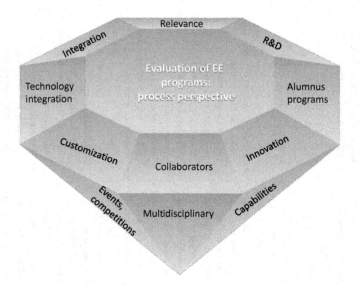

FIGURE 12.2 A 'diamond-sided' evaluation of the EE process

TABLE 12.2 Evaluating the process through different views

The process perspective by:	The learner	The instructor	The business*	The players
EE program indicators				
Customization—the EE program is engaged with each tenant company, by tailoring the content, experts and delivery methods to the entrepreneurs' and tenant companies' needs	The degree to which the program fits the learner's needs	How can the instructor gain information on the tenants to customize his/her deliveries for each portfolio company (rather than deliver general KSAs)?	What is the balance between customization and the program's structured activities? How can the EE program satisfy all involved players (impossible to customize for each player)?	How can customization be best used by the tenant company toward its success?
Technology integration—technology is presented in the communication in introducing new knowledge, enabling mentoring beyond time and location, and using technological tools and practices	• Simplifies logistics of time, place, fixed hours, duration, etc., of the program • Access to: cutting-edge knowledge, databases, platforms, educational material • Easier connections to international mentors and experts, simpler to share, connect • Consistent with real-world dynamics	• Simpler to communicate with the mentored companies, experts, other mentors, in terms of time and place • Ongoing learning from technologies integrated in the EE program, including applications, games, simulations, etc.	• Attracting more entrepreneurs by offering hybrid programs (logistic considerations) • Introducing innovation and cutting-edge methods • Attracting more stakeholders	• Easier connections to the various players • Easier way to introduce the portfolio companies to other stakeholders, regardless of time and place • More confidence in the tenant companies' preparation for real life
Capabilities—the EE program focuses on 'soft' skills and formatted capabilities, and endeavours to provide a 'sense and feel' emphasis, rather than 'just' knowledge	• Focusing on emotional and psychological aspects of the individual, the entrepreneur, the team, communication with stakeholders • Gaining sustainable value by expanding and deepening competencies, rather than a short-term, practical solution • Understanding other stakeholders, and improving communication with them	• Expanding the scope of the involvement with the tenant companies to long-term capabilities • Improving communication with the mentees • Demand for more specializations, e.g., psychologists, experts in negotiations, behavioral science specialists	• Offering a richer program, that touches more existing and potential entrepreneurs • Opportunity to expand the network with more corporate, government ministries, projects that emphasize capabilities	• Many stakeholders consider the team of entrepreneurial companies as most meaningful to a company's success; such focus raises their confidence in the EE program's relevance to attain this

Multidisciplinarily—the resources of the EE program derive from various disciplines, including experts, tools, mentors, corporate involvement	• Consistent with the entrepreneurial business as multidisciplinary, involving business topics, technology, design, psychology • Access to knowledge, mentors and experts from various fields • More exploitation opportunities, stimulated by the variety of disciplines	• Opportunities for instructors and mentors to meet with more specialists from different disciplines • Higher demand for instructors, as more disciplines are needed, tough stretching the need • Feeling of pride in contributing to the EE program	• Offering more value • Differentiated from competitors that focus on limited specialties • Expanding the scope of potential stakeholders, investments • Expanding the community around the EE program; creating spin-off communities • Higher efficiency in running EE programs • Expanding the impact on the ecosystem • Attracting more and a higher range of companies for the next cohort • Creating more programs under one roof	• More confidence in the EE program's robustness • Opportunities to collaborate with different stakeholders from different disciplines through the EE program's platform • The EE program attracts companies from various disciplines, hence, enabling stakeholders be the first to consider these companies for investments, collaborations, etc.
Collaborators — the network, contacts and strategic collaborators of the EE program are integrated, and complement each other	• More opportunities for support, networks • Inspiration from collaborators • A model for the tenant company to collaborate with 'competitors', merge, and share	• Collaborating with the ecosystem, creating innovative courses and projects for the mentees • New opportunities for the instructors and mentors	• Leading the trend of EE programs	
Innovation — the program introduces innovative tools, models, collaborations	• Acquisition of high-quality KSA • Role model for the tenant companies to embrace more innovation in their business pursuit • Generating a competitive advantage through innovation	• Requires constant improvement from the instructor; an ongoing learning process • Exposes the instructor to innovative applications, platforms and projects		• Can be useful for the stakeholders' practices (to be embedded in their companies, for example) • More interesting, can bring more interest in the EE program

(continued)

TABLE 12.2 (continued)

The process perspective by:	The learner	The instructor	The business*	The players
EE program indicators				
R&D – the EE program allocates more resources to develop more material, content and delivery methods		• Allocation of time, resources, knowledge sharing • The instructor is a part of the R&D and hence should constantly expose his/her added value		• Can be integrated with the stakeholders' R&D • The EE program and its portfolio companies can become the stakeholders' suppliers of R&D • More and higher quality tenant companies can be attracted for investment
Integration – the EE program is responsible for assembling, in a reasonable, practical way, the resources that it holds, so that stakeholders see a comprehensive place to develop entrepreneurship	• Translation of the multiple resources so that the entrepreneurs can understand them • Gaining the benefits of a one-stop shop that is simultaneously comprehensive and specialized	• Easier to work and collaborate with other instructors and stakeholders • Simple to work with the mentees		• A more straightforward understanding of the EE process • More efficient, practical, resourceful ways to operate the EE program (some stakeholders invest or sponsor the program)

Events, competitions exposure, challenges, media	• Exposure to the ecosystem • Hands-on experience with trends, other developments • Opportunity to win prizes, gain acknowledgment • Opportunity to attract investments • A way to dedicate all efforts toward a goal (for example, for an event, a pitch night or a competition) • Managing FOMO	• Exposure of the instructors and their specialties to the ecosystem • A way to gain more knowledge of trends and developments • A mentoring 'technique' – dedicating joint efforts with the company for a goal and a deadline • Managing FOMO	• Business models (charging money, attracting sponsorships; internet traction for online competitions and events) • Media exposure • Opportunity to raise awareness of specific companies, and of the EE program as a whole • A way to praise the portfolio companies	• A most important networking opportunity • A way to give back by sponsoring/financing an event • Opportunities to gain more knowledge on trends, developments • An occasion for exposing the stakeholders' contribution to the entrepreneurship ecosystem • Managing FOMO
Alumnus programs—long-term support in the companies and constant value introduction to alumni by making connections with the growing network, introducing new trends and enabling potential support	• Confidence in being taken care of after program completion • A chance to interact with alumni while still a tenant company • A role model	• More demand for instructors in subsequent programs • Opportunity to learn from successes, through the alumnus programs	• Sustaining the connection with alumni to support them • Opportunities for getting support from alumnus companies: mentorship, sponsorship, financial support	• Confidence in long-term EE support of tenant companies, to be supported/financed by the stakeholders • Teams and companies change; a 'second chance' to connect with alumni for strategic collaborations • A path for networking and collaborating
Relevance—being up to date, aligning with the new trends	• Being updated on new trends, tools, applications • Gaining a competitive advantage over other companies in different EE programs	• Improving the material, structures and tools through accountability for being relevant • Learning through other instructors' relevant material	• A way to continually be relevant to the stakeholders, innovate and reinnovate internally • A competitive advantage compared to other EE programs	• Being hands-on with new trends • Being more confident in the tenant companies' (mainly those to be supported) relevance to the market

* Referring to the EE program, for example, the incubator, accelerator, university hub, co-working space, etc.

The question is, what are we targeting now? In other words, how do these developments converge into a rigorous framework that is agile, yet can lead the entrepreneurial ecosystem to flourish, create and innovate?

Beyond the Here and Now

Like mushrooms after rain, EE programs are springing up everywhere. The case studies presented throughout this book describe a wide range of programs developed in different countries, with specialties that are greatly differentiated from each other; these examples prove the need not only for EE programs, but also for their response to new emerging needs. Yet, we still lack an understanding of what EE programs entail. At a more basic level, there is no one established term or expression for EE programs, and even the term 'program' is inaccurate, as not all of them are actually programs (i.e., co-working spaces, virtual communities). In research, many terms are employed for this phenomenon, for example, EE programs, EE venues, facilitating systems—referring to programs aimed at facilitating the entrepreneurial activity, support systems, or the use of specific programs, such as accelerators, centers of innovation, and co-working spaces. These also lack accuracy, as in some cases the characteristics of a program and the program's title do not complement each other; for example, a co-working space (by its characteristics) that is called an accelerator, yet mainly provides a place for work, not necessarily for entrepreneurs, and without a cohort basis, structured mentorship, etc. Such mismatches nourish the continual fuzziness and incoherence on the heuristics and practicalities of these programs.

The significance in delineating the programs, and assiduously demarcating them by names/terms, characteristics, processes and outcomes, is twofold. Research-wise, existing analyses focus on accelerators, mainly based in the US, followed by research studies on incubators and some others on their ecosystems, though not necessarily on EE programs; hence, comprehensive research on the various programs is still lacking. In fact, research on new, active programs other than accelerators or incubators is still scarce. In addition, the existing studies on accelerators and incubators are predominantly descriptive; few comparative assessments have been conducted, and there is a deficiency of available and reliable data. Therefore, research results are inconsistent; for example, while a great deal of research associates companies' success with their participation in business incubators, other studies show the opposite. The lack of in-depth research on the business models of EE programs, limited attention to the role of other stakeholders in shaping and affecting EE programs, and lack of evaluative studies demand more robust, global and comparative research (Grimaldi & Grandi, 2005; Hackett & Dilts, 2004, 2008; Scillitoe & Chakrabarti, 2010). From a practical perspective, the proliferation of EE programs proves that not only is there a need and place for the variety, but also that EE programs seem to 'invent' themselves, bringing new, and more customized value to entrepreneurs. The new forms of EE programs complement, but do not eliminate, the existing forms; as evidence of this, entrepreneurs gradually move from one program to another, until they feel confident enough to find their way by themselves. According to the managers of EE programs, the new wave of enrolling entrepreneurs is typified by a more experienced, mature entrepreneur, running businesses in more advanced stages, as compared to past cohorts who were typified as inexperienced and just starting their first project. Such 'bottom-up' evidence clearly reveals entrepreneurs' continually changing need for support.

Enabling systems seem to encompass a wide range of EE programs, including shared spaces and communities. This term echoes the mission of EE programs, and is grounded in most EE principles, that is, sharing, value generation, impact distribution, etc. It also reverberates the dynamic needs and expectations of tenant and potential entrepreneurs, which are agility, space, enabling rather than instructing, opening doors, and easing the way.

Sharing and Mapping

Entrepreneurship requires conceptualization and organization of the realm of enabling systems. This section suggests a conceptual framework, formed through an open platform, to capture the ecosystem's involvement in its construction. The platform calls for placing any enabling system on a map, such that the different enabling systems will be added by the users of the platform according to categories that they have developed, such as location, classification (e.g., incubator, startup factory, co-working space), number of portfolio companies, as well as 'qualitative' factors describing the experience, activities, challenges, etc. This dynamic mapping, developed bottom-up and, thus, originating from the users' terminology, views, and needs, can grow into a *smart mapping* of enabling systems worldwide. It should recap the pillars upon which this book is based:

- *Sharing* knowledge, information, feedback and views.
- Capturing *multisided* knowledge, information, etc., that is, beyond knowledge or information that is provided by the managements of the enabling systems; but also, from tenants, alumni, mentors, etc.
- Establishing *open platforms* as the norm, not the exception; the FOMO rule.
- *Sustainability* should apply, by guaranteeing that the smart map will evolve harmoniously with the phenomena, to confirm that the exponentially accumulating 'data' on the various enabling systems are documented, stored and open to everyone.
- *Multifaceted* approach, which encourages the 'sense' and 'feel' information, rather than only hard data, that is, numbers, analytics, on the enabling system.
- *Ecosystem* involvement to gain a wide-ranging overview on each enabling system.
- The role of *intuition*—smart categorization based on intuitive operation of the smart-mapping platform, so that information can be easily seized.

- *Spin-offs* of specific verticals, locations or activities, are encouraged, as they mainly represent the healthy development of trends, and hands-on capacity for further specialization, which still derives from the same core and represents the same spirit.

An illustration of a smart-mapping skeleton is presented in Figure 12.3, followed by Table 12.3, which details the facilitating, shared smart-mapping platform.

As demonstrated, the smart map is an easy mapping activity that is intuitively constructed. As such, it is appealing and value engendering for the various players in the ecosystem. To gain a deeper understanding of the conceptual organization of enabling systems and how an open platform of smart mapping resolves a real need, see Table 12.3.

Summary

The second part of this chapter assembles the principles that have been presented and debated throughout the book, to provide a conceptual organization of the enabling systems' realm. By amassing the introduced innovations and developments in the different enabling systems, such as shared knowledge, agility, the ecosystem's active involvement, facilitation rather than teaching and training, space—both physical and experiential, among others, that stem from the ground, bottom-up, the foundations of smart mapping are established. By probing the heuristic deficiencies in knowledge, information and data, the inconsistency in data gathering and the associated biases, the suggested smart map is an endeavor to respond to a real need that is arising in an intensified field that seems to continuously grow, develop and create spin-offs.

Takeaways

General:

- Be aware of the lack of, and biases in, existing information on enabling systems.
- Prioritize the information gained on enabling systems, and evaluate its quality.
- Map the criteria for assessing enabling systems' function, mission, success.
- Encourage entrepreneurs that are/have been involved in enabling systems to share their insights, comments and ideas for improvement.
- Encourage mentors, instructors, and program developers to be part of an active ecosystem that can continually contribute to entrepreneurship sustainability and dissemination.
- Document enabling systems, to monitor, learn, share knowledge and experiences, and enable a more effective decision-making process.
- Be an active player in formatting a community that can contribute to smart mapping.

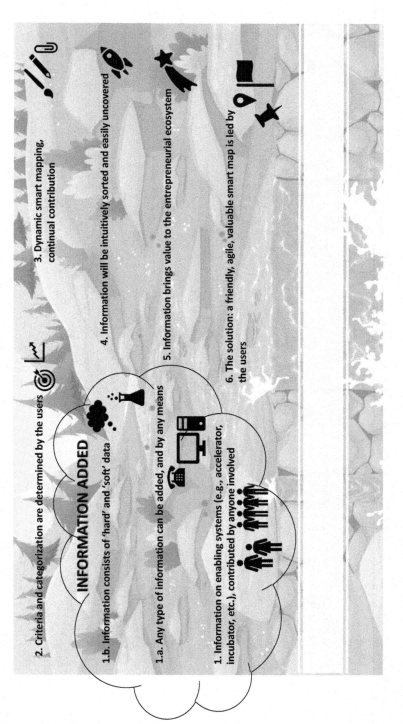

FIGURE 12.3 A smart-mapping skeleton

TABLE 12.3 A summative framework for enabling systems' conceptual organization—creation of a smart map

	HOW (means, time, resources)	*BY WHOM* (contributors, users)	*WHY* (value delivered)	*WHICH* (characteristics)	*WHO* Who is in charge (responsibility)?
Information	✓ Added on an ongoing basis ✓ Technological platforms and applications can sort information based on frequency of topics raised ✓ Intuitive and user friendly	✓ People managing an enabling system ✓ Tenants ✓ Alumni ✓ Mentors ✓ EE program developers ✓ Researchers	✓ Document ✓ A one-stop shop ✓ Enabling information for decision-making on EE programs ✓ Enabling smart scouting of enabling systems ✓ Research ✓ Comparative assessments ✓ Regional, national, global assessments on the quantity and quality of enabling systems	✓ 'Hard' data—numbers, analytics, figures ✓ 'Soft data,'—sharing experiences, feedback, comments ✓ Quantitatively based: following a template of questions and topics to address ✓ Qualitatively based: open discussion, chats, blogs	✓ Users ✓ Technology: developers, support ✓ Cyber and security-based monitoring ✓ Establishment of a new role: smart-mapping spotlighter, suggesting content-based prioritization of information flow (supported by technology)
Criteria	✓ Basic criteria set in advance ✓ Following criteria (where traction and more content allow) are formed technologically	✓ Basic criteria set by smart-mapping managing team ✓ Then, it will be technologically formatted through the frequency of appearance of words, topics ✓ Can be suggested by contributors	✓ Criteria will be evolved bottom-up, and echo reality ✓ Will be easier to search and find ✓ Will create knowledge, rather than adapt knowledge to existing criteria only	✓ Basic criteria will include several well-established factors ✓ Criteria contributed by users and 'technologically based' criteria will be determined on the go ✓ Criteria will be visibly exposed to enable easy use	✓ Users ✓ Establishment of a new role: smart-mapping community leader ✓ Technology: developers, support

Categorization	✓ Created by technology	✓ Technological platforms and applications	✓ Easy for scouting ✓ Easy to find any related information ✓ Useful to all stakeholders in their decisions on entrepreneurship and EE ✓ Imperative for research	✓ By location ✓ By sector of portfolio companies ✓ By success factor of the enabling system ✓ By the enabling system's methods ✓ By best comments from investors, mentors, etc. ✓ By qualitatively based analyses of the most typifying word (e.g., professional, connected to the industry)	✓ Technology: developers, support
Contributions	✓ Continually added ✓ Can be adjusted	✓ Contributions come from the various players	✓ Represent a large scope of views, information, etc., thus enabling being hands-on regarding trends, needs, etc. ✓ A decision-making enabler ✓ Urges diversity ✓ Fosters tolerance to a multiplicity of approaches and views	✓ All types (hard, soft), personal: blogs, chats, interviews ✓ External: from media, research, statistics, national reports	✓ Smart-mapping community leaders for denial-of-service (DoS)-related attacks, shaming, fairness, etc. ✓ Smart-mapping spotlighter

(continued)

TABLE 12.3 *(continued)*

	HOW (means, time, resources)	*BY WHOM* (contributors, users)	*WHY* (value delivered)	*WHICH* (characteristics)	*WHO* Who is in charge (responsibility)?
Value creation	✓ Updated information synchronously displaying trends ✓ Providing fair exposure to any enabling system ✓ SM is a platform that can be disseminated	✓ By all contributors ✓ Being appreciated by the users (who are not actively contributing) ✓ By serving as a focal point, a one-stop shop, where all needed information is actively stored and used	✓ Knowledge on enabling systems is lacking, biased or inaccurate; this is an opportunity to assemble knowledge in the users' way and through their mindsets	✓ Accuracy of knowledge ✓ Easy to track knowledge sources ✓ Addition of knowledge that is atypical, such as emotional and creativity-oriented information ✓ The formation of two important new roles, smart-mapping community leader, and smart-mapping spotlighter, as well as development of specialists in technology-based demands	✓ Users ✓ Contributors ✓ Smart-mapping community leaders ✓ Smart-mapping spotlighter
Solution	✓ Easy to contribute and use ✓ Sharing-based business model (crowdfunding) ✓ Open source, technology is friendly and easy ✓ Users help each other on how to navigate, contribute, etc. ✓ An agile, thus potentially growing platform	✓ Entrepreneurs in different stages of their business' development ✓ Managers of enabling systems ✓ EE developers ✓ Mentors ✓ Investors ✓ Private institutions ✓ Financial institutions ✓ Research institutions ✓ Teaching institutions ✓ Government institutions ✓ Global institutions for innovation, grants, reporting ✓ Innovators ✓ Media	✓ Responds to a real need ✓ Agile – transforms and retransforms through its accumulated content ✓ Constantly renewing ✓ Corresponding entrepreneurs' mindsets ✓ Enables exposure of anything to anyone ✓ Easy to navigate ✓ Independent, hence not affected by special interests		

Case Study 12 – Accelerating Startups for the Chinese Market: Beijing, China[5]

A six-month accelerator program, providing free co-working space, training and networking, opened in the Sanlitun area of Beijing, with the support of the Israeli government. This program was intended to enable high-tech startups from Israel to penetrate the Chinese market, then grow and scale up in China. This is a brand new program of the Israeli Ministry of Economy and Industry, established with the support of DayDayUp, the leading innovative business community in China, and Shengjing, a leading consultant and investor in China. Meanwhile, Shengjing has become the very first Chinese investor in Israel, proving the need to intertwine the immense Chinese market with the innovation introduced in Israel under the same roof. According to Xinbei Zhang, the senior trade officer of the Trade & Investment Mission at the Israeli Embassy in Beijing,

> In China, high-tech companies are shifting from business model innovation to the integration of technology innovation and business model innovation. For example, we have the O2O services such as Elema, Meituan Dianping. O2O is a kind of business model innovation, but combined with advanced technology such as positioning, coupon stimulating, order optimization, etc. The company has achieved huge development. That said, we believe that it is time to introduce Israeli technologies to the Chinese market. We believe that Israeli technology has been hugely successful in the US market. Using the case studies of how US companies have acquired Israeli technologies, we believe that we have attracted target audiences within the Chinese market. In addition, Israel is known as a startup nation in China. Some Chinese firms go to explore Israel by their own initiative.

The program offers training lectures, monthly report discussions, mentor meetings and service partner office hours—crafted around the challenges revealed on both sides: "Challenges include language, geographical and cultural differences: it is much easier for Chinese companies to work with local suppliers. From the Israeli companies' side, it is hard for them to locate suitable partners" says Zhang. The program is operated under the Israeli Ministry of Economy and Industry. "We see the advantages that we provide by offering the most comprehensive services to Israeli companies: training, business development services, matchmaking, and *ad hoc* handling; we work as the arm of their team. We have quite a few success stories," attests Zhang. The accelerator's mentors include Wanqiang Li, co-founder of Xiaomi, Hang Zhou, founder of Yidao, and Xiao Wang, founder of Unity Ventures, among other renowned individuals. They help the tenants understand Chinese culture and business. Thus, the accelerator aims to attract startups that, in Zhang's words, "are keen to penetrate the Chinese market, already have products, can work on their own initiative and are result-driven but patient." The challenges are concentrated around customization: "Companies within the accelerator come from a very wide range of subsectors, and it is very challenging for us to provide customized services," says Zhang.

Questions on the Case Study

1. Zhang and her team are interested in evaluating the outcomes of the acceleration program. What are the 3–4 main factors that you would recommend she assesses? Explain your choice.
2. The Chinese government is interested in assessing the accelerator process to suggest it to corporations in China. Choose 3–4 factors associated with content evaluation; explain how these factors can be leveraged and how they can apply to Chinese corporations.
3. Suggest a model to continually evaluate the accelerator, thereby enabling better access to its activities and successes.
4. In your opinion what are the 3–4 major challenges that Zhang and her team should be attentive to?
5. Suppose that Zhang wishes to form a ranked list of accelerators in China. Based on the smart-mapping concepts, create a template for such a list. What are the 3–4 main factors discussed in this chapter that you have included?

Reflective Questions

In this section, the rules of the game have changed. The questions will be contributed by *you*! Based on your ideas, internet search, brainstorming with colleagues, please complete the following blanks; make sure to carefully align them with the topics presented in this chapter.

1. Look on the web for _____ in Europe and in Asia, and compare_____.
   What are the main similarities and differences that you have located? Indicate which two topics you used for this question.
2. A governmental association asks for your consultancy to create a smart map of _____.
   What are the three main questions that you wish to ask the association to plan your work? Indicate which two topics you used for this question.
3. Search the internet for a template on evaluating education programs, and adjust it to _____ entrepreneurial programs. What are your main conclusions? Indicate which two topics you used for this question.
4. Watch _____ on an innovative initiative that corresponds to the topics of this chapter. What are the three main questions

on this initiative that still need to be discussed? Indicate which two topics you used for this question.
5. Now it's your turn to develop a smart, valuable and contributing question:

_____

_____

_____

_____

Notes

1 Stipends refer to budget provided by the accelerator to entrepreneurs to support their activities.
2 See at: www.surveymonkey.com/r/P5QH52N
3 See at: http://home.zcu.cz/~vacekj/SyKaPo/reg_scan_quest_cz_v2.pdf
4 A memorandum of understanding is a legal document outlining the terms and details of an agreement between parties.
5 I interviewed Xinbei Zhang over the phone.

References

Carey, C., & Matlay, H. (2010). Creative disciplines education: A model for assessing ideas in entrepreneurship education? *Education+ Training*, *52*(8/9), 694–709.
Edwards, L., & Muir, E. J. (2005). Promoting entrepreneurship at the University of Glamorgan through formal and informal learning. *Journal of Small Business and Enterprise Development*, *12*(4), 613–626. https://doi.org/10.1108/14626000510628261
Fehder, D. C. (2016). Essays on the evaluation of entrepreneurship programs. PhD Thesis. Massachusetts Institute of Technology.
Grimaldi, R., & Grandi, A. (2005). Business incubators and new venture creation: An assessment of incubating models. *Technovation*, *25*(2), 111–121.
Hackett, S. M., & Dilts, D. M. (2004). A real options-driven theory of business incubation. *Journal of Technology Transfer*, *29*(1), 41–54. https://doi.org/10.1023/B:JOTT.0000011180.19370.36
Hackett, S. M., & Dilts, D. M. (2008). Inside the black box of business incubation: Study B—scale assessment, model refinement, and incubation outcomes. *Journal of Technology Transfer*, *33*(5), 439–471.
Hannon, P. D. (2005). Philosophies of enterprise and entrepreneurship education and challenges for higher education in the UK. *International Journal of Entrepreneurship and Innovation*, *6*(2), 105–114. https://doi.org/10.5367/0000000053966876
Hochberg, Y. V., & Kamath, K. (2012). *2012 Seed Accelerator Rankings*.
Honig, B. (2004). Entrepreneurship education: Toward a model of contingency-based business planning. *Academy of Management Learning & Education*, *3*(3), 258–273.
Hytti, U., & O'Gorman, C. (2004). What is "enterprise education"? An analysis of the objectives and methods of enterprise education programmes in four European countries. *Education+ Training*, *46*(1), 11–23.
Pittaway, L., & Cope, J. (2007). Entrepreneurship education: A systematic review of the evidence. Retrieved from https://papers.ssrn.com/sol3/papers.cfm?abstract_id=2815321

Pittaway, L., & Edwards, C. (2012). Assessment: Examining practice in entrepreneurship education. *Education+ Training*, *54*(8/9), 778–800.

Scillitoe, J. L., & Chakrabarti, A. K. (2010). The role of incubator interactions in assisting new ventures. *Technovation*, *30*(3), 155–167. https://doi.org/10.1016/J.TECHNOVATION.2009.12.002

Vij, V. (2014). Exploratory study into entrepreneurship education: Awareness and impact upon science, engineering and technology (SET) undergraduates. Unpublished PhD thesis. Northumbria University, Newcastle, UK.

Vij, V., & Ball, S. (2009). Exploring the impact of entrepreneurship education on university nonbusiness undergraduates. *International Journal of Entrepreneurship and Small Business*, *9*(1), 86–109.

Yu Cheng, M., Sei Chan, W., & Mahmood, A. (2009). The effectiveness of entrepreneurship education in Malaysia. *Education+ Training*, *51*(7), 555–566.

INDEX

Page numbers in **bold** refer to information in tables; those in *italics* refer to figures.

500 Startups 207

abilities 90–91, 94
academia: accelerators 55–58, 139–142, 164, 169; effect on/from EE **96**; incubators 151, *152*; new breeds of programs 129–137; open innovation platforms (OIPs) 187; venture labs 191
academic accelerators 55–58, 139–142, 164, 169
Accelerated Learning Cycle *63*, 76
Accelerator Ventures 207
accelerators: academic 55–58, 139–142, 164, 169; activities 165–167, **166**; business models 167; corporate 173–174, 204; development trends 153; examples 86–87, 100–103, 139–142, 176–179; financial models 168–169; growth trends 8, 163–164; institutional 174; models and approaches 163–172; process of *171*; research 2; scaleup 172–173; virtual 135–136
AccorHotels 188
action research *63*, 76
advice 146
affect 89
agile culture *65*, 102
Akirachix 192
ALACT model *63*, 76
Alchemist 168

Alscher, Henrietta 25–26
Amazon AWS Marketplace 212
Angel Capital Association 207
AngelPad 163–164
angels 167, 206–208
appreciative inquiry 50
apprenticeships 28
Arar, Raphael 103
Arslanian, Henri 220
Art Thinking Lab 34
artificial intelligence 103
artist-entrepreneurs 32–34
Ashoka 214
asynchronous learning 136, 137
attitudes 84, 91, 94
Azevedo, Rivanda 202, 204

Banga, Kalyan 157
banks 208–209, 218–220
Batavia Industrial Center, New York 1, 147
behavioral traits 85, 92
beholder's views 229
benchmarking 227
Bennett, R. 28
Berkeley, recognition of Startup Grind 16
Betaworks 189
Blank, S. 50
blended-value: approach to learning 72, *75*; framework 64–68; in shared spaces 115; venture builders 77–79

Blue Man Group 79–80
boot camps 191–193, 207
Brown, David 176–179
Brush, C. G. 64–65
Buccheit, Paul 102–103
business 42–43, *44*
business innovation centers 148
business look 229
business model canvas 50
business models 167
business perspectives in EE 22, 23
business services *148*, 170
business simulations 70
business- to-business contracts 101–102

Caldwell, Dalton 102–103
Call9 100–103
capabilities: inflow process 62; knowledge, ability and skills (KSA) 84–85; personalized approach 69–70, *75*
capacity-building 23–24, 66–67, *75*
career choices 30
case studies: academic accelerators 55–58, 139–142; accelerators 176–179, 243–244; artist-entrepreneurs 32–34; banks 218–220; communities 14–16; co-working space 123–125; customer needs 100–103; incubators 156–159; open innovation platforms (OIPs) 195–197; venture builders 77–79
Centre for Digital Innovation (C4DI) 147
Chase 208
children and entrepreneurship 34, 211
China: accelerators 243–244; venture builders 77–79
Cisneros, Luis 123–125
cities 214–216
classroom education 23, 119–120; *see also* teaching
coaching 146–147
co-creation 54, 67, 72
cognitive traits 84, 89
Cohen, David 176
Cohen, Maor **116**
co-labs 191
collaboration 183–187, 218
communities: accelerators **167**; entrepreneurial cities 214–216; for entrepreneurs 14–16; impact hubs 190; open innovation platforms (OIPs) 187; shared spaces **117**, 118
community outreach teaching methods 27–28

community-based economy 109
community-shared assets 109
comparative assessments 227
computer-mediated communication (CMC) 71–72
conferences 14–15
conservative teaching 26, 27, 28, 53–54
construction 77–79
constructive stress 89–90
content: digital 110, **110**, 112–115; education context 10–11; of EE programs 13, 49–50, 135–136
content-based building 65–66, *75*
corporate accelerators 167, 170–174, 177, 204
corporations: accelerators 167, 170–174, 177, 204; entrepreneurship support 212–213; financial models 168; innovation factories 187–188; J. P. Morgan's In-Residence Program 218–220; open innovation platforms (OIPs) 183–187; venture labs 191
Coursera 79, 113
co-working space: accelerators **166**; entrePrism 123–125; examples 8, 87; as shared spaces 115–119, 148; startup factories 189–190
Creative Bazaar Model 204
creativity: artists and 32–33; boosting 27; mentoring 9; teaching 53
critical positivity ratio 53
cross-cultural differences 9, 10, 13, 48
crowdfunding 111, 119–121
customer needs 100–102
customer–supplier relationships 146

data **166**, *226*, 228–229
DayDayUp 243–244
Deloitte 142
design thinking 50, 94
destructive stress 89–90
Dew, N. 50
Digital Business Academy 113
digital content: learning and teaching 135–136; sharing economy 110, **110**, 112–115
digital entrepreneurs 108–112
digitalized learning 134–135
discipline-based perspective in EE 22
discussion boards 136
disruptive innovation 42, 47, 48–49, 108–109
do–learn–think 64

Dorf, B. 50
dumb money 109

early education boot camp 192
eBay StartUp Cup 212
economic stimuli for EE programs 10
ecosystems: education context 7, 9–10, 12; entrepreneurial cities and communities 214–216; entrepreneurship support 206–213; impact of learning on 25; impact on/from EE **96–97**; impact on/from entrepreneurship 200–201; international outlooks on 213–214; learning about 42–43, *44*; models 204; structure and processes *205*; value creation 201–205
Edspace 119
education: educational forms 71, *75*; innovation in 14–16; models 20–21; relationship with industry and government 10, 13; role in enabling entrepreneurship 21–23
edu-preneurial learning 67, 72, **73–74**, *75*, 76
effectiveness 48
effectuation 50
Ek, Daniel 48–49
e-learning 70
ELM model 76
emotions: AI and 103; as entrepreneurial traits 85, 89, 92; in learning 15; as outcomes 94; positive and negative 53
employability 23, 24
employee innovation 140–141, 188
Empower Orphans 103
enabling platforms *see* innovative enabling platforms
enabling systems: beyond here and now 236–237; evaluation of 225–226; smart mapping 237–238, **240–242**; terminology and research 2–3
entrepreneurial competencies 29
entrepreneurial education (EE) programs: for or about entrepreneurship 10–11, 30; accelerating 20–21; 'bubble' of 162, 175, 197; contextual overview 7–14; digital content 113; evaluation of 225–226, 229–235; fundamentals of 45–48; future 236–237; learning areas of 42–45; mainstream education and 48–49; outcome outlooks 94–95; process-driven 91–94; psychological perspectives 87–91; reasons for enrollment 85–87, **88**; shared spaces and 119; stakeholders in 95, **96–97**; terminology and research 2; *what, why* and *how* 42, 49–54
entrepreneurial teaching 26, 29–30
entrepreneurs: acknowledgement of 210; diversity of 21–22; process- and outcome- views of EE 91–95; psychological traits 87–91; teamwork and 93–94; traits of 85–86
Entrepreneur's Club 214
Entrepreneurs' Organization 214
entrepreneurship: as a career choice 30; changing role and impact 7; complexity of teaching 21–23, 49, 53–54, 62; institutionalizing 149–154; processes and outcomes 42, **43**
entrepreneurship centers 55–58
entrepreneurship education (EE) 23–24
entrepreneurship learning (EL) 23, 24–26, 129–137
entrepreneurship teaching 23, 26–29, 30, 129–137
entrePrism 123–125
Ernst and Young 204
European Commission 8, 214
evaluation: of educational process 229–231; of EE and enabling systems 226–227
expectations of EE 86, 94
experiential learning: boot camps 191–192; effectiveness 15; models of 10, 63–64, *63*; practice, internship 133–134; service learning 50; whole-person pedagogy 11–12
experts: accelerators 167, 177; feedback from 20; role in sharing economy 113–115
exposure **166**
externships 28

F10 147
Farcet, Alex 192–193
Feld, Brad 176
fellowship programs 28
financial advice 146
financial models 168
FinTech 218–219, 220
flexibility of programs 45
FOMO! **110**, **116**
Fortify.vc 219–220
Foster, Kenneth 32
Franklin, Guy 115, 195–197

Fredrickson, Barbara 53
free interpretation 48
Fry, R. *63*, 76
funding: accelerators 168; startups seeking 109
FusionAnalyticsWorld.com 157

gains 225–226
game-allocated teams 70
gamification: ecosystems 201; teaching 70, 130–132; virtual reality (VR) technology 134
Gardinier, Ives **117**
GBL (game-based learning) 70, 130–132
'geeks' 89
Georgia Tech's Venture Lab 191
Gill, M. D 147
Global Accelerator Report 8, 162
Global Entrepreneurship Bootcamp 192
global entrepreneurship learning (GEL) 48
goals of programs 45
Goldman, Matt 79–80
Google documents 137
Google Startup 212
government: accelerators 167, 174; impact on/from EE **96**; incubators 151, *152*, 153; participation in entrepreneurship 209–212; relationship with education and industry 10, 13
Greene, P. G. 64–65
group work 71, *75*; see also teams
Gupta, Neha 103

HablemoS 220
hackathons 67, 135–136
Hard Valuable Fun 189
Hargadon, A. 188
healthcare 86–87, 100–103, 202, 210
Herold, Cameron 34
Hewlett Packard Enterprise 187
Hiltz, R. 71–72
Hochberg, Y. V. 226
holistic view of learning 11–12
horizontal accelerators 169–170
Hult International Business School 47

IBM 187, 191
idea generation 50
IdeaLab 188
idea-thons 91–92
IDEO 188
imagined knowledge 42
impact hubs 190

incubators: government 153; institutionalizing perspective 149–153; journey 149, *150*; landscape of 145–146; models and approaches 147–149; Neotec Hub 156–159; origins and evolution 1–2, 8, 147–148, 162; resources 146–147; strategic connections 151, *152*; virtual 135–136, 148; World Food Program 154
individual look 229
individual perspectives in EE 22, 23
individuals, learning about 42–43, *44*
individuals' personalized platforms 187
industry: bridges to *148*; impact on/from EE **96**; relationship with education and government 10, 13
inflow entrepreneurial process 62, 76
information **166**
infrastructure 146, *148*
in-house innovation 140–141
INNOVATING Accelerator Program 139–142
innovation: in education 14–16; education context 10; embedding 187–188; as principle of EE 13; routinizing unconventional processes 71–72; see also disruptive innovation
innovation factories 187–188
Innovation Outpost as a Service (IOaaS) model 94
innovative enabling platforms: boot camps 191–193; evolution of 183, *184*; impact hubs 190; individuals' personalized platforms 187; innovation factories 187–188; open innovation platforms (OIPs) 183–187; startup factories 189–190; startup studios 190–191; venture builders 189; venture labs, co-labs 191
In-Residence Startup Program 218–220
institutional accelerators 167, 169–170, 174
institutional look 229
institutionalizing entrepreneurship 149–154
intellectual property **110**, 146
international outlooks: education context 10, 12–14; on entrepreneurship support 213–214; global entrepreneurship learning (GEL) 48
internships 27, 133–134
interpretation of problems/solutions 48
investment look 229

investors: accelerators 167; contact through incubators 146; impact on/from EE **96**; venture capital 206–208
Isenberg, Daniel 200–201, 209–210
Israel: NOVUS Center of Entrepreneurship 55–58; sFBI (small Factory Big Ideas) 69

J. P. Morgan 208, 218–220
Jam Central Model 204
Jones, C. 30
Jones, Peter 201

Kahneman, D. 227
Kamath, K. 226
KantoorKaravaan 119
Kaplan, Oren 89–90
Kauffman Foundation 169
Kessels, J. 76
Khan Academy 8–9
Kirby, D. A. 28
Klandt, H. 30
knowledge: academic and disciplinary 49–50; accelerators **166**; acquisition of 64; EE-accelerating models 20–21; feasibility and 90–91; imagined 42; knowledge, ability and skills (KSA) 84–85, 86, 94; sharing economy **110**; spillovers 210
knowledge-brokering cycle approach 188
Kolb, D. A. 10, *63*, 76
Korthagen, F. *63*, 76
Koster, B. 76

Lagerwerf, B. 76
Lal, Suman 197
lean models 48–49
lean startup 50
learner-centered education 68–72
learning: blended-value approach to 64–68; by doing 54, 133–134; cycles 62–64; dashboards 8–9; entrepreneurship 22–23, 24–26; personalized approach 68–72; process- and outcome-driven 91–95; shared spaces **117**; styles 24, 53, 62–63; tools 129–137, *139*
'learning about' map 42–43, *44*
legal advice 146
Lengnick-Hall, C. A. 12
letters of interest (LOI) 101–102
Lewin, Kurt *63*, 76

location: government and 210; shared spaces **116–117**; synchronous learning 136
loneliness **116**
losses 225–226
Lucent Technologies 191

Martinez, Luis **116–117**
MassChallenge 165, 168
massive open online courses (MOOCs) 70
Matlay, H. 30
Matorin, Shahar 14–16, 201
mentoring: accelerators 164–165, **166**, 167; incubators 146–147; NOVUS Center of Entrepreneurship 57; open innovation platforms (OIPs) 185; Y Combinator 102–103
messages 137
meta-modeling 29
Microsoft accelerator 168, 170, 173, 213
Microsoft Innovation Centers 34–35
mini boot camp 192
mobile apps 103
MOD Station Model 204
models: ecosystems 204; EE-accelerating 20–21; incubators 147–149; 'learning about' maps and 43–45; of learning cycles 62, *63*
Mokrin House 119
Molino, Diego 180
MOOCs (massive open online courses) 70, 79
Moonshot Horizon 93–94
Mosaic Smart Data 219
motivation 85, 89
multidisciplinary approach 66, *75*
multifaceted approach 67, *75*
musician entrepreneurs 32–33, 156–159

Nagai, Diantha **116–117**
Nambisan, S. 204, 220
Nay, Robert 103
Neck, H. M. 64–65
Neotec Hub 156–159
Neotia, Ambuja 156–159
Neotia, H. V. 156–159
networking: accelerators 164–165, **166**; government roles 210; incubators 146; shared spaces **117**; as skill 47; Startupbootcamp 86–87; Y Combinator 102–103
Neumann, Adam 126
New Enterprise Associates (NEA) 207

New York Times 212
Newlands, M. 51
Nillson, Liam 33
non-profit 168
NOVUS Center of Entrepreneurship 55–58
nursing homes 100–103

Obvious Corp 189
Ohlsson-Corboz, A.-V. 50
oneself, learning about 42–43, *44*
open innovation accelerators 142
open innovation platforms (OIPs) 183–187, 195–197
OpenEducation Challenge 142
'open-source' practice 29
opportunities: identification, exploration, creation 50, 129–130, **131**; outflow process 62
Orchestra Model 204
Osterwalder, A. 50
outcome perspectives of EE 94–95, *226*
outcomes, value of 226–229
outflow entrepreneurial process 62, 76

Pasricha, Mukul 118
Peck, Tim 100–103
pedagogy: personalized approach to learning 68–72; whole-person 11–12
personal skills *111*
personality 12
personalized approach 68–72, *75*
physical goods 111
Pigneur, Y. 50
Pipeline Angels 207
planned behavior 87
platform economy 109
Plug and Play 168
Polis, Jared 176
positivity 53
practice: EE-accelerating models 20–21; teaching 133–134
pre-boot camp 192
private sector *152*, 212–213
process perspectives *226*, **232–235**
process-driven education 91–94
project-based learning 29–30, 43–45, 185, 191–192
psychological traits 87–91, 94
public sector 209–212
push/pull factors 86, **88**

Read, S. 50
ready-to-work boot camp 192
real-world challenges 29–30

reference points 227
reflective practice 64
reflective questions: accelerators 179–180; context of EE programs 16–17; education for entrepreneurs 34–35; entrepreneur's perspective 103–104; evaluation, implications, future avenues 243–244; incubators 159; innovative enabling platforms 197; role of the environment 220; sharing economy 125–126; there is no 'one size fits all' 79–80; *what, why* and *how* of EE 58
research incubators 148, *152*
research into EE 2–3, 7–8
Research Triangle Park (RTP) 215
resources of incubators 146
returns on investment (ROI) 51
Ries, E. 50
RockaLabs 8
Rocket Internet 189
Rosa, P. 30
routinizing unconventional processes 71–72

Sanders, M. M. 12
Saras, S. 50
Sarda, Sanjay 156–159
satisfaction 86, 92–93, 94
scaleup accelerators 170, 172–173
Schmitt, B. 11
Scott, M. 30
Seed Acceleration Rankings Project 163
seed investment **166**, 170, 207
self-efficacy 89
Sense, Feel, Think, Act, React 11
Senses Wines 67–68
service learning 50
sFBI (small Factory Big Ideas) 69
shared spaces 115–119, *148*; *see also* co-working space
sharing economy: crowdfunding 119–121; digital content 112–115; entrepreneurial context 108–112; inspirational course on 25–26; opportunities, hurdles, challenges 110, **111**; shared spaces 115–119
Silicon Valley 215
Silicon Valley Bank 208
simulations of businesses 70
Singaram, Muthu 79
skills: acquisition of 64, 71; digital entrepreneurs *111*, *114*; knowledge, ability and skills (KSA) 84–85, 94; personalized approach *75*
smart mapping 2–3, 237–238, *239*, **240–242**

Smilor, R. W. 147
Smith, Alistair *63*, 76
social networks 20–21, **96**
social stimuli for EE 10, 13
social support 85, 91–92
society **96**
soft data 228–229
SOSA, New York City 115, 195–197
'spaces' 63
specialization in EE 22
Spotify 48–49
Spring House Coworking 118
Square Capital 208
stakeholders 13, 90, 95, **96–97**
standalone incubators 148
Stanford's Startup Garage 58
StarterSquad 189
startup communities 14–16
startup factories 189–190
'Startup for Enterprise' approach *171*
Startup Genome report 204
Startup Grind 14–16, 190, 214
startup studios 190–191, 197
startup tenants 167
Startup with Google 212
StartupBlink 159
Startupbootcamp 165, 180, 192–193
Station F, Paris 58
Steidl, Ed 34–35
stress 89–90
Strieter, Christopher 67–68
student consulting projects 28
success **46**, 47, 226–227, 236
summaries and takeaways: academia and the new breed of program 137–139; accelerators 174–175; context of EE programs 12–14; enabling systems 238; entrepreneur's perspective 98–99; evaluation and implications 230–236; incubators 154–156; innovative enabling platforms 193–195; role of the environment 216–217; sharing economy 121–122; there is no 'one size fits all' 76–77; *what, why* and *how* of EE 54–55; what education entails for entrepreneurs 30–31
sustainable value 13
Sutton, R. I. 188
synchronous learning 136–137

Tahoe Mountain Lab 119
tailor-made learning 47, 49, 51
takeaways: academia and the new breed of program 138–139; entrepreneur's perspective 99; incubators 155–156; innovative enabling platforms 194–195; role of the environment 217; sharing economy 122; there is no 'one size fits all' 76–77; *what, why* and *how* of EE 55; what education entails for entrepreneurs 31–32
teaching: blended-value approach to learning 64–68; classroom education 119–120; entrepreneurially 26, 29–30; entrepreneurship 21–23, 26–29; gamification 130–132; methods 22, 23–24, 27, 29–30, 53–54, 71; practice 133–134; virtual learning 134–137
teams: digital entrepreneurs' skills *111*; individual's view 93–94; psychological perspectives 89–90
TECH U 139–142
technological innovations 108–109
Techstars 164, 176–179
TED talks 137
terminology 2–3
thinking styles 47
T-Hub 147
timing 45, 92–93, 170
Tong, Wyatt **116**
traction 109, **110**
traditional teaching 26, 27, 28, 53–54
training 146
transferable knowledge/skills 64
transformational learning 20, *21*
Turoff, M. 71–72

Ubiqua 180
Udacity 113
Udemy 113
unconventional processes 71–72, *75*
United Nations 190, 213–214
universities 20–21, 148; *see also* academia
user–client relationships 95

value: blended-value approach to learning 64–68, **73–74**; creation of 24, 50, 201–205, 227–229; of EE programs 50–53, 94; gained from EE 86; of outcomes 226–229; sharing economy 110, **110**, **111**
value 'buffet' 51, **52**, 53
VamosA 192
Vasalos, A. *63*
venture builders 8, 77–79, 189
venture capital 168, 189, 206–208
venture labs 191
venture studios 190–191

vertical accelerators 169–170
verticals 192, 208–209
VibaZone 79
video games 70
videos 137
Virgin Startup 212
virtual accelerators and incubators 135–136, 148
virtual learning 71–72, 134–137, 187
virtual learning environments 136
virtual reality (VR) technology 134

Watson, Vinitha 32–33
webinars 136
Wessell, Rebecca 204–205
WeWork 8, 118–119, 125–126, 148
whole-person pedagogy 11–12, *11*, 13, 28–29

wikis 136–137
Wiltbank, R. 50
World Bank 8, 208
World Food Program 154
Wubbels, T. 76

XL-Africa 159

Y Combinator 100–103, 163–164
Young Entrepreneur Council 214
Young President's Organization 214
YouTube 137

Zahra, S. A. 204, 220
Zegans, Marc 32
Zhang, Xinbei 243–244
Zimbabwe:Works 17
Zoo Labs 32–33